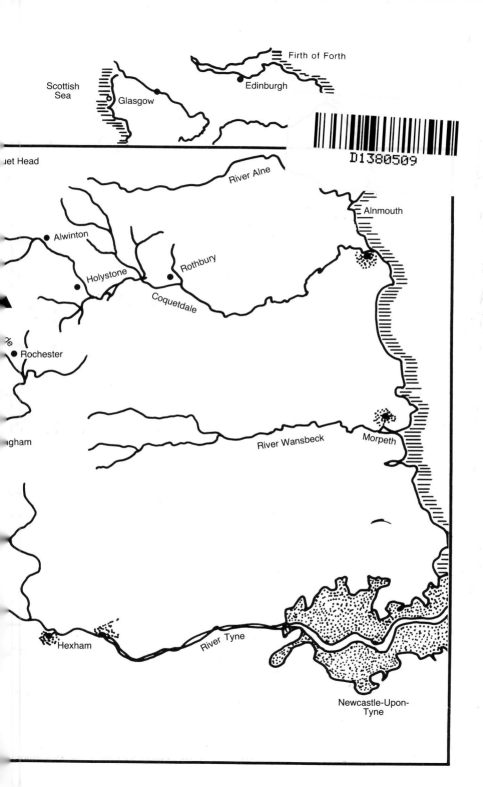

Scottish Sea

Glasgow

Firth of Forth

Edinburgh

...et Head

River Alne

Alnmouth

Alwinton

Rothbury

Holystone

Coquetdale

...e

Rochester

...gham

River Wansbeck

Morpeth

Hexham

River Tyne

Newcastle-Upon-Tyne

D1380509

About the Border Terrier

A view of its history and breeding
Walter J. F. Gardner

T. C. FARRIES
AND CO. LIMITED

Dumfries and Hinckley

Publishing history

1st edition published 1985 in the United States of America by Bradford Press, Box 224, Bradford, Massachusetts 01830 (no ISBN)

2nd, revised, edition published 1991 by T. C. Farries and Co Ltd, Irongray Road, Lochside, Dumfries DG2 0LH

ISBN 0 948278 15 3

Printed in Great Britain by Headley Brothers Ltd The Invicta Press Ashford Kent and London

To my wife Joy,
whose love for little creatures
is surpassed only
by her love for her family

Portrait of Mr. William Jardine, painted 1820, showing probable Border Terrier (lower right).

On Stamina in Horses, Men and Dogs; Some Lore
About the Gypsies of Yetholm—Dog Breeders and
Pipers; The Reality of Rabies; Telegony, or Maternal
Impression; Border Country Agricultural Shows of
Interest

"Toast To The Border Terrier:
Never a better worker in the field
Never a better companion by the fire"

—*Anon.*

Foreword to the 2nd Edition

The early evidences of the Border Terrier are scattered through a multitude of sources—in stories and impressions handed down through the years, in the private records and diaries of huntsmen and farmers, in paintings and photographs and letters, in breed club and agricultural show records, in newspaper articles, and in a very few small-circulation monographs and pamphlets, most of them long out of print and hard to find.

Few people devoted to the Border Terrier are as well placed and as well suited by experience and interests to gather such evidences together as Walter J. F. Gardner. The son and grandson of Dumbartonshire and Ayrshire veterinarians, he has shared the Border Terrier's rural world—in his childhood, in his career as a livestock genetics specialist, and as a long-time Border Terrier breeder. Luckily for his interest in Borders, he began breeding them at a time when the long memories and experience of many influential early breeders were accessible to him. And luckily especially for those of us more distant in time and place from the Border's original world, he distilled a lifetime of informed experience into his *About the Border Terrier,* first published in America in 1985 and now out of print.

This new edition not only makes *About the Border Terrier* available to readers once again but its much expanded Appendixes will add substantially to their knowledge and understanding of the unique qualities of the breed. This edition reprints two rare early publications, Montague Horn's much prized monograph *The Border Terrier* (1943), reprinted with the kind permission of Mr. Plummer of Gatheral and Co. Hexham, and "Border Lines", a collection of information articles by early Border Terrier breeders which was originally compiled in 1948 by Jim Schiach. Also included among the treasures of the second edition are further early photographs and an early reference and explanation on the phenomenon of kinked tails in Borders.

It was a privilege and a pleasure to serve as editor for the first edition of *About the Border Terrier.* It is even more satisfying to witness the publication of this expanded second edition, which makes accessible to many an accumulated wisdom about a modest and remarkable breed heretofore available only to few.

Kate Murphy
Bradford, Massachusetts, USA
April 1991

Foreword to the 1st Edition

We quickly consented to Kate Murphy's request that we write a fore-word to Walter Gardner's *About the Border Terrier: a View of its History and Breeding*. The book gives the reader a uniquely personal view of the origin, the nature and the purpose of the Border Terrier. It is all too easy for the breeder and competitor in the show ring, so far distant from the origins of the breed, to forget the original goals and purposes for breeding the Border Terrier. And it is important to remember that we are breeding the Border Terrier, which originated in the Border Country, not the Australian Border Terrier, the Swedish Border Terrier or the American Border Terrier. To under-stand the Border Terrier Standard we must understand the Border's history, its origin, and the characteristics its original breeders were attempting to select and breed for as the Border, the Bedlington, and the Dandie Dinmont Terrier evolved in their different ways in the latter half of the 19th century.

We see Walter Gardner's book as an important means for doing this. Knowing personally so many of the famous figures associated with the breed, having worked most of his lifetime travelling the Border Country between England and Scotland, and being a breeder of Borders for many years, Mr. Gardner is in a unique position to bring all of his knowledge and insights together. This book is a per-sonal document, but also an historical document. We are grateful to Walter Gardner and to his editor Kate Murphy for providing us with this valuable source book.

Robert Naun
President
Border Terrier Club of America

Ruth Ann Naun
American Kennel Club Delegate
for the Border Terrier Breed

Author's Note to the 2nd Edition

I was very encouraged by the interest from Border Terrier breeders from all countries where the Breed is to be found. This response kindled the thought of a 2nd Edition of the book, and this became a reality when in discussion with Mr. Plummer of Gatheral & Co., Hexham, who kindly offered me the copyright of the book by Mr. M. Horn as an appendix should I decide to produce a 2nd Edition. It was Mr. Plummer's father who as owner of the company originally published the book.

To Mr. Plummer and his co-directors I record my appreciation of this gesture from them in the interest of the history of the Breed at the time of Mr. Horn's writing.

Mr. Horn (Monty as he was known to his fellow exhibitors and breeders at that time) was a journalist and in this capacity he contributed to the column "Border Terrier Notes" in *Our Dogs* every week, for many years, after World War 2.

We made a courtesy call on Mrs. Horn who is still in residence at the same address as when Monty was writing for *Our Dogs*, some 40 years ago. In the course of our discussion Mrs. Horn expressed appreciation of the fact that her late husband's book was being republished at this date, thus adding to the knowledge of the newcomers to the breed some history of the breed at the date of his writings.

In expressing these sentiments she considered that these would be the feelings of her late husband. Monty died 12th December 1965. Mrs. Horn informed me they were married in 1943, and at that date Monty had Borders, obtained from Adam Forster. His best known dog was Ch. Hepple (2475 AF) (called after the village in the Borders of that name) Br. Mr. M. Horn, b. 21st April 1948, S. Fearsome Fellow d. Happy Day c. Red.

I remember Hepple well when he was being exhibited by Monty. He was an upstanding type, solid red in colour, with dark mask and ears. This solid red colour is sadly lacking in Borders today. Mrs. Horn showed us a trophy won by Hepple in 1950. This trophy, donated by Capt. Blumberg, O.B.E. and inscribed for the best Border Terrier 1950, was won outright by Ch. Hepple. I must admit that I had never seen any reference to this trophy in any record of trophies up for competition in any of the shows. I record my appreciation of Mrs. Horn's good wishes and encouragement in relation to this project.

Border Lines

This pamphlet, published by Mr. J. Shiach in 1948 when he was in the publishing business in Carlisle, and edited by Mr. T. Lazonby, is a most informative little document.

The articles contained therein were compiled by the leading breeders, from the date of recognition by the K.C. until after the last War. At the time of our own entry into the exhibition side all those who contributed articles were exhibitors or judging. I knew them all and have discussed the various aspects of the standard with them and listened to their views. The early Champions and Blood lines by Miss Hester Garnet Orme take us back to the early blood lines when the Breed was recognized by the K.C. To the younger members who have come into the Breed, who are either wishing to establish a kennel of their own, or who are ambitious enough to wish to judge the breed, I say study the pamphlet, read it well and commit to memory the views of these judges, because they all had a lifetime experience of the Breed, both in the field and as exhibitors and judges.

Jim Shiach I knew well, as a ken speckle figure with his deer stalker type hat and his Sherlock Holmes type pipe. Jim was involved on the organization side either as show manager at the club shows or organizing shows for charity. He died some 13 years ago.

I discussed with Mrs. Shiach the probability of including this pamphlet as an appendix; she was very pleased and wished me well in this project.

I wish to record my appreciation and grateful thanks to Mr. A. Forster's two daughters, Mrs. Jane Langley and Mrs. Ena (Christina) Nixon for the photographs of their mother, Mrs. A. Forster, with Ch. Ranter and for the photographs of their father's dogs. Also to Mr. Jeff Carruthers for the photograph of his father and sons, with the Border Bitch Nell.

Finally I record my appreciation of the suggestion and encouragement from Dr. K. Murphy, Robert and Ruth Anne Naun, and to Bradford Press, the publishers of the first edition.

Walter J. F. Gardner
Greencleuch
Torthorwald
Dumfries

Author's Note to the 1st Edition

Many fine and responsible breeders have contributed to the Border Terrier breed. In this book, however, I have confined my observations to those older Border Terrier breeders whom I came to know personally at the time of our own entry into the exhibition side after World War II.

By and large, the older breeders of that time had established their kennels in the twenties and thirties. Most had been active in the breed from the era when the Border Terrier was a hunt terrier with the Border Hounds to the time of the breed's recognition in 1920 by the Kennel club. The Border Terrier breeders of that era were (and in the case of those who are left to us, are) great characters. They are part of a period in the history of this country unlikely to be seen again.

I wish to acknowledge with very warm thanks the help I have received from many people in writing this book: to Kate Murphy, who has given so much of her time to editing the work and on whose initial suggestion I have endeavored to put my thoughts into writing; to Miss Margaret Edgar, who typed a considerable part of the initial manuscript; to Mrs. K. Twist, who gave me so much information about the Border Terrier at the time she came into the breed and provided such helpful photographs; to Mrs. S. Mulcaster, who contributed her knowledge of the breed at that time; to the editors of *The Field* and *Our Dogs*, for permission to use their published material; to Mr. H. L. Plummer, of J. Catherall and Company, Hexham, for permission to use material in *Border Sports and Sportsmen* by Ferguson; to Longman and Co. for the use of material in their *Fox Hunting on the Lakeland Fells*; to Gilmour for allowing access to early editions of the Ayrshire Agricultural Association catalogues; to Mr. J. Patterson, Terrona Farm, Langholm, for his help from the records of the Langholm Agricultural Society; to Mr. Brian Stavely, Secretary of the Border Terrier Club, for his valuable suggestions and help; to the Kennel Club, for permission to reprint the Standard of the breed; and fundamentally to my family, for their steady and warm support of the project.

Walter J. F. Gardner, Greencleuch,
Torthorwald, Dumfriesshire, 1985

Introduction

One time as a schoolboy I came across two little red dogs of a kind I had not seen before; they were owned by the local grocer. My father, who was a veterinary surgeon, told me they were Border Terriers and that they were worked at the foxes by the hunting people. Although over the years lots of dogs came to my father's surgery to be given veterinary attention, I never saw Borders other than those mentioned. Borders, not a popular breed, were in the hands of estate owners, those who lived in the country, and most of all those who had some connection to the hunt. At this first sighting of Border Terriers, I did not know how important to me this remarkable breed of dogs would later become.

I was brought up among dogs and stock. My father had an extensive practice among the livestock breeders in the Carrick District of Ayrshire, and travelling with him as a boy I met and listened to many breeders of all kinds of stock, from the mighty Clydesdale to Ayrshire cattle and hunting horses. It was a great interest and treat then to sit and listen to the long conversations about the different traits of the various breeds. It was while listening to these discussions that I learned about the great Clydesdale stallion Dunure Footprint. This horse proved to be one of the outstanding sires of all time and was most prepotent, stamping his type on all his progeny. I learned at that time that Footprint was father-to-daughter-bred, sired by the famous Baron of Buchlyvie out of Dunure Ideal by Baron of Buchlyvie. At a later date, having studied genetics, I remembered the prepotent Clydesdales and established Maxton Border Terriers on a similar basis.

After I returned from the war, I joined the professional staff of the Department of Agriculture for Scotland. My first assignment was at Hawick in Roxburghshire. It was in this area that my interest in Border Terriers really developed, and I met some of the older Border breeders—the Crozier brothers, Tom and Jim, and Willie Barton, for instance.

I also met Joy, who was to become my wife. Through her I really became so interested in the breed that I decided that when we were married I would purchase a Border bitch. Joy's family had long owned Border Terriers, but just before the war her brother had taken the family's Border on a hunting trip along the banks of the River Tweed. The dog had gone to earth and was never seen again. Joy's parents were so distressed at the loss of the dog that it was never replaced. At the time Joy and I were engaged, I travelled a lot to visit farms in the county, and in the course of my travels I came across a well-bred litter of Borders in the village of Newcastleton, which lies south of Hawick. The owner was a Mrs. Nixon and the pups had been sired by Ch. Rising Light, owned by Mr. Wattie Irving, one of the best known of the early breeders. Joy's mother knew Wattie, because her late husband had been Station Master at Maxton, and Wattie, who also worked on the railway, had from time to time been Relief Station Master. Through the purchase of the Rising Light pup, whom we named Kim, I later came to meet Wattie and to visit him at his home in Musselburgh.

At that time I also encountered many Borders on the farms in the area, for it was well-known hunting country, the hunting grounds of the Buccleugh Hunt. This Hunt's foxhound kennels are at St. Bos-

Hounds of the Morpeth Hunt 1983 (Jean Clark photo)

well's, not far from Maxton, the village which is the basis of our pre-fix. In the course of my duties I met Mr. A. Douglas of Saughtree Farm, who was at that time running a hill pack of foxhounds. He always had a good Border about the farm, as did the Douglases of Gatehousecote and many other farmers and shepherds in that area. Mrs. Tweedie of Middlethird Gordon, who bred Ch. Ranting Fury, was a keen Border enthusiast though to my recollection she did not exhibit much.

Another person important to Border Terriers I first met as a boy, when I was exhibiting rabbits at the Agricultural Shows: the late Jimmy Garrow was an expert at judging Borders and all types of live-stock. On one occasion I exhibited Ch. Maxton Mannequin and Maxton May Queen under him in a large Any Variety Brace class. He placed a Borzoi brace first and my Borders second. Coming down the line writing up his judge's book, he looked over his glasses in his characteristic way and said, in his broad Scots accent, "They're no show dugs but they are a pair o' braw Borders." On another occasion when I met him after he had been judging Borders, he said, looking over his glasses, "You did na' dae sae weel today. I weel remember when you had a better day with your Borders—aye, and a' weel remember when you showed rabbits as a boy."

Jimmy Garrow's remarks illustrate two important points in the exhibition of livestock. All dedicated breeders who exhibit stock will have days when they do better and days when they do worse. Breed-ing a truly fine animal in any species of livestock takes careful plan-ning, time, and patience. There can be sudden setbacks—by way of example my loss of fine well-bred bitches like Maxton Red Princess and Ch. Maxton Mannequin. When my Ch. Maxton Monarch proved sterile, it was well nigh a disaster, because I had a small kennel. One must shed despair, however, for in time one will regain lost ground and make satisfactory advances toward one's ideal.

Garrow's other comment, that he remembered when I showed rabbits as a boy, demonstrated his memory, as at the time it must have been some 25 or 30 years since I had exhibited rabbits under him. Memory is a very important asset to the good judge of stock, as it is to the breeder. To be able to commit to memory the overall virtues or failings of particular dogs is a treasured gift that not all breeders of stock have received. If the breeder has this gift, he or she can commit to memory those lines of breeding that produce good stock and those that produce otherwise.

I have spent a lifetime listening to great breeders express their views about the judging of stock, and I have bred Border Terriers for over thirty years. By conveying in this book what I have come to know about breeding livestock in general and Border Terriers in particular, I hope to help novice breeders dedicated to the Border reduce their setbacks and speed their advances toward their ideal. I also hope that my detailed discussion of the Border Terrier standard may assist them in judging the result of their efforts.

I would be deeply gratified if, as well, this discussion of Border Terriers adds further dimension to the strong affection in which the breed is held by those fortunate enough to know them.

Walter J. F. Gardner
Greencleuch, Torthorwald, Dumfriesshire

1

Some general aspects of animal breeding history; Border Terrier origins and development

Man's domestication of animals began so far back in history that its specific origins can only be guessed at. But clearly the domestication and care of stock began because of man's close association with and specific needs for such animals as the dog and the horse. From very early on, therefore, their breeding with particular functions in mind appears to have received close attention. The many breeds of dogs apt for specific purposes no doubt evolved through this attention, just as the Arab horse, because of the particular ways the Arab tribesmen depended on it, came in for a lot of consideration for specific kinds of improvement. It is noteworthy that these early tribesmen kept breeding records for consultation as good livestock breeders at every period seem to do.

In England the systematic improvement of domestic animals would seem to have begun when Robert Bakewell (1726–1795) took over the Disley Grange estate, Loughborough, Leicester, about 1760, and became the most famous of the English improvers of stock. His method was to collect and breed together animals he considered to be near to his ideal within a general type—that is, he bred like-to-like from selected animals in order to produce superior Long-horned cattle, Leicester sheep, and other animal breeds he was interested in. Like the Arab tribesmen, he kept careful records and sought to produce quality and performance rather than numbers and size alone. He inbred closely, best-to-best, to achieve the ideal of his breeding programme. He also lent out well-bred sires to others to prove his animals' worth as breeders. The excellent results of these breeding experiments were probably the key factor to his success. It must be remembered that he followed his radical breeding programme against a background in which the general population would strongly disapprove of such close matings. One can imagine the talk and the mutterings about the goings-on at the Disley Grange estate, only at length to be followed by strong admiration for the improved stock and emulation of Bakewell's methods.

5

We must bear in mind that only 75 years before Bakewell's birth, the greater part of Britain was still cultivated on the open system. Although the enclosure of the land began about 1450, it progressed at different rates in different parts of the country, either by Act of Parliament or by local agreement. Bakewell's breeding programme would not have been possible before enclosure, because only through enclosure could he control the sires to be used on his females. With an open grazing system, which provided that all villagers had a right to graze their animals on land owned in common, one can easily picture a variety of cattle grazing together, the males of any type mating with any female in season. Before enclosure, stock breeding appears to have been the haphazard union of "anybody's son with everybody's daughter".

Because enclosure made it possible, Robert Bakewell was able to breed systematically for traits he admired, and stock improvement advanced. He was able to concentrate in a single subgroup of animals the characteristics or qualities he admired which were already present in the available stock but which were dispersed over a great many individuals.

As Bakewell's efforts demonstrate, all improvement in livestock arises because the breeder has a particular preconceived object in mind, whether it be high performance in milk or beef production, or, in the case of a racehorse, speed or stamina or both.

The success of the Collings brothers, whose effective application of Bakewell's methods to the breeding of Shorthorn cattle eventually drove the Longhorns, improved and unimproved, from their established grazings in England, demonstrates another crucial point. In beating their master Bakewell at his own game, using a systematic approach to breeding, the Collings brothers had the advantage over Bakewell of having a better gene pool to select from in the first instance, and an improved environment, in the form of better grazings, in the second instance. This grazing improvement too was made possible by enclosure.

In all forms of animal breeding, it would seem, success depends on the gene pool on which your foundation is laid and the environment in which your stock is maintained.

Many informal records suggest that improvement in the Border Terrier followed the same lines as those influencing other livestock.

Joe Bowman, Huntsman to Ullswater Hounds, about 1870. From Foxhunting in the Lakeland Fells.

Breeders having a mixed type would select for breeding those animals showing the traits best suited to their needs. Initially, this choice would probably be based on the dog's ability to defend itself. (Borders would also be selected for their colour.) Some breeders in a given area would use other breeds for work, and some would favour the Border. Concentration and refinement of type would follow this choice. It is related by the older breeders, for instance, that the late Mr. John Carruthers of Barrow Mill (the late Adam Forster's father-in-law), who was associated with Borders from his childhood over a period of 60 years during the initial stages of establishing the breed, would never cross his Borders but kept within his own kennel. This individual application of the concept of enclosure would fix a terrier type, or concentration of preferred traits.

Enclosure, that great revolution in British agriculture, made possible rotational systems of crop production; this in turn stabilized farming and animal keeping. Further developments in its wake much speeded up all domestic breed development. The introduction of the turnip crop, for instance, increased the farmer's ability to carry stock over the winter, leading to a more prosperous rural economy. In the early part of the 19th century better transport facilities increased contact between communities, and that increased breeders' opportunities for discussion. Newspapers grew common, and that too increased the interchange of ideas; local agricultural shows were formed and grew gradually to much larger shows which stimulated ideas and interest in livestock improvement. The broader agricultural community which was being generated, moreover, contained a mixture of occupations. It was a real capitalist world, whose members were free to express in their own way those things they wished to do. Landowners, joiners, blacksmiths and tenant farmers shared a common interest in the rural life and its pursuits. Their discussions would no doubt range from the lord of the manor's racehorse down to the local blacksmith's dog. There is little doubt that, in the great era of stock improvement in Britain the dogs of the community, a mixed bag of all sorts and sizes, would like other domestic animals come in for close scrutiny and interested examination with improvements in mind.

I would like to conclude these general remarks by noting that those committed to the improvement of cattle and other farm livestock have an important advantage in speeding the improvement of their animals over those of us interested in the breeding of dogs. In livestock breeding in general, the success or failure of the breeder is demonstrated not only by success in the show ring but more basically by events in the open sale ring, where other breeders bid for a particular breeder's surplus animals. A potential dairy industry customer, for instance, guided by official (and therefore consistent and accurate) milk records of the animals for sale or their near relatives, bids for that animal what he feels it is worth to him. A beef industry customer, guided by an official record of live weight gain, does likewise. The reputation and success of the cattle breeder and his herd thus depends on the accumulated opinion of the other breeders, expressed in how much they are willing to pay for his animals. If other breeders show a keen interest in his stock and it makes a high average, the cattle breeder can infer that he is achieving herd improvements, in the eyes of others interested in the same goal. If on the other hand his stock makes a low average in open sales, the breeder recognizes that there is something wrong.

In the breeding of dogs there are no broad-based and responsive indications of achievement as reliable as the open sale ring in cattle breeding. Progress in stock improvement is indicated formally only by the award of prizes or Challenge Certificates by an individual judge. All breeders will confirm that there have been good and bad champions, made up by good and bad judges. In the breeding of dogs, unfortunately, outward success may be importantly influenced by Lady Luck.

Border Terrier origins and development

The tracing of the origin of the Border Terrier is fraught with difficulty. To trace the history of income-generating or food-source farm breeds is a much easier task, because all manner of official records exist pertaining to farm and farm stock, many of which were in the hands of members of the same family for many generations indeed. Furthermore, the custom of keeping farm stock records was established much earlier than keeping breeding records of dogs, because it was clear to the farmer much earlier that a herd book is an economic necessity. So is a council of the breed association, made up of breeders who have the interest of the particular breed at heart. The local breeders, through committees, express their views to the breed council, who decide matters at issue, promulgate information, and make a record of their activities. In this way, the breed progresses (or falls by the wayside, if for some reason it is uneconomic as a breed). On the other hand, those who are interested in the breeding of dogs are entirely in the hands of the Kennel Club, whose decisions they are not organized to influence. Only the Kennel Club has the power to declare a breed eligible for registration by the Kennel Club, for instance. Initially only breeds quite heavily established were registered. Breeds not officially recognized as a breed are included under the category, "Any Other Variety"; that is, they are not classified. For such breeds, record keeping beyond a minimal level is left to the individuals interested to keep in any way they choose. Thus, for a less well-known breed like the Border Terrier, whose breeders did not seek Kennel Club recognition as a breed until 1920 and whose first championship show was held at Carlisle on September 30, 1920, we must seek out the evidence available in letters, in memory, in pictures, and in private records.

In presenting the breed's history, then, I do so in the knowledge that much of that history has been lost in the dim and distant past, or has become distorted over time. Some of the old breeders laid claim to the fact that the Border was one of the oldest indigenous breeds in Britain, for instance. Some even claimed that their families had the breed for some 400 years. However, from the short account given earlier of what the state of livestock breeding was before enclosure took strong hold in Britain in the 18th and early 19th centuries, I do not think breeding dogs would be any more systematic in character than was the breeding of cattle. Surely there would be all sorts and sizes of dogs, and the local blacksmith, the joiner, and the farmer would have their own ideas as to their particular ideal type of terrier or gundog.

Written histories of British dogs are not specific enough to shed much light on particular breed development. One of the earliest writers about English dogs was a Dr. Caius, a professor at Cambridge, who in 1530 published, in Latin, a general description of domestic dogs (*Englishe Dogges*). In 1667 one Gervais Markham touched on terriers, mentioning two small dogs that go to ground after game. Markham does not describe them in detail. Neither does his contemporary, Nicholas Cox, who describes the work of the terriers, without giving any description of their appearance. In 1760, Daniel, in *Field of Sports,* makes a slight advance when he differentiates between the rough coated terrier and the smooth and also deals with colour.

Despite these obscurities in formal written record, however, there is a good deal of other evidence that in the area of the Border's origin there were numerous specific breeds of terriers who have taken their names from villages in the Border country. The Bedlington, for instance, was formerly known as the Rothbury Terrier, and was also called at times the Northern Counties Terrier. (Rothbury is the largest town in the Coquetdale area, and Borders as well as Bedlington Terriers have been associated with that place.) I have heard the older breeders say that in the early years of this century the Border was called the Coquetdale Terrier, after the valley in the Rothbury area.

There were those who claimed that the Border was closely related to the Redesdale Terrier—in fact, so much related that they were one and the same. There could well be some justification for their opinion, as it is but walking distance between the Rede and the Coquetdale rivers.

Another claim is to association with the Ullswater and Ellterwater Terriers. These take their names from the Lake District, where such terriers were raised. There is some evidence for the claim that the Borders and these two breeds are one and the same, or at least that the Border comes from them. We know that a Mr. Joe Bowman, who was huntsman to one of the Hunts in the Lake District, had two dogs of the Ullswater breed, named Ullswater Jack and Ullswater Nellie, who were the sire and dam of a bitch called Wasp. Wasp was the dam of a dog called Geof (sired by a dog called Flint). Geof sired a dog called Gyp, whose name occurs in many of the older Border pedigrees. He was later registered as North Tyne Gyp. Gyp's dam was a bitch called Wannie of Tynedale.

North Tyne Gyp was a much admired dog in the 1920's, as reported by breed columnist F. W. Morris. It appears that he was in considerable demand at stud, as many of the Borders at that time are descended from him. (It should of course be remembered that in part his popularity might arise because there would not be many dogs of the type the Border breeders wanted.)

While in many cases we are able to establish the lines of descent, in some we are not so fortunate. For instance, for the important bitch Gowanburn Bess (unr), bred by Willie Barton, the sire is unknown but the dam is his old bitch Bess 1 (1900). It's a case of "anybody's son with everybody's daughter".

Sir Walter Scott, who was the Sheriff of Selkirkshire as well as a world famous author, was familiar with the Border country. In *Guy Mannering* (1814) he introduces the reader to a Border farmer whom he calls Mr. Dinmont. In his notes to the novel, Scott explains that "Dandie" Dinmont could be any of the number of stout Liddesdale farmers whose hospitality he enjoyed while in that district. ["Dinmont", it may be of interest to note, is a Border term for a male sheep between his first and second shearing. Two shears means clipped twice and is roughly equal to two years of age. The connection of the term to the dog called the Dandie Dinmont is probably to the Dandie's topknot, which is in length similar to the coat length of a dinmont.]

Scott specifically mentions in his notes a Mr. Davidson, who farmed Hindlee, a wild farm on the very edge of the Teviotdale mountains in the parish of Southdean, Roxburghshire, bordering close on Liddesdale. Those who knew Davidson, who died in 1820, assumed he was the person in the tale, because Davidson had a breed of terriers which he had the humour to name by the generic name of Mustard and Pepper, depending on their colour. As Mr. Dinmont explains it to Mr. Brown in *Guy Mannering*, "There's auld Pepper and auld Mustard and young Pepper and young Mustard and little Pepper and little Mustard. I had them a' regularly entered, first wi' rottens—then wi' stots or weasels—and then wi' tods and brocks— and now they fear naething that ever cam wi' a hairy skin on't." The association of Davidson with Scott's Dandie Dinmont gave Davidson's breed its name. It is unfortunate that Scott did not give us a description of these terriers.

In another note to *Guy Mannering* Scott describes the isolated Liddesdale area at that time. Roads were non-existent and the district was accessible only through a succession of tremendous morasses. Scott states that 30 years earlier (i.e., 30 years before the 1814 publication of *Guy Mannering*) he was "the first person who ever drove a small carriage in these wilds. The people stared in no small wonder at the sight, which many of them had never witnessed in their lives before."

The Dandie Dinmont breed was identified with Davidson on the publication of *Guy Mannering*, but it is clear that Davidson was not the first to have these terriers; records suggest that the gypsies of that area were known to have them. Among the gypsy tribes or families who bred terriers at that time were the Allans, the Andersons, the Camells, and the Faas. The Allans of Holystone on the Coquet Water, near Rothbury, were regarded at that time as having the purest strain. Since Allan was a piper, the animals were first known as Piper Allan's strain. (Piper Allan, who died in 1779, is buried in Rothbury churchyard.) While this purity of strain might have arisen as a result of selection for type, it seems more probable that it came about because the wild and rocky terrain made travel difficult and would have led Allan to use as a sire the nearby dog who was closest in traits to his needs.

An early letter suggests that the custom was to choose the animal for courage and work ability rather than type. This letter, published in *The Field* in 1878, also suggests that the type of terrier identified in *Guy Mannering* with "Dandie" Dinmont did not closely resemble the modern breed of that name and was not confined to any one person but in fact was owned by the greater number of the "muggers" or gypsies frequenting the Border area. The letter (published with permission by *The Field*) follows:

Sir,

I, as rather more than a sexagenarian and a Border man, and one who almost in his childhood took up with Dandies, can, I think, throw some light on the origin of the Dandies possessed by Mr. Davidson. The Border "muggers' were great breeders of Terriers—Andersons on the English side and the Faas and Camells on the Scotch side. In their perambulations they generally met once or twice a year at Long Horsley, Rochester (the ancient Bremenmnium of the Romans), Alwinton, or some other Border village. If they could not get a badger, they got a foumart, wild cat, or hedgehog at which to try their dogs.

The trials generally ended in a general dog fight, which led to a battle royal amongst the tribes represented. This afterwards led to a big drink and an exchange of dogs.

Jock Anderson, the head of the tribe, once had a red bitch, who for badger drawing, cat, foumart, or hedgehog killing, beat all dogs coming over the Border. Geordy Faa, of Yetholm, had a wire haired dog terrier, the terror not only of all the other terriers in the district, but good at badger, fox, or foumart. They met at Alwinton, where Willy and Adam Bell (noted terrier breeders) had brought a badger they had got hold of at Weaford, near the Cheviots. Both the red bitch and the black terrier drew the badger every time they were put in.

"Jock Anderson," says Geordy, "the dogs should be mated; let's have a grand drink, the man first doon to lose his dog."

"Done," says Jock.

They sent for the whisky, which never paid the king's duty, to Neviston's, at the little house, having agreed to pay two shillings a quart for it. Down they sat on the green, fair drinking. In eighteen hours Jock tumbled off the cart-shafts, and Geordy started off with the dogs. They were mated and produced first peppers and mustards, which were presented by Geordy to Mr. Davidson (Dandie Dinmont of *Guy Mannering*). Strange to say the produce were equally the colour of pepper and mustard. The last pair I saw of what I consider perfect Dandies were Robert Donkin's at Ingram, near Alnwick, just before I left the North in 1838.

I have been at shows, but could never identify any Dandies shown as at all like the original breed belonging to the Telfords of Blindburn, the Elliots of Cottonshope, the Donkins of Ingram, and other Border farmers. I am not a doggy man, but like to see all old breeds kept distinct.

J. Davidson, Andover, Dec. 2, 1878

Other details suggestive of Border Terriers appear in the records. For instance, at the time Mr. Davidson entered into the lease of the farm of Hindlee, there was another farmer who was interested in terriers, a Mr. Stephenson of Plenderleigh Farm who, it appears, obtained a small terrier from someone at Rothbury. His Rothbury dogs were described as dark and roughcoated and small. Other figures are mentioned who were closely connected with Davidson of Hindlee and his terriers. One was gamekeeper Ned Dunn of Whitelee, Carter Bar (at the top of Redesdale Valley) only about two and a

The Dandie Dinmont "Doctor" with Dr. Hemming's Bedlington Terrier "Geordie".

half miles north of the farm of Byrness, for many years the home of Jacob Robson, of Border Terrier fame, master of the Border Hunt.

C. M. Ferguson's *Border Sport and Sportsmen* (Hexham: Catherall and Co., 1932) contains an interesting piece of information. In 1875, on February 3rd, the Border Hounds were hunting the farm of Hindhope. Ferguson quotes Robson as follows:

> The famous terrier Flint, weighing 12 pounds, could bolt foxes out of holes which had hitherto been considered impossible places. (My brother once saw him put three foxes out of the Little Dome.) [Flint] is often mentioned in my brother's diary.

Left: John Jardine of Dandie Dinmont fame with one of the Terriers.
Right: Miss M. Edgar with her Border.

He is without doubt the best terrier ever seen in the Borders since the days of Robbie Potts' "Flint", by one of Ned Dunn's dogs. He [Ned Dunn] was contemporary with Dandie Dinmont. Robbie Potts was an old and popular shepherd at Kielder, and one of the keenest hunters I ever saw. Nailer, bred at Catcleugh, was another splendid terrier but had not the constant hard work "Flint" had. The latter once bolted four foxes out of Parlour, one of the strongest holds at that foxy place Cottonshope Doure.

The possibly very close link between Border Terriers and the old Dandie Dinmont may be reflected in the fact that a dog called Flint was sired by a dog belonging to Ned Dunn. Dunn was associated with the foundation of the Dandie Dinmont Terriers, and his dog was working with the Robson's Border Hunt.

The Border Foxhounds at that time had been in existence for 120 years, having been originally started by the brothers Robson, at the farm of Kielder, in North Tyne. From the records there were hounds hunting in the Kielder district in the early days of the 19th century. The Border Hunt was founded in 1857, when Mr. John Robson came from Kielder to Byrness, bringing his hounds with him. There he joined forces with Mr. John Dodd of Catcleugh, whose pack of hounds hunted the hill foxes up and around the Carter Fell. In 1869 Mr. John Robson Jr. of Newton Farm took over the horn until 10 years later, when Mr. Jacob Robson assumed the office and held the mastership for 54 years. In this long period he had Mr. John Dodd as joint master from 1879–1887. Mr. Dodd went to Riccarton at that time to take over the Liddesdale Hounds. Dodd was married to Mr. Robson's sister, so there was a bond between the two families. Their names constantly crop up in the hunting history of that area. In over one hundred years, no one other than a Robson or a Dodd held the mastership of the Border Hunt.

Because of the close association of the Robson family with the Border Terrier breed, quite a number of the older breeders felt that the animals should have been called Robson Terriers.

The writer of the 1878 letter to *The Field* mentions the name of a terrier breeder called "the Donkins of Ingram". Ingram also was probably a focal place for Borders. In the diaries of Jacob Robson, for instance, we note the following description of a hunt in 1883:

> The fox went to ground at Carry Burn on Kielder. We put the terriers Flint and Jack in, but the fox not bolting and darkness [setting in], we had to make the best of our way down Scalp Burn to Kielder [i.e., Kielder village]. Going out next morning with a spade we got the fox and Flint out dead and Jack alive. Flint was a very bonny Border Terrier and belonged to David Hall of Ingram.

Ferguson, the author of *Border Sport and Sportsmen,* in giving an account of his first visit to this area about ten years after the death of Flint (1885) refers in his account to the Border Terrier *as a breed:*

An essential asset to this pack [was] the terriers. In a wild country like this, full of peat holes, rocky strongholds and unstoppable earths, the terrier plays a very important part. At the kennels and in fact at nearly every shepherd's house there is a terrier which will go to ground and face anything. These are of all sorts and conditions but the breed most in vogue is naturally the Border Terrier. (He has only been so called for the last thirty years.) At Hindhope, Kielder and Catcleugh, and Byrness they have always had real working terriers worthy of the name.

Ferguson goes on to suggest that the Border was an original cross between the old fashioned Dandie and the Bedlington. The prevailing colour is mustard, he notes, but blue often crops up, showing the strong blood of the old Bedlington. Ferguson reports further that being small they can creep in anywhere and are game to the last. He adds:

Mr. Robson likes them just a bit on the leg so they can keep up with the pack, and with not too punishing a jaw, as he has had so many mutilated or killed. The late Mr. Tom Robson, his brother and M.F.H. to the North Tyne Foxhounds, really evolved and improved the type of this now famous breed of terrier. The breed has become very fashionable of late years, and it is to be hoped the show bench will not destroy the qualities for which it was produced and develop it into a ladies' lap dog, as the show bench has a subtle way of doing. Border folks have no use for lap dogs or any which cannot do the job expected of them.

The word breed used by Ferguson and others in referring to the Border Terrier of this period must have had some foundation. The term, particularly when used by huntsmen, farmers, and stock breeders, would hardly be used in an indiscriminate way. If dogs of two different breeds were mated, the progeny would be referred to as crossbred. Before the word breed was used, the animals referred to would have to breed true to the type they represent. This would seem to be true of the Border Terrier extant in the 1880's and probably considerably earlier.

At some stage in a breed's development a group of breeders, selecting for the particular characteristics desired in their terriers, would probably look around for an animal expressing a characteristic desired but not present in the original group. We know that at some point in the history of the Border Terrier breed a white terrier, or a terrier carrying a factor for white, was introduced, no doubt for a characteristic other than his colour. It is well known that in some strains there were numerous puppies born with white feet and white chests. This was in evidence even at as late a date as our own introduction to the breed. It was one of the factors that the older breeders selected against.

The reader might question what evidence we have that this introduction of a white terrier or one carrying a factor for white actually happened. One evidence is inheritance patterns. If for some reason something distinctive turns up regularly in livestock breeding, it is usually accepted as a genetic factor. The white on the feet of pups, the splashes of white that regularly appeared on the chests, thus can most likely be traced to an early ancestor.

Another support for this view is that at the time the Kennel Club recognized the breed, the then secretary of the Border Terrier Club, Mr. Hamilton Adams, sent a letter to the Earl of Lonsdale, one of the great sportsmen of his time, who was among those who had taken an interest in the founding of the breed club. The Earl replied to Mr. Hamilton Adams as follows:

> Thank you very much for your little booklet re the Border Terrier. I note in the first page under the description of "colour" that you restrict the colour to "red, wheaten, grizzle, or blue and tan".
>
> I do not know if you are aware that we had these terriers at Lowther since 1732 and have a continuance of pedigree from the date and that we have a continuance of them white. I have often wondered whether the rough haired terrier was not originated from this breed. There is a picture here (Barley Thorpe) of two of these terriers with the Cottesmore Hounds on their way down to Lowther in 1693; they were blue. I have this year two white puppies as beautiful rough haired terriers as ever you saw that are direct descendants of these very two animals. I have owned them now for fifty years and the whole of the

1870's Ullswater Terriers Jimmy (top), Pincher and Myrtle (bottom).

These terriers were by Joe Bowman, huntsman to the Ullswater hounds around 1870. Bowman's terriers Ullswater Jack and Ullswater Nellie were the sire and dam of Ullswater Wasp (unr.), dam of Geof. Geof, mated to Wannie of Tynedale, gave the Border Terrier breed the much-used sire North Tyne Gyp, born 1917. North Tyne Gyp sired many dark-coloured dogs. Photo from Fox hunting in the Lakeland Fells *by R. C. Chapman. (Longmans, Green & Co.)*

predecessors of the two white ones were blue, very light tan or dark brindled. There is no earthly chance of any accident having arisen over the birth of them or the parentage because they are in the kennels and enclosed park and the time and the mating and everything are kept in detail. My reason for drawing your attention to the fact is that it is apt to occur, and has occurred to me several times, and some of my best terriers were white. I send this for your information as I do not register my terriers. I record them in books like Hounds. We have always called these terriers Ullswater terriers and there is a place at Whale Moor, which is in Lowther Park, where there were at one time elaborate kennels for breeding them and where the Cottesmore Hounds used to go for summer. These terriers have been bred most persistently so I am sure there is no mistake about them. However, I only send this for what it is worth and it may be of interest to you.

The Earl of Lonsdale mentions in his letter a picture in his family's possession of two of these terriers. In discussion with the older breeders about the origin of the breed, mention was made of a painting by an animal artist, Abram Cooper, done in the 19th century. The picture depicts the breed of terrier used by the Cottesmore Hunt. All who have seen it do not agree that the dogs in it resemble the Border Terrier.

The earliest painting I have seen which in my view resembles a Border is one in the book *The Thistle and the Jade,* published in London in 1982 by Octopus Books to celebrate 150 years' existence of the famous trading firm of Jardine, Matheson and Company, based in London and Hong Kong. On page 13 of the book is a painting by the British artist Chinnery of William Jardine, the founder of the company. At the subject's feet lies a small terrier. This in my opinion could not be mistaken for any breed other than a Border Terrier. The painting was done in 1820. Jardine was born on a small farm near Lochmaben in Dumfriesshire, Scotland, and was known to be associated with hunting. The fact that the artist lived for many years in the Orient and was not likely to have seen Borders there leads to the view that Jardine had at least one Border with him in the Far East, perhaps one sent out to him, for he left Scotland for the Orient in 1802. This picture, at least to me, is evidence that the Border Terrier as a breed was in existence by 1820.

21

As far as I am able to ascertain, however, the first Border Terrier was registered at the Kennel Club only in 1913, in the Any Other Variety (unclassified) section. The dog was owned by a Miss M. Rew and was called (The) Moss Trooper, by Sly (unr) *ex* Mr. J. Robson's Chip, b. 2/2/12.

Though Borders do not appear on the Kennel Club register until 1913, records indicate that they were shown at some of the agricultural shows held in the Border country at a much earlier date. Classes for the breed were held at the Langholm Show as early as 1900 and, from evidence, probably earlier. The catalogues earlier than 1900 appear to be lost; however, Mr. John Paterson, whose family have farmed Terrona Farm for three generations, was able to show me farm records of the stock exhibited from the early days of the Langholm Agricultural Society. There were several Border breeders in that area around the turn of the century, one of whom was his father, Mr. J. J. Paterson, whom I met in 1946 when I was in that area. The elder Paterson had Borders in 1900, as did Miss May Paterson, also of Terrona Farm, and a Mr. W. E. Annandale, of Hopsrig Farm near Langholm, who was, I believe, married to a sister of Mr. Paterson. The Dodd family, who were at Riccarton, just over the hill from Langholm, had Borders by 1892, as did Mr. W. Bell, also of Langholm, and a Mr. W. Irving, Whitshields, near Langholm. (Although there may be a family connection, this Mr. Irving should not be confused with Wattie Irving of more recent date.) It seems very likely that the Border Terrier was exhibited at the Langholm Show, therefore, previous to 1900, especially since the Langholm Agricultural Society has traditionally catered for the breed.

The Ayrshire Agricultural Society catered for dogs at an early date after its formation; there were classes for gundogs and "Skye Terriers". All other terrier breeds were classified as Rough Haired terriers or Smooth Haired terriers.

Another evidence for the establishment·of the breed long before Kennel Club registration lies in the history of the Border Hunt. Here the name of a Mr. Hedley appears. He would seem to be the same Mr. Hedley who exhibited the first Border Terrier that I can trace, named Bacchusin, who was shown at an agricultural show in 1870. (Agricultural livestock shows were established about 1833, so it is natural that those interested in dogs would in time have dog shows in conjunction with the local agricultural show.)

As Border Terrier breeders interested in breed history we are indebted to Mr. F. W. Morris, of Bardon Mill on Tyne, for his report in *Our Dogs* of one of the first Championship shows, held at Carlisle on September 30, 1920. His account of that show also includes the names of the founders of the Border Terrier Club and the breed standard they drew up. I reprint it in its entirety, with the kind permission of the editors of *Our Dogs:*

The awards of the Border Terrier classes at the Carlisle show will doubtless give many of us food for thought but first let me congratulate Mr. W. Barton on his great success. This old and tried breeder won the bitch championship with Liddesdale Bess, 3rd with Red Gauntlet, and he also bred Miss Bell Irving's Tinker, the winner of the dog championship.

Now let us look at the decisions and at the same time bear in mind that Mr. S. Dodd also officiated as judge at Bellingham on the Saturday, where he placed Mr. A. Forster's dog Dan first. At Carlisle Dan notched two firsts and two seconds, and in the open class did not "touch". Now I wish fanciers to compare his type with Mr. J. Dodd's North Tyne Gyp, a beautiful type of Border Terrier, and Mr. Hamilton Adams' Ivo Roisterer, and The Wooler Sensation, a dog we all admired at Hexham. At Carlisle I. Roisterer was awarded two seconds and two reserves; Mr. T. Lawrence's Teri, the Hexham and Langholm cup winner, had two 3rds to his credit at Carlisle. When fanciers get the chance to see these dogs all together, let them compare them and then I should like to hear which type they prefer.

Mr. T. Lawrence is the judge elect for the Borders at the forthcoming Kennel Club Show. Mr. T. Lawrence is quite a new hand in the show bench world, for it seems only the other day he wrote to me to say he had found a dog paper called *Our Dogs*. Mr. T. Lawrence is keen and enthusiastic and his decisions will be awaited with much interest. For the first time Border Terriers will be classified at the Newcastle New Year Show, where with Bedlington Terriers they will certainly be a great attraction.

Signed F. W. M.

We have been favoured by the Hon. Secretary of the Border

Terrier Club Mr. Hamilton Adams with a list of officials and the Standard of points adopted by the club. They are as follows.

Vice Presidents: The Duke of Beaufort, M.F.H.; the Lord Charles Bentick, M.F.H.; the Lord Chesham, M.F.H.; the Duke of Northumberland; the Lord Poltimore, M.F.H.; the Lord Southhampton, M.F.H.; the Lord Tredegar, M.F.H.

Committee: Messrs W. Barton, W. Bell, J. Carruthers, Jasper Dodd, H. T. Elliot, J. R. Haddon, T. Hamilton Adams, T. Lawrence (Moorhouse), T. Lawrence (Scawmill), J. Howit, G. Sordy, and J. M. Strother.

Hon. Secretary and Treasurer Mr. T. Hamilton Adams; Hon. Assistant Secretary Mr. J. M. Strother (Wooler).

Standard of points: The Border Terrier is essentially a working terrier, being of necessity able to follow a horse, and to combine activity with gameness.

N.B. The points following are placed in order of their importance.

Size: Dogs should be between 14 and 17 lbs weight and 13″ to 16″ at the shoulder. Bitches should not exceed 15 lbs in weight and 15″ in height at the shoulder.

Head: Like that of an otter, moderately broad skull with short strong muzzle, level teeth, black nose preferred, but liver and flesh coloured not to disqualify.

Eyes: Dark, with keen expression.

Ears: Small V drop.

Body: Deep, narrow, fairly long, ribs carried well back, but not oversprung as a terrier should be capable of being spanned behind the shoulder.

Forelegs: Straight, not too heavy in bone.

Feet: Small and catlike.

Stern: Undocked, thick at the base, then tapering. Set high, carried gaily but not curled over the back.

Hind Quarters: Racing

Coat: Harsh and dense, with close undercoat.

Colour: Red and Wheaten, Grizzle, or Blue and
Tan.
Disqualification: Mouth undershot or overshot.

Because my own Borders are in some lines descended from his
strain, it is a pleasure to me to see the name of Mr. J. Carruthers as one
of the founding members of the Border Terrier Club. The late Adam
Forster, on the many occasions when I discussed the breeding of the
early Borders with him, often mentioned the dog Barrow Jack, bred
by his father-in-law Mr. Carruthers. The dog was born 10/3/13, sired
by Mack (unr) *ex* Nettle (unr). Barrow Jack, mated to a bitch called
Nailer II (unr) produced Adam's bitch Coquetdale Vic, b. 27/2/16. It
was on this line of breeding that he founded his kennel. From
Coquetdale Vic in female line came Little Midget, b. 2/8/22. Midget
was the dam of Revenge. This line of breeding, along with that of
Rival, has had a big influence in the establishment of the breed.

At this stage of our tracing we have reached the point where someone registered the breed with the Governing Body, although the
Kennel Club did not cater at this time for the Border Terrier breed as
a breed. It can be taken for granted that someone was interested
enough at this time to register a dog of a particular breed, then there
were among the owners of that breed a considerable number of
people aiming in their breeding programmes for a strain of dog that
was their ideal within that breed, as Mr. F. W. Morris's remarks about
the Carlisle show of 30/9/1920 also attest. This activity would be
taking place in other breeds as well.

It seems clear from the evidence that the improvement of dogs
came fairly late in the movement in Britain systematically to improve
farm livestock. Robert Bakewell's efforts in 1760 and the Collings
brothers following work preceded by half a century the publication
of Sir Walter Scott's *Guy Mannering,* in 1814, with its portrait of the
Dandie Dinmont, an at that time little-known breed. The first Kennel
Club recognition of the Dandie Dinmont as a breed followed Scott's
recognition of its existence by some 66 years, for the Kennel Club
itself was not organized until 1873. The Dandie appears in Volume 1
of the Kennel Club registration list, issued in 1880. Recognition in
such a formal record followed, then, many years after the facts of
breed existence.

For Border Terrier fanciers, the distance between the time of formal recognition of the breed and the breed's establishment is even longer than the Dandie Dinmont's. The recognition of the breed at agricultural society shows is perhaps more closely reflective of their length of existence as a breed. It is only natural that in an area where you have members of the community interested in hunting who have a breed of dog called Border Terriers that those breeders would sponsor classes for their breed at the local show. Because of the number of Border Terrier breeders in the area, the Bellingham Agricultural Show became the mecca for the Border Terrier breed. Through the influence of Mr. Tom Robson, the breed was scheduled at that show in 1881.

These early exhibitions of Borders would be, for the modern exhibitor, an extraordinary sight. In those days, the Kennel Club was not involved in show organization, so the exhibitors did not have to pay a large entry fee to cover the costs of modern benching, tenting, and other expensive requirements. The dogs were simply tied to a post or fencing stob. One of the unfortunate economies of that time, however, was that the pedigree of the dog was not recorded, so this source of information is not available to the researcher in the breed.

After World War II, the Bellingham show developed into a large agricultural show catering for a number of breeds of dogs. In the eyes of the older breeders Bellingham (not Crufts) remained THE show for Borders, and winning at Bellingham was the end-all of their aims in the breed. For some reason Bellingham Show lost its popularity in the dog world, and for a number of years there was no dog section. Some enthusiasts have endeavoured to revive it, but as far as Borders are concerned, it is not the show it was in the days of Carruthers, Forster, Renton, Barton, and Irving.

Borders in those earlier days were somewhat different from the current show version. The earlier Border, who was bred for work rather than exhibition, was certainly smaller then many Borders we see winning today, who can reach 16–18″ at the withers and weigh 20–24 pounds. Ivo Roisterer, for instance, Mr. T. Hamilton Adams' famous Border, is recorded to have weighed $14\frac{1}{2}$ pounds and to stand $12\frac{1}{2}″$ at the withers. Jacob Robson's Flint weighed 12 pounds.

In reconsidering this history of the Border Terrier, I realize how true it is that there are lots of things we do not know. But there are

Jacob Robson, Esq, M.F.H., The Border Hunt. One of the founder Breeders of the Border Terrier. From Border Sports and Sportsmen, *C.M. Ferguson (1932).*

Three all-time Border Terrier Breed stalwarts and Breed Club officers.
 Shown at the 1983 Newcastleton (Liddesdale) show, Left to Right, the late
J. Renton, with his dog Ch Happy Day, who went Best of Breed that day; the
late Adam Forster, who judged the show (it was the last show he judged); and
Wattie Irving.

also an astonishing number of things we do know, from both formal
and informal sources. For instance, Mr. Montagu Horn, in his book
The Border Terrier (published by Catherall and Co., 1943 and repro-
duced here at Appendix I, page 207) gives us an interesting piece of
information about Border Terrier names. He mentions that one hunt
in the district could have a dog called, say, Ginger. This dog could
pass to another hunt and be renamed Jock. To quote an instance of
some interest, a dog purchased by Mr. J. Carruthers was called Rock.
Mr. Carruthers renamed him Mick, and exhibited him at a small
show in the North. The dog passed to the then Secretary of the
Border Terrier Club, Mr. T. Hamilton Adams, who showed the animal at the Carlisle show and eventually made him up as the well
known champion Ivo Roisterer. Border Terriers exist today whose
ancestry includes this dog under either of these two last-mentioned
names.

2

Memories of some earlier Border Terrier breeders and their dogs

James Garrow, F.Z.S.

Jimmy Garrow's name is not likely to ring any bells with the younger generation of Border Terrier breeders, but older breeders will probably remember him, and some may even have exhibited under him. In my view no book on the breed would be complete without a note on "the Grand Old Man of dogs", as he was known when I started to exhibit Borders. I had met him much earlier as a schoolboy, when I was exhibiting rabbits. In those early days Jimmy was often seen judging some form of livestock.

There are no characters like Jimmy Garrow in dogs today and none who have his all-round knowledge of domestic animal breeds. He was the true all-rounder. Border Terriers were his favourite breed of dogs and no one knew the Border better than he. He spoke in a broad Scottish accent and had the voice of a trained actor. (He was, at one time, associated with that profession; he was also a playwright, journalist, schoolmaster and a contributor to the "Caledonian Chat" column in *Our Dogs* for many years. He was in addition a well known orator and speaker, much in demand in that field at functions connected to livestock.) If he met me at a show he would say "Aye, maun, did ye dae weil the day?" If I had not got a ticket, he would add, "Aye, it hasna been your day." He often noted that "the heid o' the Border has all the all-rounders beaten."

He would often speak of Tommy Lawrence's dog, Ch. Teri. With a twinkle in his eye, he would remind me that it was the Ayr Agricultural show that first catered for Borders after the Kennel Club recognised them as a breed. "Aye, and dina forget that I handled Ch. Teri to win his 2nd C. C. under Baines."

On occasions he would mention Newminster, Sir John Renwick's prefix, and remind me that he had recommended to Sir John that he buy Ch. Grakle.

Jimmy wore a large broad brimmed soft hat with his long hair curl-

"The Grand Old Man of Dogs" Jimmy Garrow.

An early photograph of
Mr J. CARRUTHERS WITH TWO OF HIS SONS

Mr J. Carruthers of (Dodd & Carruthers) with his two sons. The youngest of the family is next to him, Mr Jeff Carruthers of Leahall Farm, Northumberland, who at the time the photograph was taken, 1912, was three years old. The bitch in front of him is NELLIE, b. 1/5/1908. Bred by Nr. N. Crozier, S. Flint (unr, unt) ex Wasp (unr). Jeff Carruthers remembers her well as she used to follow him round the farm, and when she went away hunting he was sent to look for her.

The other bitch is NETTLE, Br. W. Barton, b. 23/11/1909 by Wasp (unr, unt) ex Birkie, Nettle was the dam of Wannie of Tynedale. In the early days of the breed one could have a dog or bitch called Wasp.

Nettle was also the dam of Barrow Jock (unr) who was born March 10th 1913 by S. Mack (unr unt).

Barrow Jock was a dog much used by A. Forster and his father-in-law Mr. J. Carruthers, of Barrow Farm, Upper Coquetdale (no relation of J. Carruthers in the photograph).   (Photo courtesy Mr. J. Carruthers)

ing out from under the brim, and favoured hard shirt collars with high outspread peaks and a large cravat. He was the picture of the Shakespearean Actor.

There was only one Jimmy Garrow and there will never be another. He was probably the most popular man in British dogs. This was demonstrated in 1946 when in public testimony through the good offices of *Our Dogs* he was presented with a cheque for £1,132.

The late Walter Irving (no prefix)

I came to know Wattie through my wife Joy's mother, who knew him as a young man. Joy's father was Station Master at Maxton and Wattie came there from time to time as a relief Station Master. When Joy and I were engaged to be married, I bought Joy a Border Terrier pup by Wattie's dog Ch. Rising Light. At this time, I was transferred to Edinburgh Headquarters and as I was interested in the Border Terrier I decided to call on Wattie at Marine Cottage. We became very good friends and when I was in Edinburgh at the weekends I could always depend on receiving a very friendly welcome from him and Mrs. Irving. I enjoyed listening to both reminiscing on the breed and the older breeders. Wattie had spent the earlier part of his railway service at Riccarton Junction, which was then a railway village. The only way in and out was by train. Apart from the school master, all other dwellers there were railway employees. In such an environment, no one could have a better hobby than having a few dogs and as Riccarton was in the heart of the Liddesdale Hunt country there could be no better choice than the Border.

Wattie was associated with the breed since early 1924. He obtained a bitch from Tommy Lawrence, who was a Station Master at Hawick and then St. Boswell's. This bitch, Station Masher, Wattie made a Champion. The foundation of his kennel, she was bred by Mr. Fox (b. 11/4/24) by Oxnam Picher *ex* Jed (unr). On many occasions when I was quizzing him about the dogs of the past, Wattie would describe here as "saddleback". This marking he described as dark sides, extending over her withers and along her back like a saddle on a horse.

Miss Bell Irving had a dog, the first certificate winner in the breed, called Tinker. This dog is sometimes referred to in pedigrees as a

Champion, but as Wattie informed me, two of the three certificates he won were by the same judge. Tinker, mated to Ch. Station Masher, bred a dog called Arnton Billy. This dog Wattie regarded as "big enough" at that time. Arnton Billy, mated to a bitch bred by Willie Barton called Tiot Fancy, gave a dog registered as Ch. Heronslea, born 1930. Heronslea Wattie though a lot of; he regarded him as one of the better dogs of that era. On many occasions Wattie mentioned the bitch Ch. Joyden. This bitch he bred in 1930. She was by Whitrope Don (Red Rock *ex* Liddesdale Nettle, br W. Barton, b. March 18, 1928). In her show career Joyden won some 10 C.C.s. She won her last C.C. at the age of nine. This win gave Wattie a lot of pleasure.

It was from Wattie I learned about Willie Barton, one of the oldest breeders. It was obvious that they worked closely together in their breeding plans. On many occasions Wattie spoke about a bitch called Din Sheila who was mated to Willie Barton's Whitrope Don. Wattie bred a resulting dog called Knowe Roy to a bitch called Brandy Snap, producing a dog called Rab O'Lammermuir (bred by a Miss M. Dobie). This dog Wattie owned. Mated to a bitch called Traquair Gypsy, Rab gave the breed probably the best known Border of all time, Ch. Fox Lair, bred by Mr. A. Stevenson. Wattie considered Fox Lair to be the ideal in Border Terriers. Fox Lair, owned by Mrs. Twist, laid the foundations for the modern Border Terrier. He was born 26/5/1934. He was coming to the peak of his prime in 1939 when the war started. As Mrs. Twist lived in the centre of the bombings, he was evacuated with Ch. Aldham Joker and Ch. Wedale Jock to Miss Duthie, in Aberdeen.

Among the post war dogs Wattie had was Ch. Rising Light, with whom he won some 10 C.C.s. This dog was a great shower and would show for anyone. Wattie used to say the dog was a champion before he ever handled him. This was due to the fact he was unable to attend the shows at that time. The dog was put into a box and sent to a friend who handled him, looked after him, and returned him to Musselburgh by train with the C.C.

The railway company in those days was a different organisation from that of today. The personnel were a human set of individuals and it was remarkable the number of dog owners you met who were railway folk. That was a fortunate thing for me. On several occasions

Circa 1927 Dubh Glas (487 H.H.), one of the first registered Border Terriers. Bred by Willie Barton, b. 5 May 1923 s. Ch. Grip of Tynedale (1216 C.C.) d. Liddesdale Bess Ch. (842 A.A.) c. Red Grizzle (1 C.C.)

when Wattie and I were together we left our dogs in the care of a railway porter, signalman, or any railroad person Wattie happened to meet on the platform when we were looking for some place to leave the dogs to go for a meal. It did not matter to Wattie whether we were in London or Birmingham, there was always someone who knew him.

We had a close liaison in the showing of our dogs. He used to phone me to say he was entering for a certain show and that I should enter. Once we had arranged to go to the L.K.A. show in London, but I had to call off for some reason. Wattie said to send my bitch to him and he would look after her. He was second with this bitch, Maxton Mannequin, in the open bitch class. The judge withheld the C.C. from the bitch that beat her, but awarded the Reserve C.C. to Mannequin. He phoned me from London informing me about this decision and advised me to write to the Secretary; he felt you cannot have a reserve C.C. unless you have the C.C. awarded. He had already handed the reserve C.C. to the Secretary.

Circa 1936 Ch. Fox Lair. Bred by Mr. A. Stephenson, born May 1934, by Rab O' Lammermuir ex Traquair Gypsy.

Wattie also had Ch. Bright Light, Ch. Alexander, Ch. Rob Roy and Ch. Briery Hill Gertrude, the latter three bred by Miss Galbraith. He had another dog called Alton Lad. This dog he regarded as his Saturday afternoon dog. He was always afraid someone would give it a Certificate, thus making it ineligible to compete at the Saturday shows he so much enjoyed. He also had a greyhound which was quite useful in this way and quite capable of breaking the track record, but Wattie said you could not get a good price on it, so he wanted its record slowed. Once he filled it full of the best pies and anything it would eat and set off for the track, feeling quite confident that on this occasion it could not win. He handed the dog over to the track official and went to the stand to watch the race. His dog won and broke the track record. When he went to the kennels to collect the dog, the kennel boy handed over the dog and in doing so said to Wattie, "Boy, was that dog of yours sick just after you left me! I have never seen a dog as sick as that one ever. He brought up a basinful of food."

Wattie only said, "I wish you had come and told me."

During a railway strike once we agreed to meet at Carlisle to drive to the Leeds (benched) Championship show. After the judging it was announced that there was a train for the North leaving at two o'clock, hours earlier than one could ordinarily leave the bench unless excused formally. Wattie proceeded to obtain the passes to leave the show early because of the train schedule. However, the chap in charge of the removals asked to see the return part of our tickets. Wattie asked him if he thought we were daft. "Who would buy a return, not knowing if they could get a train?" We obtained the removals and collected the dogs without creating too much attention among the rest of the exhibitors. On reaching the car and about to put the dogs into the boxes, one got loose after a cat. There were the two of us trying to catch a dog and expecting all the time for the removal man to lay his hand on us. With all the dogs safely in the boxes, we got started. Wattie was certain we could get out of the park down a back lane. At the end of the lane in the middle of the exit was a post. Wattie was quite sure we could make it; and we barely edged our way through. Having got clear, he said, "You know, if you had painted this car last night, we would not have made it." On our way across from Scot's Corner near Brough Garage, which then was a tin shed, we had a blowout in the rear wheel. At the tin shed I purchased the only tyre available. Wattie's comment was "That's what we get for telling the removal man all the lies."

The exhibition of dogs was to Wattie a dedication; after he retired from the railway, it was his recreation and life. There was nothing allowed to interfere with this activity. The following two tales illustrate this matter.

He had arranged to attend a Championship show in the South, which meant he had to get a train at Waverley Station, some miles from Musselburgh. Sometime earlier he had been approached by someone to get a mating to one of his dogs. It happened to be the dog he had entered for the show. The owner of the bitch had arranged to be at Wattie's house in time to have the bitch mated before Wattie left for the show, but through some unforetold difficulty was delayed. He arrived with just sufficient time to have the mating completed before Wattie left for the train. At least that is what they thought but they did not consider the dog or the bitch.

The mating was successful, so much so that the dogs were tied so long Wattie thought he would miss the train. The situation would have stopped a less keen exhibitor, but not Wattie. When the taxi arrived to take him to the train, he had one of his family accompany him to the station with the tied dog and bitch. Wattie was convinced that by the time they reached the station all would be well.

It happened that this was so. It did not appear to occur to Wattie that by some coincidence of nature it might happen that he would require to take them both with him in the train.

On another occasion he and his youthful grandson set off for Hawick show in a borrowed vintage van that to say the least had seen better days. Wattie like many of his generation was more acquainted with trains than he was with cars. They proceeded fine until something started to happen. Youthful driver, who had recently passed his driving test, informed Grandad that things were not going well. Grandad's reply was, "Tut, man, it's going like a bomb", and as youthful driver said, from the noises coming from the engine one could hardly disagree. On reaching Jedburgh, the driver called at the first garage to have the ancient model looked at. Wattie meanwhile made for the telephone and called the Show Secretary to inform him he had been slightly delayed.

Everyone at the show was by this time wondering what was the cause of the delay. We all realized what it was when Wattie arrived in the ring, saying to everyone, "THE SHOW CAN NOW COMMENCE!" I thought one of the lady exhibitors was going to have a heart attack.

Wattie was a great character, jovial, win or lose made no difference. He was helpful to any novice who made any approach for advice. When I got my first judging appointment, his prudent advice to me was, "If there should be a good dog in the ring you think you cannot span, don't try, for if you do and find you are unable to span it then you will have to put it out the tickets." Wattie had a long association with Border Terriers, and did a lot for the breed, having at one time held most of the important offices of the breed club.

The late J. Renton (no prefix)

I met John at one of the early shows we attended in Edinburgh, and later we became very good friends indeed. He came into Borders in

1915 A group of Willie Barton's early Border Terriers. Left to right: Bess I, Willie Barton's first Border, b. 1900 Br. Mr. J. T. Dodd of Riccarton; Viper (lying) and Venom, by Nailer ex Venus; Piper, also ex Venus; and Venus. Piper was grandsire of Ch. Liddesdale Bess, dam of Dubh Glas.

the late 1920's. Among the first of his champion dogs would be Ch. Tod Hunter; this bitch he exhibited at the Ayr show as a puppy in 1931. At the same show he exhibited a dog called Dandy Warrior in the working class, which it won. However, it was the following year he showed one he considered to be one of the great Border bitches, Ch. Happy Mood. She was beaten in the Limit class by her litter brother, Ch. Blister. (The limit class in those days appears to have been a mixed class.) Later she won the open bitch class. On many occasions he spoke about the famous litter Ch. Blister, Ch. Happy Mood, Ch. Tod Hunter (all by Revenge *ex* Causey Bridget).

John and his wife Hazel were both very keen on the dogs. In his period of association with the breed, stretching well over 40 years, Renton owned many good Borders. He had a type of dog of his own, and he never deviated from this type. It was a racy dog, on the leg, with good coat and not heavy in the bone or coarse in the head. On many occasions he said to me, "If the present day judges are not careful we will lose the 'otter' type head." He also considered there was an increasing tendency in modern Borders to lose the rich red colours of, e.g., Adam Forster's great bitch Romance, and Revenge. He also considered that the so-called "blue" dogs exhibited today were much too black. The dark colours he considered came from a cross of the Manchester Terrier at some time in the past. This cross in his opinion had been introduced to improve the fronts and give more height. He also expressed the view that Borders were becoming far too big and coarse of their bone, with skulls too broad and muzzles too short.

On one occasion he was exhibiting at the Ayr show and stayed with us at Maybole. We had quite a large house then and a big garden. There was in addition to the stables (where we had our own kennels) a range of brick buildings, the end one being a wash house. This building contained a large basin for washing clothes, a large window on the external wall, and opposite it a boiler with a flat lid. John agreed that with a good box and well bedded, the wash house was an ideal kennel for his dog.

The dog was put into this kennel at bedtime and we retired for the night. About 1 a.m. I woke to hear a dog barking in the yard, and went down to investigate. When the dog saw me in the bright moonlight, he took off down the garden and I followed, as I did not think he could get through the fence at the bottom of it. However, he managed to do so and was outside our premises on the main road, barking furiously. I called Mrs. Renton and he came to her without any trouble, as she was a great favourite of his. He spent the remainder of the night in the Rentons' bedroom and won the C.C. next day.

The following morning we had a look at his method of escape from the washhouse. He had come through the window, which was in very good condition before he broke the glass. We came to the conclusion that to get the impetus to break the glass, he must first have jumped up on to the lid of the boiler, and sprung from there to the window, thinking no doubt because of the moonlight that there was a space. Only his thick coat could have have saved him from getting torn in the effort both from the glass and the garden fence barbed wire. To go on the next day and win the C.C. said a lot for his temperament.

John Renton had many good Borders in his period in the breed: Ch. Barb Wire, Ch. Rona Rye, Ch. Happy Mood (12 C.C.s), Ch. Rantin Rover, Ch. Vic Merry, Ch. Happy Day, Ch. First Choice. The fact that he won the Bellingham show three years in succession gave him a lot of pleasure, as it was the only time it had been achieved.

On another occasion when John stayed with us we were invited to see through Drumlanrig Castle, with Jim and Mrs. McKnight, whom we were visiting. On leaving John said to me he was very short of petrol and asked me to stop at the first petrol station. (Our family was young at the time, which made it a necessity to take two cars.) I proceeded to the nearest filling station in the adjoining village, thinking that John was behind me. We waited for some time, and I thought he must have run out of petrol, when he appeared all smiles. He had taken the wrong turn on leaving the castle and proceeded north. He realized he was wrong and drew into the first layby he came to. He was soon joined by a petrol tanker. He asked the driver where and how far it was to the nearest petrol filling station. The driver informed him, "You are right now as near to an oil well as ever you will be. If you want your tank filled there is sufficient in that hose to fill the tank." So the tank was duly filled. I said to him, "How can I compete against you for C.C.s with that kind of luck?"

It gave me great pleasure after I got to know him really well that I won the C.C. at Crufts with Ch. Maxton Matchless, a dog he really liked. I also was very pleased to hear John tell George Leatt, the year George judged the Glasgow Championship show and my Ch. Maxton Mannequin won the C.C., that in his opinion the open bitch class was the best class of bitches he had seen for a very long time.

John Renton was connected with the breed for 40 years. He not only owned many good Borders, but also held the post of club treasurer and was a member of the committee. He was a man of few words, particularly in company, but when you could get him talking on Borders he was worth listening to.

The late Adam Forster (no prefix)

Adam Forster was an active breeder of Border Terriers from around 1916 to his death in 1964. He was a lean, tall man of upright posture and athletic build. In his youth he had been a wrestler in what is known as the Cumberland Style of rules. This interest he still retained in late years. He was a keen exhibitor at the local agricultural shows where there were classes for Borders. After the judging was finished, you would find him at the ringside of the wrestling area. Although he was not a regular exhibitor at the Championship shows, he was always present at the Bellingham Show which so many Border

Mrs Adam Forster with Ch. Ranter (1060 J.J.) Br. Mr. A. Forster, b. 1 June 1927, s. Rival (1479 F.F.), d. Coquetdale Reward (1488 E.E.), c. Brindle.

exhibitors favoured. Hexham was another such show, as was Alwinton, and in fact all the local shows in the area where the Border was first established.

Joy and I met Adam at one of the first Championship shows held after World War II in Edinburgh. On many later occasions we visited him at his home in Harbottle, Morpeth. At the time of these visits I took the opportunity to ask him about the Borders of the past. The first bitch he had was Nailer II. This bitch he purchased from a shepherd who had exhibited her at a local show but was disappointed so wished to part with her. Adam recognised her potential as a brood bitch and purchased her at the modest price of two pounds.

This bitch he mated to his brother-in-law John Carruthers' dog, Barrow Jock (unr). From this mating he bred a bitch called Coquetdale Vic, b. 27th Feb 1916. Also in this litter was a bitch he called Gippy who was in turn the dam of Ch. Titlington Tatler. Gippy was a favourite of his, as was Coquetdale Vic.

He often spoke about Coquetdale Vic's gameness. When she was quite a young bitch, she was out one day with the Border hunt, and went to ground in one of those foxy places which are so numerous in that country. The huntsmen could hear her giving tongue but could not get her out of the hole, and as night was approaching they decided to leave her and return the next day. The earth was a rocky hole and it took the members of the hunt digging for three days before they came on her. The hole behind her had filled up with a fall of rocks and small stones.

She recovered but was in an exhausted state. When they came on her there were the bodies of two foxes and four cubs. She must have had a hard time with that lot.

Adam regarded Coquetdale Vic as one of his best brood bitches, and he often spoke about her litter to a dog called Ch. Ivo Roisterer—Dash, Winnie and Flint. Col. Appelyard took Dash and Winnie, and Adam's brother-in-law John Curruthers took Flint. Though in the early days the older breeders seldom exhibited their Borders, Winnie won two C.C.s, one at the Crystal Palace in 1920 (Mr. Tommy Lawrence judging) and then again at the SKC show at Edinburgh in 1921 (Mr. J. Robson judging).

However, probably Vic's greatest contribution to the breed was through her daughter Little Midget b. 12/12/1919, by Titlington Jock. Little Midget, who was red in colour, mated to a dog called Buittie gave the breed the great sire Revenge.

Revenge was the sire of Ch. Tod Hunter, Ch. Benton Biddy, Ch.

Happy Mood, Ch. Bladnock Raider, and Ch. Blister. Blister in turn sired Ch. Not So Dusty and a dog called Stingo. Bladnock Raider sired Ch. What Fettle and Ch. Gay Fine.

On the other hand Mr. J. Carruthers bred the famous dog Rival. Rival's contribution to the breed was also considerable. Neil McEwan and Dr. Lilico founded their kennel on the interbreeding of these two dogs. Rival was by Rab of Redsdale (br. Mrs. Speirs b. 24/2/1924 by Flint *ex* Dinkey (unr unt).) Flint was the son of Coquetdale Vic by Ch. Ivo Roisterer. Rival sired Ch. Ranter, who sired Ch. Grakle, who in turn sired Ch. Gem of Gold, who sired Ch. Dinger. Dinger sired Ch. Brimball of Bridge Sollars and Ch. Barb Wire.

The older breeders often spoke about the five major lines in Borders as the A line (Revenge), the B line (Rival), the C line (Ch. Grip of Tynedale), the D line (Ch. Blister) and the E line (Whitrope Don). The A and B lines were regarded as being those that gave the greatest number of Champions. This is understandable as the two exponents of genetic breeding at that time (no doubt because of their training) were Dr. Lilico and Neil McEwan, M.R.C.V.S. These breeders very successfully combined in the Bladnock dogs the Revenge (A) and Rival (B) lines. Mrs. Kathleen Twist has told me in the letters we have exchanged over the years what struggles she had exhibiting against the Bladnock dogs in the hands of Mr. J. Johnson.

Adam was a keen worker of his dogs. On one occasion when pedigrees were mentioned he said, "the best pedigree a Border can have is the marks on its face." His Coquetdale Vic had all the flesh torn from her underjaw while working. In the period of the Original Northumberland Border Terrier club (the records have all unfortunately been lost) she won a challenge cup three times in succession. In winning this trophy, she was the first Border to win the cup outright. At that time one of this club's rules was "if any part of a terrier's face was missing through legitimate work, that part was to be deemed perfect". The last time Vic won the challenge cup she had lost part of her underjaw.

From another of his early bitches, Little Midget, Adam got one of the great pillars of the breed, Revenge. In a way one can regard the great influence of Revenge on the breed as being in livestock parlance an "accident", as the following stories make clear.

FIGHTING FIT (1284 UU). Br. Miss Ena Forster, b. 20th August 1937, s.
Ch/Blister (1020 M.M.), d. Finery (85 VV), c. Red

When Adam told these stories, he had a twinkle in his eye indi-
cating great satisfaction with the transactions. The story about

Adam Forster's Coquetdale Vic with Cup "The Deucher" at N.E.T.C. about 1922–23. Underjaw bitten by fox. Born 1916, by Barron Jock (unregistered) ex Nailer II (unregistered)

Revenge is that Adam had a friend who wished a puppy for working about the farm, and as Adam had a litter of pups he gave the friend the opportunity to pick one. The friend chose a dog pup, but some time later he returned with the request that he would like to exchange his dog pup for a bitch. When Adam saw the pup, he said, "I need a dog pup for future use and already have some good brood bitches", so the deal was made. The dog pup was Revenge.

The other story concerns his brother-in-law, with whom he had a friendly rivalry. On one of his visits to his brother-in-law's farm, he saw a litter of pups by the dog called Rab of Redesdale, who was by Adam's homebred dog Flint. Adam referred to the pups by Rab as "mangy little pups" (in those days a farm dog's environment was not always of the best). Adam exchanged a bitch puppy of his own breeding for one of the dog pups in the litter by Rab. Each breeder no doubt thought that he had the better deal over the other. The dog was named Rival and the bitch puppy was called Suzanne. They were exhibited on several occasions and one would win one day and the

QUARTETTE OF WINNERS AT ALWINTON SHOW

RTH MAIL AND NEWCASTLE CH

COMRADES IN ARMS of Miss Ena Foster, of Harbottle, are four Border Terriers, all first prize-winners at the Alwinton Border Shepherds' Show, yesterday.

Christina Forster, Alwinton Show, prior to the 1939 War. The dog highest in her arms is Fearsome Fellow (see pp. 46-47).

other the next time out. Rival was the sire of Ch. Ranter (b. 1/6/1927), bred by Adam *ex* Coquetdale Reward. The latter bitch won the C.C. at the Scottish Kennel Club show in 1924 (Mr. T. Wallace judging). Adam's other bitch, Miss Tut, was second to her.

Ch. Ranter won five C.C.s, one in 1929 at Birmingham under Mr. Watson, and four in 1930: the National Terrier under Mr. J. J. Holgate; Crufts under Mr. D. Black; Darlington under Mr. T. Holmes; and the Scottish Kennel Club under Mr. G. Sordy. He was badly cut up working in later days.

At a show in 1938 Forster's dog Fighting Fit won all the classes from puppy to open, and the following year his dogs won all the dog classes, with Frugal Friar in puppy, Fearsome Fellow in junior and novice, and Fighting Fit in the open class.

Adam regarded Fearsome Fellow as one of his best dogs, but as far as exhibition was concerned he was born at the wrong time (4/11/1938), just prior to the last war. He was by Furious Fighter *ex* Finery. He also proved to be another good worker.

In the conversations I had with Adam Forster, Finery's name was regularly mentioned. She was bred by Capt. Hamilton, and Mr. Forster picked her from a litter at eight weeks of age. She won Bellingham in 1938, and the C.C. at Harrogate under Sir J. Renwick.

At the Annual General Meeting in 1952, when Dr. Lilico tendered his resignation as chairman due to his ill health, Mr. Mitchell, who had served as acting Chairman since the resignation of Dr. Lilico, proposed Mr. A. Forster as Chairman. This proposal was unanimously accepted by the members of the club. It was a fitting tribute to one who had been associated with the breed for such a long period of time.

Adam Forster's death in April 1963 at the age of 83 years was a great loss to the club in particular and to the breed overall. He had over the years established a very good strain of dogs, of the correct type, with the ability to do the job they were bred to do.

The late Willie Barton (no prefix)

I was fortunate in being sent to Hawick in my initial period with the Department of Agriculture. I could have been sent to any other part of Scotland. If this had happened, then I would have missed the opportunity of meeting one of the oldest of the old brigade in Borders at that time. Willie Barton had Borders from around 1900. His first was Bess I, bred by Mr. J. J. Dodd, of Riccarton, by Dodd's dog Twig *ex* Dodd's bitch Fury. This took place a long time before the breed was officially recognized by the Kennel Club.

On one of my early visits to the late Wattie Irving's home, while Wattie and Mrs. Irving were discussing some of the older dogs of the breed (I was doing the listening), the name of Willie Barton came up. Wattie asked me if I had met him; as I had not at that time, he suggested I go and see him. Willie was at that time living at Teviot Head, a small village on the Hawick-Langholm-Carlisle road, a few miles south of Hawick.

At the time of my visit he had retired from his job as a hill shepherd. He had spent his life on the hills in the open and like all of his age group he could recount many tales of experiences with the weather on the high hills.

The first thing that was noticeable about Willie Barton's dogs was their untrimmed appearance, their hard top coats, and soft undercoats. Above all they looked like doing the job they were bred to do; they were a hard-bitten lot. Like other breeders of stock that spent considerable periods of time on the open hill, Willie Barton required that his dogs have a good coat to keep out the elements.

Also like all the older breeders of Borders, he considered the agricultural shows the important shows. To him none were as important as the shows around the Borders, like Langholm, Bellingham, Falstone, Jedburgh, and Yetholm. All were important, and all were more or less within a radius of the country in which the Border was originally bred.

Like many of the older breeders, Willie never travelled more than 50 miles to a show even when the breed was recognized by the K.C. and C.Cs were offered. The breeders who did travel were those who lived near a railway station as this was the means of travel in those days.

Willie was a great walker and was known to travel long distances on foot. There was a legendary story related to me by Wattie that Willie had been known to trail a fox in the snow through four counties. (As the boundaries of four counties meet in the Border area, although some distance would be covered, it is within the capabilities of a fit, able person to accomplish this feat.)

Many of Willie Barton's dogs were unregistered. Like many other breeders of his time, he did not consider registration important. (For most of these breeders, registration was probably the last of their thoughts; in fact many were against the idea at that time.) One of his dogs which Willie Barton spoke highly about was Venus (unr), whose dam was Bess (unr). Venus was shown regularly at the Border country shows. The first trophy offered for competition in the breed was won by her in 1913. She was the dam of Daisy and Piper. Daisy in turn was the dam of Tinker, Rip and Clincher (1919), sired by North Tyne Gyp.

The Dumfries Otter Hunt obtained many of their terriers from

Willie Barton. Tinker and Rip both went to that Hunt, as did the dog Rock at some earlier point. Rock was one of the Hunt's first Borders. A game dog, he lost an eye while working.

After the breed was officially recognized by the K.C. in 1920, Willie Barton was the first to win the C.C. and to own the first Champion in the breed. This was his bitch Liddesdale Bess (unr), bred by J. Davidson. She was by Barton's dog Liddesdale Nailer (unr), *ex* Pearl (unr) and was red in colour (b. August 1917). Bess won her first C.C. at the Carlisle Championship show on September 30, 1920, under Mr. J. Dodd, and took C.C.s thereafter at Birmingham, under Mr. E. Bagley; at Ayr, under Mr. R. T. Baines; and at Edinburgh, under Mr. G. Davidson. She won her fifth C.C. under Mr. T. Lawrence in 1924, at the age of seven years.

When Willie was describing some of his terriers he would say, "grand little bitch, short-coupled, dark red, with a short thick-set coat, and stood on her feet and legs like a thoroughbred; tight feet like a cat and a flat otter skull."

I did not know the Standard of the breed in those days but often thought later about the comment "short coupled". On reflection I can only assume that Willie Barton meant they were shorter coupled than some of the originals he saw in the earlier days of the founding of the breed. He would speak about Liddesdale Wasp as being high on the leg and thus better able to follow a horse. This bitch was never beaten when a Master of Fox Hounds was the judge.

Mr. Barton's Liddesdale Wasp was the dam of Tiot Fancy (b. June 26, 1927, sired by Arnton Billy). Tiot Fancy was the dam of the late Wattie Irving's Ch. Heronslea (b. June 26, 1930, sired by Styrrup). Liddesdale Wasp was by Redden *ex* Colterscleugh Betty, b. February 12, 1925.

Another of Willie Barton's bitches was Liddesdale Wendy, bred by W. Irving, b. October 10, 1925, sired by Tinker *ex* Station Masher. Wendy, mated to a dog called Whistler, was the dam of Willie's Liddesdale Nettle, b. March 7, 1927.

Nettle was exhibited three times, twice at Newcastle where she won her class and again at Falstone where she was second to Liddesdale Wasp in a big class. Willie considered her to be his best brood bitch. She was the dam of Whitrope Don, bred by him, b. May 18, 1928. Don was the great-grandsire of Ch. Fox Lair. Foomert, in the same litter, was the dam of some useful winners and workers. She was granddam of Epigram (2 C.C.s) and maternal granddam of Ch. Rising Light.

Liddesdale Nettle became the property of Mr. T. Sedman and bred Ch. Oakwood Pickle, Halleath's Piper, and Miss Grakle (by Ch. Grakle), and later, by Ch. Blister, bred Stung Again, who was the dam of Ch. Share Pusher and Finery. Later Nettle was owned by Miss E. Forster and mated to one of her dogs, Furious Fighter, was the dam of Adam Forster's dog, Fearsome Fellow (b. April 11, 1938). This dog was important to most of the modern Border Terrier families.

Nettle comes into the pedigree of most of the dogs born in the early 1930s. She is the dam of Foomert, bred by W. Barton, sired by Red Rock, b. May 1928. Red Rock was another of Barton's dogs, born May 18, 1926, sired by Burn Foot Jock (unr) *ex* Rags (unr).

Mr. Barton also bred Sheil Law, the paternal granddam of Ch. Rising Light (i.e., the dam of Rock Sand, the sire of Ch. Rising Light). Rock Sand was also the grandsire of Portholme Magic.

Mr. W. Barton judged the Borders at the Edinburgh Championship show in 1923 and Durham in 1928. Like most of the older breeders, he did not have a registered prefix. He used Liddesdale, an area of the Borders through which the River Liddle runs, and he also used Whitrope, a farm on which he was shepherd for a number of years.

Miss Helen Vaux (prefix: Dryburn)

At the time we came into the breed in the late 1940's, Miss Helen Vaux had probably been in the breed longer than anyone else other than the three stalwarts Adam Forster, John Renton, and Wattie Irving. Her prefix was Dryburn and although she was not enthusiastic about the exhibition side of the game, she certainly had considerable success with her stock. She also had a good eye for a Border. Her kennel was established in the late 1920's with Dryburn Kutchuk, bred by Mr. D. Jackson out of his good bitch Ch. Daphne, sired by Ch. Barney Bindle. Kutchuk was grizzle in colour.

Miss Vaux followed this foundation by the purchase of Ch. Oakwood Pickle, bred by Mr. T. Sedman, b. March 9, 1932 (by Ch. Grakle *ex* Liddesdale Nettle), thus bringing in the oldest strains of the breed. (Ch. Grakle was bred by the old breeders Dodd and Carruthers, and Liddesdale Nettle by the veteran breeder Willie Barton.)

Miss Vaux purchased a dog carrying Sir John Renwick's prefix, Newminster Rab. This red dog was bred by Mr. F. Corbett, b. April 22, 1935, and was by Furious Fighter *ex* Nop. The dog had one C.C. to his credit. However, I rather suspect that Miss Vaux in purchasing this dog did so not for C.C.s but to bring into her strain some of Adam Forster's dogs, as Furious Fighter was sired by Ch. Ranter *ex* Adam's famous bitch Romance.

One of Miss Vaux's last purchases was the good bitch Ch. Vic Merry bred by Mr. T. Crozier, b. January 2, 1948, by Why Not *ex* Dinger Queen.

In all good strains of livestock, if the right foundation has been laid, good stock turns up from time to time. Miss Vaux had laid her foundations on the right lines. This was demonstrated in the later years of her breeding activities, when she successfully exhibited and made up Dryburn Devilina, and from her Ch. Dryburn Dazzler, and a C.C. winner under George Leatt's prefix, Leatty Linty.

After her retirement from the show ring, Miss Vaux continued her breeding activities. Mrs. Sneddon purchased from her the bitch Ch. Newsholme Modesty and Mrs. Bulmer purchased a blue and tan dog she made up as Ch. Easingwold Rascal.

Mrs. Kathleen Twist (prefix: Hallbourne)

I met Mrs. K. Twist at the first show I attended in the south, Crufts. At that time she was the Secretary of the Southern Border Terrier Club; the success of that club in the early days was due to her efforts. The outbreak of World War II interfered with her breeding plans probably more than those of most other breeders, as her home was in the south and in the range of Hitler's bombers and V2 rockets.

Kathleen Twist registered some good Borders under her Hallbourne prefix. Her most famous dog of the pre-war era was Ch. Fox Lair, bred by Mr. A. Stevenson, b. February 26, 1934. He was by Rab O'Lammermuir *ex* Traquair Gypsy. This dog Wattie Irving used to speak a lot about. Fox Lair was a red grizzle, a great shower, the only dog to my knowledge to win three C.C.s in succession at Crufts.

Mrs. Twist informed me in one of her letters that the first time Fox Lair saw a rat he did not know what to do. It was after the rat bit him that his instincts were aroused. Those rats that came after the biting were soon dispatched.

Ch. Fox Lair was the sire of the very good breeding dog Callum, *ex* Dipley Dinah, born April 10, 1938. Callum was a big winner in the few shows in which he was exhibited pre-war. His stud card records some 28 First prizes at Championship shows and five reserve C.C.s, including a Junior Warrant. The older breeders all agreed that had it not been for the war he would have obtained his title. It is of interest that his stud fee was four pounds four shillings plus return carriage. Another of Mrs. Twist's good dogs was Ch. Aldham Joker, bred by Miss V. Smither, b. June 24, 1937, by Ch. Barb Wire *ex* Country Girl.

Ch. Aldham Joker, mated to Daphne's Dream (by Ch. Wedale Jock *ex* Delight), gave the breed the good breeding dogs Ch. Boxer Boy, Ch. Swallowfield Garry, and Mr. D. Black's Ch. Tweedside Red Biddy. Mrs. Twist also owned Ch. Wedale Jock, another of Wattie's favourites and, from the photographs I have seen of him, a dog of good type.

Ch. Wedale Jock was by one of the best of the early Champions, Ch. Heronslea, bred by Wattie Irving, b. June 26, 1930, by Styrrup *ex* Tiot Fancy. Wedale Jock's dam was Shaw's Lady, who was by Ch. Blister *ex* Patchwork.

In purchasing these three dogs, Mrs. Twist showed considerable foresight and a knowledge of genetics. If the reader considers their pedigrees, it should be apparent how they proved such a valuable stud force and how they did so much for the breed: Ch. Fox Lair's paternal granddam, Brandy Snap, was by Revenge *ex* Causey Bridget. The dam of Wedale Jock, Shaw's Lady, was by Ch. Blister, a full brother to Brandy Snap. Ch. Heronslea's sire, Styrrup, was by Ch. Ben of Tweeden and Ch. Fox Lair's dam, Traquair Gypsy, was by Bladnock Twink, who was sired by Ch. Ben of Tweeden. Ch. Aldham Joker was by Ch. Barb Wire *ex* Country Girl. Barb Wire's dam, Ch. Tod Hunter, is a full sister to Ch. Blister and Brandy Snap.

Ch. Fox Lair and Ch. Wedale Jock spent the war years with Miss Duthie (Todearth prefix) in Perthshire. Mr. D. Black had Ch. Aldham Joker in the latter part of his life. Joker became a foundation of Mr. Black's breeding.

The war years robbed many breeders of the potential of these dogs, who were earlier made available through Mrs. Twist's foresight in establishing them together in the south. Any breeder establishing a bitch line through Ch. Fox Lair and then using the other two could not go wrong on the law of probability.

Although her contribution to Borders in breeding terms was very important, probably Mrs. Twist's greatest and everlasting contribution was in the gathering of all the information required to help Miss Hester Garnett Orme to compile the first book on Border Terrier Champions and Certificate winners. It was through her efforts and writing to the older breeders that this book containing such interesting information was put together.

The late Dr. Lilico (prefix: Bladnock)

I first met Dr. Lilico when I was working in the Wigtownshire area. I was visiting the late Neil McEwan when the Doctor called. They were very good friends and very close associates in the breeding of Borders. After our initial meeting I visited him frequently when in that area if it was convenient to him; because he had an extensive country practice, he never knew when he would be called out.

He was very interested in his dogs and any newcomer to the breed could expect help in any problems likely to come the way of the novice. The doctor's Bladnock prefix comes into many of the older pedigrees. His first show Border in the 1920's and from memory one of his earliest Borders was Bladnock Gyp, b. January 7, 1928, by Quick Work *ex* Bailey Head Brownie.

Bladnock Gyp was mated to Ch. Ben of Tweeden and from this mating a dog called Bladnock Twink was retained. Neil McEwan had a bitch called Taynish who was mated to B. Twink. From this breeding Dr. Lilico retained a bitch called Red Gold (bred by N. McEwan, b. November 9, 1929). This bitch was mated to Revenge, Mr. A. Forster's good dog, and to him she bred Ch. Bladnock Raider, b. April 29, 1932, and registered as a grizzle and tan. Although the doctor was able to make up the dog Bladnock Raider, his professional life did not often allow him the time necessary to make up dogs.

Although his professional life did not allow him to attend many shows, he judged some of the Championship shows as and when he could get away. His bloodlines did a lot of good to the breed. The dog Bladnock Twink mated to Neil McEwan's bitch Taynish resulted in the bitch Traquair Gypsy. Gypsy, mated to Rab O'Lammermuir, was the dam of the great modern dog Ch. Fox Lair.

Another of Dr. Lilico's early foundation bitches was B. Ginger, b. July 13, 1920. She was by Ch. Ben of Tweeden *ex* Blacklyne Wasp and was bred by Mrs. Armstrong. Dr. Lilico mated Ginger to Ch. Ranter and obtained the bitch B. Nippy, b. February 11, 1932.

B. Nippy was mated to the famous dog Ch. Blister and from the mating Dr. Lilico retained the bitch B. Beatrice, b. June 13, 1933. This bitch was mated to Dandy Warrior to produce the famous stud dog Brownie O'Bladnock, b. June 24, 1935. Brownie helped to lay the foundation of the Portholme dogs owned by Mrs. Phyllis Mulcaster. The Doctor's final triumph in the breed he loved so much was the breeding of Ch. Bladnock Spaewife, b. May 1, 1945. She was by Dipley Dusty *ex* Bladnock Jinty. The bitch he exhibited himself to championship status. She won her certificates from the late W. Irving, J. Renton and P. R. Smith.

Mrs. Lilico was also a shrewd judge of a Border and always made a person very welcome to their home. It was for this reason that on purchasing our foundation bitch, Red Hazel, the first breeders to see her were Dr. Lilico and Mrs. Lilico and Neil McEwan and Mrs. McEwan. We had a private dog show in one of the side streets in Wigtown, at the doctor's house, and I obtained the views of the judges. I found their judgements most helpful in later days among Borders. I appreciate how fortunate I was in being advised by such a dedicated group of breeders. No beginner could have wished for better advice.

At that time I had acquired Red Hazel, my foundation bitch, and Dr. Lilico had a young dog which he offered to me. I sometimes regret I refused the offer. I did so on the basis that I had not the accommodation for a dog, and I preferred to have two or three bitches. He understood my views on this matter.

Dr. Lilico was a member of the Border Terrier Club for many years and was Chairman of the Committee at the time we came into the breed. I have always regarded it as a compliment that it was he who proposed me as a member of the Committee when he resigned the Chairmanship and Club activities on the grounds of his busy professional life and the fact that he did not enjoy the best of health in later years.

The late Neil McEwan, M.R.C.V.S.

Neil McEwan in his youth was quite an athlete, and the night before his wedding, as is customary in Scotland, all the bachelors in the district were out to get him. The result of this if he was lucky might be to get his feet blackened. Neil was determined that the local youths would not do unto him what he had done unto others. The night before his wedding when he got wind of what was in store for him he took refuge in a place nearby, thinking he was safe from the mob. However, they were soon on his trail and arrived at the front door of the "safe house" just as he was making his exit from the back door.

(I should explain that the area of land around Wigtown is tidal, and is made up of a low-lying alluvial type plain, where the burns that run into the River Bladnock are in places very deep and in many cases wide because of the tidal erosion.) So, leaving by the back door of the house, Neil made for the carse, hoping to lose the mob, who were by this time in full cry not many yards behind. Being the athlete he was, he steadily outdistanced them, but he found in his course one of the many burns that run into the Bladnock. It so happened that the burn in question was not only wide but also very deep. There was no alternative other than to jump or to surrender to the mob. Accelerating in time, he jumped the burn, knowing full well that none of the others would attempt the crossing and there was no other way for the mob to pursue him. Afterward he simply ambled along the carse until it was dark enough to return to a "safe house".

Those who knew about this athletic feat are all agreed it was a pity the jump was not measured and recorded at the time. All are agreed it was some jump!

Neil McEwan's and Dr. Lilico's thoughtful breeding of Borders put this breed a jump ahead as well.

George and Phyllis Leatt (prefix: Leatty)

I first met George Leatt in my early days of exhibiting dogs (in the early 1950's). He was a jovial character who could see the funny side of life. The fact that he had an interest in dogs is understandable as both his father and grandfather were interested in terriers and gundogs. Apart from that, his first breed was Cocker Spaniels, followed by Bulldogs. George, along with his wife Phyllis, has had many good Borders. One of the first I remember was a bitch, Raisgill Rhona, bred by Miss Garnett Orme.

They had many good dogs. Among those I recollect were Ch. Leatty Lace (by Bladnock Brock of Deerstone *ex* Leatty Sadie) and Ch. Lily of the Valley. (This bitch I thought was one of their best.)

Leatty Lace was mated to Ch. Future Fame and was the dam of Leatty Lass, who was the dam of Ch. Leatty Lucky. The Leatts had one of the most successful stud dogs of that time, Ch. Leatty Druridge Dazzler. However, it is probably as an all rounder that George Leatt has come to the fore, being recognized to award C.C.s in some 100 breeds.

In his early days in dogs, George Leatt was secretary of the Yorkshire Bulldog Club and the Silsden Agricultural Show Society. (In the 1950's the latter association held the largest one day show in the North.) He also had a long interest in the Craven Canine Association. In the early days, with Phyllis Mulcaster he was one of those who helped to establish and was secretary of the Southern Border Terrier Club. For many years he served as breed contributor to Border Terrier Notes in *Our Dogs,* keeping us all well informed about day to day happenings in our breed.

If George was asked to give an opinion as to what has been the most satisfying achievement in his life, I think he would state as far as dogs are concerned it was the invitation to judge the Working Group at Crufts. On the other hand, he might consider it his restoration of a water mill dating back to 1310. In restoring this mill, he has given a lot of pleasure to the many who have visited it. If you should attend a dog show and George is there, you will have no difficulty in recognizing him. All you have to do is to look out for a stocky, jovial figure dressed in plus fours and you have your man.

In the show ring I have won well under both Phyllis and George Leatt. Phyllis awarded Mr. R. Drummond's young dog Ch. Bargower Silver Dollar his second C.C. when she judged at the Manchester Championship Show. Under George I won the C.C. with Ch. Maxton Mannequin. It was on that occasion that the veteran breeder John Renton said in his opinion the open bitch class was the best class of bitches he had seen for a very long time.

Mrs. Phyllis Mulcaster (prefix: Portholme)

The first introduction I had to Mrs. Phyllis Mulcaster was at the first Crufts show I attended. On that occasion Phyllis exhibited Portholme Manly Boy. Later he gained his title. Under her Portholme prefix she bred many very good Borders.

Phyllis obtained her first Border in 1932 as a wedding present. This was a bitch called April Shower. This bitch was mated to a dog owned by Miss M. Long, called Randale, bred by Mr. R. D. Scott. Randale was sired by Renton *ex* Bunty (unr) and was born July 22, 1930. This dog, it may interest the reader to know, laid the foundations of one of the oldest of Border kennels, that of Miss M. Long (Winstonhall prefix). From this mating Mrs. Mulcaster obtained Portholme Jan, b. July 20, 1934.

Phyllis Mulcaster and Dr. Lilico were very good friends and if he had something worth showing and he did not have the time to go to shows, Phyllis would take the dog under her care. She obtained Portholme Merrilegs from him. This bitch she mated to Devonside Diversion and obtained P. Mab (after winning 1 C.C. this bitch was exported to Sweden).

The Portholme Kennels, since the end of the war, have had seven Champions; Ch. P. Mab (Sweden), Ch. P. Magic, Ch. P. Maire, Ch. P. Mamie (little sister to Maire), Ch. P. Manly Boy (who proved to be a very successful sire), American Ch. P. Mayduke, and Ch. P. Marthe of Deerstone. Also, P. Meroe was the best puppy at the Border Terrier Club championship show at Carlisle the year Mr. A Forster judged, and Ch. P. Maire won her seventh C.C. that day. P. Meroe won the Capt. Ridley Memorial Bowl for the best junior bitch under the veteran breeder judge Mr. R. Ogle, Sr.

Phyllis Mulcaster is one of the few remaining breeders who have been associated with the breed since the late 1920s and early 1930s era. She served as a fearless judge and critic, who judged the dogs and did not care what the owners thought of her judgement. She would often say, "Exhibitors complete the entry form to obtain my opinion, so I give it honestly. I award the top honours to, in my opinion, the top dogs on the day. That is what the judge is in the ring to do." I from experience know that what she said is true. I have had my big wins under her and I have also had my disappointments, but we have always remained the best of friends.

Phyllis now lives in Newcastleton, where many of the old breeders stayed in the early days of the breed. Although she is now an octo-generian, I am glad to say she remains very fit for her years. In good weather she comes over from time to time to see how I am progressing with the dogs.

Mr. Robert Hall (prefix: Deerstone)

I met Robert Hall in my early days of exhibiting Borders at the Scottish Kennel Club show in Glasgow, just after the war. I had heard about Mr. Hall from Dr. Lilico when I visited him on my trips through Wigtownshire. R. Hall founded his kennel on Dr. Lilico's breeding. In the days before the war, he had exhibited gundogs, and in returning to the arena he decided to breed Borders; this was in 1943 or thereabouts. His breeding activities commenced by the purchase of the Bladnock-bred bitch Mischief, bred by Mrs. M. McGuffie, b. August 10, 1943, sired by Callum *ex* Bladnock Patty. Bladnock Patty was born in 1937 and was bred by Dr. Lilico. She was by Brownie O'Bladnock *ex* Bladnock May Mischief and was a blue and tan.

The bitch was registered in Hall's Deerstone prefix, and mated to Devonside Diversion, produced Deerstone Defender, b. April 11, 1945. He won the C.C. at the Southern Border Terrier Club Show held in London in 1947. Lady Howe was the judge. At the Peterborough Championship show he was reserve C.C. to Wattie Irving's dog. Ch. Rising Light. In the same litter as Defender was Deerstone Dainty. Another dog that helped to lay the foundation of Hall's kennel was bred by Dr. Lilico, Bladnock Brock of Deerstone, b. May 1, 1945, sired by Dipley Dusty *ex* Bladnock Jinty, also a blue and tan. This dog was a full brother to Dr. Lilico's very good bitch Ch. Bladnock Spaewife, b. May 1, 1945. Robert Hall also obtained from Dr. Lilico one of Spaewife's sisters, Bladnock Tinkerbell.

B. Tinkerbell, mated to Adam Forster's good dog Fearsome Fellow, gave Mr. Hall one of his first Champions, Deerstone Driver, b. March 17, 1947. From Mrs. P. Mulcaster, Robert Hall obtained the good bitch Ch. Portholme Martha of Deerstone, bred by a Mr. A. Sanson, b. September 21, 1946, sired by Aldham Joker *ex* Portholme Ruby. He exhibited her as a young bitch and had two Reserve C.C.s. Mrs. Holmes of Wharfholm purchased her to lay the foundations of her kennel. Exhibited by Mrs. Holmes, she became a champion; in fact, I believe she won some six C.C.s.

However, probably Robert Hall's best known dog was Ch. Deerstone Destiny, b. April 15, 1955. With this dog he won some 12 C.C.s. He was sired by Ch. Portholme Manly Boy; his dam was Raisgill Radella of Deerstone. Other dogs of R. Hall's that I remember were Ch. Deerstone Realization, Ch. Deerstone Delia, Ch. Rip of Deerstone and Ch. Deerstone Douglas (in partnership with Miss Bland).

His dogs were always well put down, and were keen showers. It was obvious to the observer that Mr. Hall must have spent a considerable time with the preparation and the handling of the dogs. He was a keen and a good exhibitor. He did not grumble about the judge's decision if he did not win. Like all committed exhibitors, he had his good days and his bad days, but he was always prepared to help the novice exhibitor.

Above all he had a deep feeling for his fellow exhibitors when circumstances beyond their control fell their way, causing them deep concern and personal unhappiness. This I can vouch for personally.

Robert Hall has always taken the task of judging seriously and tried to judge according to the Standard of the breed. And if you were exhibiting against him and it so happened that the judge of the day preferred your dog to his, he would not then regard you as his enemy.

It is a great pity there are not more exhibitors like Robert Hall.

Mr. A. L. Waters (no prefix)

Another exhibitor I met at the Crufts Show in 1950 was Mr. A. L. Waters. He was exhibiting a nice bitch called Misty Dawn bred by Mr. and Mrs. W. J. E. Eccles, b. February 11, 1947, sired by Ch. Boxer Boy *ex* Sweet Sue. She was a nicely made bitch and certainly smaller than some of those exhibited today. She was the dam of his good little dog Ch. Billy Boy, sired by Callum. A number of the older breeders considered that Billy Boy was very like his sire. He was a lovely-headed dog of a rich red colour.

At stud he proved to be a prepotent sire of some good progeny. He was the sire of Ch. Winstonhall Counden Tim, a dog I always admired from the ringside, and of Ch. Full Toss, to whom I awarded her third C.C. She was a very nice type of bitch. Billy Boy was also the sire of Quartermaster, who sired Ringmaster, who won the dog C.C. the same day as Full Toss. Ch. Leatty Plough Boy and Leatty Bill Bunter were also by him. (I should mention that Ringmaster's dam was Ch. Fine Features, who was by Ch. Future Fame. Fellhouse Knap was also by him *ex* Fellfoot Lass by Ch. Future Fame.)

The Ch. Future Fame and Ch. Billy Boy lines "nicked" well in breeding good stock. By way of example, Mr. George Ion's dog

Ch. Hugill Sweep is by Hugill Ruffian, whose dam is Misty Dawn, and whose sire is Fearsome Fellow; Sweep's dam is Final Flutter, by Ch. Future Fame. (A note to the student of pedigrees: do not always accept what is written as correct. If you study the pedigree on p. 37 of the 1958 *Southern Border Terrier Year Book*, the sire of Misty Dawn is given as Ch. Billy Boy. This is not correct, as Misty Dawn's sire is Ch. Boxer Boy *ex* Sweet Sue.)

The 1964 *Year Book* notes other fine get related to Billy Boy, for example, Ch. Deerstone Debrett was sired by Klein Otti, a son of Billy Boy's *ex* Orenza. Orenza was the dam of George McConnel's good dog Ch. Girvanside Cruggleton Don, sired by Callum and bred by Mr. Tom Buchanan, Cruggleton Farm, Wigtownshire, a great friend of both Neil McEwen and Dr. Lilico. Billy Boy and Girvanside Cruggleton Don thus are half-brothers by the same sire (Callum). Kilmeny is another example. He was by Billy Boy *ex* a Ch. Future Fame dam, Tyneside Lass.

Mrs. B. S. T. Holmes (prefix: Wharfholm)

Mrs. Holmes is probably the oldest of the breeders I knew in the early days who is still exhibiting from time to time. The last time I had a word with her was at the L.K.A. On that occasion she informed me she was an octogenarian, but as one of her ancestors had lived to celebrate 100 years she hoped to accomplish that too, and I hope she will.

Over the years I have seen her exhibit some good Borders and among them I recollect Wharfholm Witchie, Ch. W. Wizardy, Ch. Mr. Tims, Ch. W. Wonder Lad, Ch. W. Warrant. The earliest bitch I recollect her showing was her foundation bitch, Ch. Portholm Marthe of Deerstone, followed by another Deerstone dog she made up, Ch. Deerstone Driver.

Mrs. D. Miller (prefix: Foxhill)

In 1956 we had a litter of pups by Grenor Max *ex* Maxton Red Honey. We had used this dog successfully in 1954 and bred the lovely bitch Ch. Maxton Mannequin. We gave Mr. and Mrs. Miller a present of a bitch pup out of this litter called Maxton Moonraker. It is of interest to mention that at the time I offered John Miller the pup, I told him that the only thing about the litter not in his choice was the name, as the litter had already been registered at the K.C. He then asked if by any chance I had a Moonraker registered, because he had owned a fine pony of that name when he was in the colonial service and hoped to have a Border of that name. We were both astonished at the coincidence that indeed I had named and registered one of the pups as Moonraker.

This bitch puppy established their Foxhill Kennel. Mated to Ch. Maxton Matchless, she produced a bitch called Foxhill Fantasy. Fantasy in turn mated to Tweedside Red Ivor (who was sired by Tweedside Red Playboy, the sire of Red Hazel) gave Foxhill Flirt. Foxhill Flirt, mated to Ch. Happy Day, produced Ch. Foxhill Firm Favourite. The sire of Ch. Happy Days was Tweedside Red Kingpin, who was by Ch. Girvanside Cruggleton Don. Kingpin and Triesta (the dam of Ch. Marrburn Morag) are half-brother and -sister.

The bitch Foxhill Fantasy, mated to Portholme Mustard, gave the Millers their first C.C. winner. Unfortunately, they lost this bitch before she gained her title.

Moonraker, mated again to Ch. Happy Day, gave Foxhill Frangipani who, mated to Foxhill Fabian, gave Ch. Foxhill Fusilier.

If the reader studies the breeding of these three bitches and the results obtained by three different breeders more or less on the same line of breeding, he/she will see demonstrated the point that you do not require large numbers of bitches to breed good dogs. Breeders who have large numbers tend to rely on numbers to give them results. Although I do not have the number of pups that the Millers bred, for instance, I do know they were not out of a large number of bitches. Mrs. McKnight had in her period in the breed only a few litters. Nonetheless she was probably the most successful breeder in the short period she was in the breed.

Mrs. Roslin Williams (prefix: Mansergh)

This lady was one who was always prepared to discuss Border Terriers with a novice as I was when I met her at one of the early Championship shows. Although she exhibited Borders frequently in the early days after the war, I am sure she will agree that her interest lay more in the working side of the breed than in exhibition. The younger breeders of today will know her better as the owner-exhibitor of the Mansergh Labrador Retrievers and as the Northern Contributor to the *Dog World*. She had contributed to this column for many years. Although she appears in the ring with her Labradors, her gundogs, like her Borders in the early days, have to perform in the field. (Mrs. R. Williams and her late husband hunted with the Kendal and District Otter Hounds.) From memory, in the early days she exhibited a bitch called Red Squill. However, as the gundogs were her real interest, the Borders were handed over to her daughter Anne. This young lady I recollect in the early days coming to the shows with her mother, dressed in her school uniform and hat with a long plait of golden hair hanging down her back.

One could not wish to meet a more helpful person than Mrs. Roslin Williams in the dog arena, one who was a good exhibitor to boot.

Lady Russell, Swallowfield Park, Reading (prefix: Swallowfield)

The first introduction I had to Lady Russell was the first time I exhibited at Crufts in 1950. I was exhibiting our foundation bitch, Red Hazel. I had won the Post Graduate Bitch Class followed by the Minor Limit. The next class was the Open Bitch and into this class came Lady Russell with a very nice bitch, Swallowfield Coramine. Coramine was rather aggressive and as she passed Hazel I was caught napping and her aggressive spirit was displayed on Hazel. Wattie Irving, who was second in the previous class with the bitch Musk Rose (bred by Mr. T. Buchanan) had just whispered to me, "stop teasing your bitch and you will win the Championship"; but after her encounter, alas, the spirit had gone out of Hazel and she ceased to show.

I did not help matters very much when the judge came along the line and queried, "What's gone wrong with the bitch?" I replied that she like me was dead tired. (I should explain that it was so late in the day that the stewards were calling for all unbeaten dogs for the best in show ring, and Borders at that time were just about to enter the ring. I had left home the previous night and had been at the show all day.) The judge indicated that I should step down from my exalted position of top of the line to be in the fourth place. We finished by winning the Special Beginners class.

Lady Russell owned the good breeding dog Callum, bred by Mr. J. J. Pawson. Callum was by Ch. Fox Lair *ex* Dipley Dinah, and I had noted one or two good types by him at Crufts.

I had subsequently several interesting letters from Lady Russell, both on breeding Borders and presenting them for exhibition. No one could prepare a Border better for showing than she.

I once tried to get a bitch mated to Callum and all was arranged. Hazel was dispatched by train to Reading but unfortunately Callum was past his day for such matters. Hazel was mated instead to Ch. Swallowfield Garry, who was by Ch. Aldham Joker *ex* Swallowfield Solo. Lady Russell did a lot of winning with this dog, including Crufts in 1948, the National Terrier Show in 1947 and the L.K.A. in 1948. A winner of some eight C.C.s, his official height was given as 13″ and weight as 15½ pounds.

Lady Russell had at that time a very strong kennel of Borders, including Ch. Swallowfield Nutmeg, bred by Mrs. E. Twist, b. February 13, 1947, by Callum *ex* Hornbeam Heatherbell; Ch. Swallowfield Shindy, bred by Miss Garnett Orme, b. April 13, 1946, by Ch. S. Garry *ex* Raisgill Rasta; Ch. Swallowfield Fergus, bred by Lady Russell, by Ch. S. Garry *ex* Swallowfield Chloe.

Lady Russell is a keen advocate of line breeding and practised it in her kennel. All her dogs were bred to the Aldham Joker or Callum-Fox Lair lines.

The late Miss Hester Garnett Orme (prefix: Raisgill)

Anyone researching into the breed or taking an interest in pedigrees could not do so without coming up against the name of Hester Garnett Orme. In our early days of breeding Borders I had many letters from Miss Orme on the breed and its past history. At that time I was very inquisitive about the past and in writing to her I found the answer to my many questions. I still retain pedigree sheets with her notes about the dogs.

A member of the Southern Border Terriers Club in the early days, she joined in 1935, and became President in 1949. She was not a dedicated exhibitor and in this fact we were both of the same mind. Her interest in the breed lay in its early history and in the working side of the breed. Along with Mrs. Twist, Miss Eccles, and Mrs. Symond, Miss Garnett Orme did an excellent job of producing *The Border Terrier Year Book*. These books contain a wealth of information about the breed and the older breeders.

During the war years, along with Mrs. Twist, Miss Orme produced the little book *Border Terrier Champions and Certificate Winners*.

She also produced *Border Tales.* Along with her associates in these works, she proved that there is more in breeding Border Terriers than the winning of Challenge Certificates.

Hester Garnett Orme had a dedicated interest in the working side of the breed. In one of her letters she was of the opinion that some of the show stock and their descendants had lost the "nose for scent" and indeed now followed the hound or the quarry by sight. In other words, if they lost sight of the hounds they were literally lost. In this hereditary factor I agreed with her conclusions, for in Borders, as in hound breeding, "nose" and the ability to "speak" to a cold trail are very important hereditary factors.

Another of her genetic theories was that there was a chance of the undershot jaw becoming a dominant factor in some strains and as a result it might be that bitches with the defect could not sever the umbilical chord at whelping. In this theory I did not agree, as in my view the jaw abnormality is not due to any single recessive gene. The head, including the jaw conformation, I believe is a combination of several multiple genes.

The war years upset Miss Garnett Orme's breeding programme as it did that of all the breeders of that era, and caused her to reduce her kennel considerably. At this time she kept Ch. What Fettle, who lived with her during the war years. Probably one of her best known dogs in later years was Ch. Swallowfield Shindy, owned by Lady Russell, b. April 13, 1946, bred by Miss G. Orme, by Ch. Swallowfield Garry *ex* Raisgill Rasta. Miss Orme also bred Raisgill Rasta, b. June 1, 1939, by Ch. Aldham Joker *ex* Wild Lucy, a bitch Miss Orme purchased from Mr. J. Johnson. Lucy carried the Bladnock lines of breeding (she was by Ch. Bladnock Raider *ex* Hunty Gowk).

Mr. Robert Hall purchased a bitch from Miss Orme called Raisgill Radella. She was the dam of Ch. Deerstone Destiny and Ch. Deerstone Desirable.

The younger breeders of today owe a lot to Miss Orme for the information she collected about the breed and the work she put into *The Southern Border Terrier Club Year Books.* She was a great help to any novice breeder who wished to ask her advice. Personally, she was a rather quiet, reserved person despite all her knowledge about the breed.

Mr. D. Black (prefix: Tweedside)

Mr. David Black belonged to the older school of breeders. It is not generally known but it was Mrs. Black who had the Borders in the first instance; David was a Bulldog man to start with.

Their foundation bitch was Ch. Tweedside Red Tatters bred by a Mr. G. Hope, b. December 11, 1921, by Ch. Titlington Tatler *ex* Chip. One of their foundation sires was Tweedside Red Trumpeter, bred by Mr. T. Oliver, by Ch. Dandy of Tynedale *ex* Tweedside Red Tatters.

In the war years, David had Ch. Aldham Joker from Mrs. Twist. This dog he used a lot in forming his kennel when his breeding commenced after the war. I used to visit him in his Tweedside home with the late George McConnel, who founded his Girvanside kennel mostly on Tweedside blood. They used to exchange dogs and bitches quite a lot. A feature of David Black's dogs was their good otter heads and their red colour.

David Black was quite a character in the dog world and, like us all, he liked to win. I recollect on one occasion Wattie, David and I were all in the same class, but not as far up the line as we would have wished. David muttered to Wattie and me that the judge did not know the tail from the head. Wattie, last in the line next to David (I was in the fourth place), said, "David, it's a good job there is no photographer about. If he were to take a snap it would show you at the end of the line."

David said, "But you're at the end of the line!"

"Aye," said Wattie, "but when I see him setting up the camera I'll nip out the ring and leave you and Walter in the photograph."

David Black was a keen buyer of any good dog he came across if by Ch. Aldham Joker or by one of his stud dogs or out of a Tweedside-bred bitch. As a result by careful selection he gained many Champions.

The late George McConnel (prefix: Girvanside)

George McConnel lived in the village of Straiton, some seven miles from our own home. In the early days he farmed High Garphar near Straiton but sold it and purchased the hotel called the Boar's Head. Unfortunately, he died a young man.

One of his first Champions was a dog called Ch. High Garphar

Sensation, bred by Mr. J. Welshman, b. December 23, 1947, sired by Tweedside Red Playboy, *ex* Meikledale Trixie.

But probably his best Border was the little bitch Ch. Girvanside Tigress Mischief, bred by Mr. A. McFadzean, b. October 11, 1948. She was the dam of Triesta, who was the dam of Ch. Marrburn Morag. Mischief was a beautifully balanced little bitch, too small when she was up against the larger type, but quality all over.

George purchased Girvanside Cruggleton Don, bred by T. Buchanan, b. October 20, 1949 by Callum *ex* Orenza. The first time I saw this dog was on one of my official visits to the farm of Cruggleton to inspect Beef Shorthorn Bulls. Before reaching the farm my eye caught a red coloured animal coming down a dyke back, hunting. I at first thought it was a fox, but as we came closer to the animal I realized that it was a Border Terrier dog.

On arriving at the farm it was not long before Tom Buchanan appeared with the dog at his heel. I was very impressed with the dog and enquired about his breeding. If I had been in need of a dog at that time I could have purchased him at a bargain price. I told Tom he had a very good young dog and he should hold on to him.

It so happened that there was a Land O'Burns Canine show in Ayr the end of that week at which the late Dr. Lilico was the judge. After the judging was finished we met Neil McEwan and Dr. Lilico and we were joined by George McConnel. In the course of the conversation I mentioned to McEwan and Lilico that I had seen the best young dog that I had seen for some time and that he was not a stone's throw from either of them. They made a few inquiries as to the whereabouts and the breeding. Both, of course, knew Tom Buchanan, as they had from time to time given him bitches they were finished with from an exhibition viewpoint. In fact, Orenza was by Neil McEwan's old dog Robin Hood *ex* a bitch named Madas.

The following morning the telephone rang and it was George wanting to know if I would go with him that day to see the dog I had spoken about at the show. I agreed and we set out for McEwan-Lilico country. George purchased the dog, who accompanied us home that day. I learned some time later that we had not left the farm long before the two stalwarts arrived to see the dog and much to their surprise it had gone.

The following year George showed the dog at Crufts and won the

C.C. under David Black. It was only a short period of time before the dog gained his title. George phoned the news from London to me. I could not resist phoning my friend Dr. Lilico to tell him the good news.

In due course, I mated Hazel to Don and retained a dog pup. I named him Maxton Red Raider, because he was rich red in colour and we had raided the adjoining county of Wigtownshire to get his father. Ch. Cruggleton Don died a young dog, although George never discovered the reasons for his untimely death.

3

An Interpretation of the Breed Standard of the Border Terrier

If people take up the breeding of livestock, they should aim to improve the breed, so that when they leave this worldy existence the stock they leave behind is better than the stock they inherited from breeders who have passed on to, we hope, better lands.

This is of course easier said than done in any breed where you have had sound foundation and good breeders. It is more difficult to improve on the existing material if the previous breeders were doing

The author with Ch. Maxton Monarch by Ch. Maxton Matchless ex Ch. Marrburn Morag & full litter brother of Ch. Starrburn Sultan & Maxton Mhairi. Monarch was unfortunately killed in a kennel fight.

their jobs. (This last statement requires some qualification to be fair to those breeders who were in the breed at its foundation, when there would be a mixture of genetic types.) Depending on the foundation types, the person with an eye for stock and with some grey matter, by selecting the correct brood bitch and the right type of stud dog for each ensuing litter, should make some progress towards the ideal envisioned.

Logic would suggest that, as time passed, if breeders were on the right lines the breed should have reached some degree of perfection, and the modern breeder would simply mate dog X to bitch Y to get a perfect litter of pups, all like peas in the proverbial pod. Well, if this is so in breeding dogs, we do not see these constant perfections in the Championship shows—we still see the same-up-and-down types. The monstrosities sometimes seen in the show ring are due to man's interference with Nature, which favours the animal best suited for its living conditions. Breeding dogs for exaggeration has in some breeds resulted in an animal completely useless for the purpose for which it was originally intended. A typical example is the Bulldog, a breed that once upon a time could tackle and pin a bull. Today the unfortunate creature's respiratory organs are so deformed that it appears to have great difficulty in breathing, and females of the breed, so far as I can learn, require to have their young by Caesarian section.

This distortion of a breed's carefully selected specific characteristics can occur in any breed where you have breeders and judges who have never considered the reasons underlying the Standard of the breed or observed the breed at its work, and who have a bee in their bonnets regarding certain breed characteristics to the disregard of the whole. Such individuals, who often have a considerable influence on the breed, do not realize that *the whole basis of conformation in all stock is proportion in all body parts,* nor do they recognize the importance of the breed Standard and what it implies.

An example in modern times of the consequences of selecting against an important characteristic of the breed occurred with Aberdeen Angus cattle. Between the two world wars, because some influential overseas breeders wished a small, thickset, short-legged type of animal, breeders reduced the Aberdeen Angus to a miniature of its original size. The Aberdeen Angus as a result lost favour with the commercial breeders who had been using Angus bulls to cross on to other breeds of cattle to produce an animal to finish for beef. When the Angus became reduced in size, the commercial breeders imported large continental breeds to take its place. The Angus breeders, to regain lost ground, were then forced to import larger, less well refined Aberdeen Angus bulls from Canada and New Zealand to try to regain the size they had lost by their earlier selection for small bulls.

This process demonstrates clearly how breeders and judges can influence the swing of the pendulum within a breed to its detriment. If the present trend of awarding top honours in Border Terriers to dogs oversize as defined in the Standard continues, for instance, in a short period of time it will only be these oversize dogs that will be regarded as correct by newcomers to the breed, and the Border will lose its ability to work fox and badger.

Those who are interested in the working side of the breed all say they want dogs that are not too big, that have good, weatherproof coats which do not require trimming, and, above all, dogs that have a nose with a strong scent. Says the working terrier man, there is a difference between trimming or tidying up the dog and the present-day practice of skinning them. And they add that the majority of Borders in the show ring never put their nose to the ground. A dog that has scent, they say, is always scenting about for quarry, and if his nose is not on the ground it is in the air, nostrils twitching for scent. The wise Border Terrier breeder will take note of the comments of the working terrier man.

The interpretation of the Border Terrier Standard is crucial to the breeder and judge. The following comments are offered about what the Standard says and what I believe it implies in the hope that they will aid the novice to understand what the older breeders were trying to breed their dogs to comply to. I will try to describe in detail those points of anatomy and characteristics of the Border Terrier which they felt were important.

Characteristic: the Border Terrier is essentially a working terrier. It should be able to follow a horse and must combine activity with gameness.

Clearly, there is no point in having a Border that is not game because a dog which is not game will not go to ground, even if it can follow a horse.

The Standard's requirement of following a horse probably arose because Borders were used in the hunt in the early days of the breed and to a great extent were owned by followers of the hunt. For the Border breeder, the phrase "being capable of following a horse" draws attention to the fact that a good Border requires to be on the leg. This does not of course mean that it should be as high off the ground as an Airedale or a Golden Retriever. The reason also for the words "must combine activity with gameness" no doubt was that one could generally assume that a dog on the leg or a dog with a reasonable length of leg would be more active than one with very short legs. Some will say that there are short-legged breeds which are also active; this I accept, but would ask whether these short-legged breeds would be so active if they first had to follow a horse for several miles over rough country and then go to ground and bolt the fox. It is noticeable as well that most of the short-legged breeds are also short in their backs and thick set of their bodies. How many of the world's top athletes are short-legged or short-backed or both? How many animals which go to ground or can gallop and stay long distances have a short back?

Characteristic: head like that of an otter, moderately broad in skull with a short, strong muzzle. A black nose is preferable but a liver or flesh coloured one is not a serious fault.

This part of the Standard in my view singles out the Border Terrier from all other breeds of terriers. The character of the head is so important, first of all because the head of any animal dominates that animal in the eyes of the observer. Moreover, the animal's head seems designed to impress one first in the more physical sense. In the bull, the head is where the horns are if it is a horned breed and, even if it is not, the head is still the part that hits you first. If it is a farm collie, the head is where the teeth are. I have known of people injured by a collie's teeth but never by its tail!

More significantly, in working your dogs either at fox or badger, if the dog is going to be injured it will be by the adversary teeth. Thus, the protective conformation of the head is not merely a question of taste. (Taste is certainly involved, however; if any stocksman in conversation informs you that a particular animal has "character", then he is referring to the animal's head. If he informs you the animal lacks character, then you can take it the animal has a plain head.)

Head. Like that of an Otter, moderately broad in skull with short strong muzzle. A black nose is preferable but a liver or flesh coloured one is not a serious fault.

Above: Tarka the Otter of the TV series. Photograph kindly given by Messrs Rank Films to whom I record my appreciation.

Reader. Should note black wide nostril, extending into short flat muzzle with practically no stop, extending into a moderately broad skull with considerable width between the eyes & ears. The latter very small & low set on head. Muscular neck with ample leg bone & strong claws & paws. A formidable opponent.

Below: Ch. Maxton Matchless, head study.

I have found that there is a close relationship between the height of a well-proportioned animal and the length of its head. This is not an original observation: the French hippotamists regarded the height of a well-proportioned horse to be 2½ times the length of the head, a relationship which seems relevant to Borders as well. This is not surprising if one considers that if you put a long head on a Border then you require to increase the animal's height to balance the body. If the dog is very short, you require to reduce the head, again to balance the body.

If one looks at the head of an otter, the first impression is of its clean cut and short, flat, strong muzzle. A very good book on otters by the late C. J. Harris (Weidenfeld & Nicolson) gives the overall skull length as 111.1 to 122.6 mm for males and 102.3 to 110.8 for females—that is, 4.374 inches for males and 4.027 inches for females. Unfortunately the dimensions are not subdivided into length from the point of the nose to the eye, though the nose is clearly very short in comparison to the back skull. (The "Table of Measurements" included in appendix A shows the relationships of Border Terrier heads to their own height and is presented for the reader's interest in such questions.)

Last summer I was fishing on the River Nith, on one of those beautiful days that the dedicated fisher hates and I really enjoy—nature at its best. Looking down the large pool I saw what appeared at a distance to be a shining, blackish object coming up the pool towards me. I at first thought it was a big salmon, but there was no back fin above the water. About 15 to 20 yards down the pool from me it veered towards the opposite bank, climbed out of the water, and stood directly opposite. I was looking at a large, magnificent otter some 20 yards across the pool. Mrs. Gardner, who was sitting near me on the bank, also saw it at about the same time.

We were both struck by the otter's size, its very long body, and the obvious power that such a body could unleash if required so to do. On looking at such an animal, one could well imagine it twisting and turning in a large pool after eels and the odd salmon. The clean cut head with its short strong muzzle was practically devoid of hair around the muzzle. There were a few whiskers, no doubt to act as feelers in a tight entrance or channel. The otter probably stood some eight to ten inches from the ground and would weigh some 15 to 20 pounds. In my opinion he would make a formidable foe in a tight corner, so much so that on reflection I think I would hesitate to put a dog into any hole where I was aware there was an otter present.

In suggesting or looking at how fitting for its purposes and life the proportions of an otter are, I am again struck by the fact that man had no part in its breeding or selection for breeding; the otter is another example that Nature rewards the best adaptations and that the actual height of the otter will have been arrived at by natural selection and by elimination at birth or rearing of the weaker or less well adapted of the progeny. The lesson to be taken is that dog breeders, who select and breed on traits according to their judgement, would be very well advised to consider the Standard with the greatest respect in any breeding programme they plan.

Characteristic: The mouth

In my opinion, the original Standard of the breed drawn up in the 1920s makes the most logical statement about the mouth. Let us look at what is said in that Standard:

> HEAD: Like that of an otter, moderately broad skull with short strong Muzzle, *level teeth* (my italics), black nose preferred, but liver and flesh coloured not to disqualify.
> DISQUALIFICATION: Mouth undershot or overshot.

What did the older breeders mean by the words "level teeth"? I have had in my working life considerable experience of the mouth of stock for deformities. In this context a level mouth was one in which the two jaws (in the bovine, the lower incisor teeth) were flush with the edge of the dental pad. Thus, a plumb line or the edge of a set square would be flush with the two jaws. In the level mouth, the top incisor teeth are directly above the lower incisors, and any deviation from this position is undershot or overshot.

The (new) Standard as published by the Kennel Club states:

> **Mouth:** teeth should have a scissor-like grip, the top teeth slightly in front of the lower, but a level mouth is quite acceptable. An undershot or overshot mouth is a major fault and highly undesirable.

This Standard only states that an undershot or overshot mouth is "highly undesirable". It indicates that if the judge can find a better exhibit than the overshot or undershot one, it is quite clearly his duty to place the better exhibit at the top of the line. The new Standard does not say, as the old Standard quite clearly did, that an overshot or undershot exhibit should be disqualified. Again I ask the reader to look at this from a functional point of view. The reason for trying to breed a dog with a good mouth is so that it is capable of holding and if necessary killing its quarry (although killing quarry is not the role of a Border at work). If it is accepted that a scissor-like grip is "correct" (the front teeth are slightly in front of the lower teeth), one might logically query, since a reverse scissor bite does not interfere with the function of the teeth, why is it wrong to have the lower teeth slightly in front of the upper? (Please note I am saying SLIGHTLY IN FRONT, i.e. the reverse of the correct mouth.) In the case of the old Standard of the level mouth, it is clear that the incisor teeth should be directly above the lower incisors, and any deviation from this position was an undershot or overshot.

I feel that in judging the breed under the present Kennel Club rules, the mouth as defined in the Standard places too much importance on the position of the incisor teeth, and insufficient importance on the other aspects of the jaw, in particular the canine teeth. A number of good dogs have been penalized by inexperienced judges from the position that the mouth is not correct. The judges look at the incisor teeth and if there should be one slightly out of alignment the dog, according to them, is wrong of the mouth.

Surely the important teeth in the dog (the Carnivora family) are the canine teeth. These teeth are large, well developed, pointed and sharp. The top and bottom canines interlock on either side of the jaw. It is for this reason that the dog's mouth can move only in a vertical direction. There is no lateral movement. When the canine teeth interlock correctly, there can be little wrong with the dog's mouth.

Moreover, the incisor teeth are small teeth compared to the canine teeth. They act only as minor holding teeth. Nature evidently intends the canine teeth to be the important teeth. Note in support of this view that the canine teeth are the last teeth to be changed from the milk teeth in the Carnivora. When the incisor teeth are shed in a puppy the canine teeth, designed to hold the prey, remain. When the second or permananent incisor teeth are replaced, the temporary canine teeth are then shed, and are *immediately* replaced with the permanent canine teeth. (Sometimes the permanent canines come in before the animal loses its temporary ones.)

In Border Collies where the dogs develop the bad habit of catching cows by the tail and in so doing sometimes damage the tail, either the canine teeth are removed or the dog got rid of. Removing the canine teeth seriously disables the dog. In nature it would be no great disadvantage to the Carnivora family if by chance it lost its incisor teeth provided the canine teeth were left. But it is a serious disadvantage to this family if the canine teeth are lost. In my opinion, when a judge questions the incisor teeth in his critique I would expect to find that the fault was sufficiently bad to put the dog out of the tickets. Yet judges will comment on this aspect of the dog where there is a thousandth part of an inch between the so called imperfect and the perfect. Often such judges will be far more tolerant of a much more serious fault, such as bad feet.

In the 30-odd years I have been exhibiting Border Terriers I have only seen one dog that I would consider had a real undershot jaw. In that case the lower jaw carrying the incisor teeth was behind the canine teeth in the upper jaw when the jaw was closed. This type of jaw in my view is what the breeders who drew up the original Standard wished to draw the judges' attention to in the breed and request judges to penalize.

In my opinion, it is unfortunate that the Standard does not define the jaw more carefully, as at no time is the word jaw used. The dictionary defines the word "mouth" as the opening between the lips of men and animals through which food is taken; or equates it to lips, as a feature; or indicates it is the cavity behind the lips containing the teeth, tongue and palate and vocal organs. Jaw, on the other hand, is "one of the two bones forming the framework of the mouth and containing teeth".

As a final point, let us note that the Standard gives the judges a guide in the allocation of points for the respective parts of the dog's conformation. If the dog has a fault in its mouth, then it should be penalized in accordance with the severity of the fault. Note the importance of the teeth in this listing in the Standard:

Points:

Head, Ears, Neck, and Teeth	20
Legs and Feet	15
Coat and Skin	10
Shoulders and Chest	10
Eyes and Expression	10
Back and Loin	10
Hindquarters	10
Tail	5
General Appearance	10

Characteristic: what should be the ideal height of a Border Terrier?

The breeders who drew up the Standard for the Border Terrier agreed to a height clause and had this written into the original Standard (see Chapter One). At some later point the Standard was changed and the height clause deleted. (When I wrote to the Kennel Club requesting to know when the Standard was changed and the height clause deleted, I was informed that there was no record of change.)

In a well-proportioned dog, height is of course related to other aspects of the body. Some time ago I made a project of measuring the height and other body measurements of the Maxton dogs, with the object of determining if there was a reasonable way to define a mean Standard for the breed in height and overall proportions. The key to the matter would seem to be, in a well-proportioned dog, whether the animal can be spanned at the heart. All the dogs measured were less than $8\frac{1}{2}$ inches, the depth which I can span, and all had a girth measurement of 19 inches or less. (Provided the dog has a flat rib cage, it can be spanned. If there is a tendency for the ribs to be barrel shaped, then the dog cannot be spanned, even if his body depth is less than $8\frac{1}{2}$ inches. In a recent judging appointment, for instance, the small thickset dog was the one I had the greatest difficulty in spanning. Both the big and the small dog who cannot be spanned are outwith the Standard.)

There will be exhibitors and perhaps judges who will say they are not going into the ring with a foot rule in their pockets or handbag. There is no need, since the Good Book many years ago gave us the measurement we care about. The Bible states that the span is "the measure from the thumb to the little finger expanded, equal to about three palms", or about ten inches. There is nothing to prevent the Breed Club's coming to some agreed measurement and using a steel tape with the maximum measurement acceptable for a Border Terrier marked on its length.

The handbreadth or palm (according to the Bible, equivalent to a man's four fingers, laid flat, or rather more than 3½ inches) is another important measurement for the Border—proper width in front. As the older breeders used to point out, if a dog standing on the table or the floor was more than four fingers wide between his front paws, the dog was wide in front. Further, if you examine carefully such a dog and extend your eye to the shoulder, such a dog will be wrong at the shoulder as well.

If the dog is narrow at the forelegs and you cannot place your four fingers between his legs, the legs will extend outwards as they reach upwards to the shoulders. Again, such a dog will be wrong at the shoulder. In motion, the legs will incline inwards from the shoulder and probably there will be a tendency to cross the forefeet, giving a "toe in" (or, better, "paws in") action. If you place your fingers between the shoulder blades, that is, at the withers (the elevated portion of the spine between the back and the neck, supported on either side by the two scapula or shoulder blade bones), and there is a noticeable space between the two bones, then the animal is wide in the shoulders. In these circumstances it usually follows that the animal is wide in front.

The other extreme to this is the too narrow chest. Since the chest contains the lungs, the heart, the oesophagus, part of the trachea, and some important blood vessels and nerves, too narrow a chest will reduce a dog's ability to function well at work.

There are varying degrees of construction between the wide coarse shoulder and the too narrow chest. In those animals where the latter defect is extreme, the head and neck are badly carried, resulting in a lack of liberty in the shoulders and restriction of movement in the forelimbs. The stockman's term for this condition is "tied at the shoulders".

Characteristic: body deep, narrow and fairly long; ribs carried well back, but not oversprung, as a terrier should be capable of being spanned by both hands behind the shoulder.

It seems clear that those involved in drawing up the original Standard had the riding or hunter class horse in mind when they wrote "Body deep, narrow and fairly long". When I see a really good Border his proportions in my mind expand in all directions and I visualize him/her with a saddle in the correct position. I then think, would I be comfortable in the saddle?

This thought reinforces the fact that to have a fairly long body with the ribs carried well back the back itself must be fairly long. As in horses, if you have a short-backed animal the front and back limbs are close together and the base of support for the larger muscles which act on the limbs from the body, particularly the propelling muscles, is diminished, as indeed are the large muscles themselves. For this reason, the animal's staying and capacity for speed are reduced, unless he has a deeply arched rib cage.

What is the ideal length of back for the Border? Measurements of my own Borders averaged 12.5 inches from the withers to the top of the tail head, which I consider a good length for their proportions. However, there are bound to be various opinions as to the ideal length of back for a Border. One useful guide available to us is the minimum length of back. All breeders are in agreement that a Border Terrier should not be as short as a Fox Terrier in length of back. Thus, the Standard of the Fox Terrier can be looked at in relation to the Border.

The Standard of the Fox Terrier requires the back to be short. Dr. Roslin Bruce, D.D., F.L.S., who contributed to a column in the *Dog Journal* for many years, suggests that the Fox Terrier back should be short and gives a measurement from the withers to the tail head of 11.58 inches. If this measurement is regarded as "short" in doggy terms, and the Border requires a "fairly long" back, we can at least conclude that the Border back must exceed in length the measurement for the Fox Terrier.

We also know that to have a dog that can go to ground, we require a body with some elasticity and suppleness. These qualities cannot be obtained with a short back. We must remember also that the length of the chest is in conformity with the length of the back which forms its roof.

On the other hand, a back of too great a length (often also associated with legginess) is a weakness. If subjected to any strain or stress, such a back tends to become hollow or dipped, particularly behind the shoulder. Hollowness behind the withers in some bitches only becomes worse with age, particularly if they are bred. When heavy in whelp, they are said to be "down in the back". The condition is worthy of note for the breeder because it is due to vertebrae lacking firmness of union and the back as a whole lacking rigidity, with the result that the animal's weight, instead of being borne by the bones, is in great part supported by the connecting ligaments. In time these yield to the animal's weight, increasing a defect caused in the first instance by some disturbance in vertebral development or by a relaxation of the ligaments by which vertebrae are united and supported. In animals with this defect, the forces transmitted to the back by the forefeet and progressing to the hindquarters are greatly diminished. Hence, animals affected by swayback lack the power and ability to follow possessed by others better constructed. (This condition is seen in lambs suffering from a lack of the trace element copper in the diet prenatally. Such lambs lose control of their rear quarters and in bad cases drag the hind legs.)

An opposite defect in the Border is the roach back, as seen in the Dandie Dinmont Terrier. Although Dandie breeders often do not accept the characteristic Dandie back as roached, the Dandie Standard calls for a "back rather low at the shoulders, slight downward curve with a corresponding arch over the loins, slight gradual drop to the root of the tail". If any breeder of horses saw a horse with a back as described above, he/she would accept it as a roach back. Anyone not familiar with the condition can examine the Dandie or the Borzoi to get an idea of what is meant.

The Loins: the loins comprise that portion of the spine interposed between the back in front and the croup and haunches behind. Below, it is in relation with the flanks. When the rib extends well back in the body, thus making the loin short, the stocksman refers to the animal as being "well ribbed up". A short, strong loin gives strength to the movement between the hind legs and the spine because there is less distance for the forces to pass. If the loin is long and weak, it separates the end of the ribs, the croup and the haunches. This increases the width of the flank and gives an appearance of slackness which does not look well in the show animal. The Standard calls for the loin to be strong and the hindquarters to be racy.

The Croup: the croup is important to consider in relation to the requirement in the Border Terrier Standard of a "strong loin" and "racy hindquarters". (The hindquarters, it must be remembered, are the part of the dog most used when getting into a hole.) The Standard also requires the Border to be "capable of following a horse" and must combine "activity with gameness". The croup and hindquarters should be judged with these important points in mind.

The croup is that part of the body situated between the loins and the tail setting. It extends to and is bounded by the upper part of the thighs and buttocks; it is the area of the dog's body which you view when standing immediately behind the animal and looking down on its rear quarters.

In a dog with a straight croup, that part of the body in front of the tail head (described above) is horizontal (parallel to the ground) when you view the animal from the side at eye level. In a dog with a sloping croup the highest point of the area of the body in front of the tail head is immediately behind the loin, where the haunch bones unite with the sacrum or the end part of the spine. From there they descend downward and backward to the tail head. If the croup is sloping to the tail head, then you have a typical example of what the older breeders called for in the Standard—racy hindquarters.

In horses, the croup is the part of the animal that has given rise to more discussion among breeders than any other. One view held is that the level croup is more designed for speed, as in the racehorse, whereas the sloping quarter is designed for power. In Border Terriers, extremes in either direction should be avoided, as too much inclination downward is just as much a fault as the croup too level. One requires to remember that in the dog, galloping, jumping, and standing up on the hind legs are all done by the action of the hind muscle of the croup on the upper and lower thigh.

The Limbs: although the Standard deals at some length with the body of the Border Terrier, it does not give much of a guide as to the limbs other than to indicate that "the forelegs should be straight" and "not too heavy" in the bone. How does one judge if an animal is too heavy or too light in bone? I remember a judge of beef cattle saying to me, "Bone can only be measured when the carcass is hung in the slaughterhouse." This leaves a lot for the judge to interpret in his/her own way.

In my view, the dog at ground level should stand, to use the stocksman's expression, "four square to the ground". This means that the four feet should be on the four corners of an imaginary square at ground level. In other words, the feet on either side of the body should be parallel to each other, the legs terminating in small feet with thick pads.

Well set limbs are crucial to sound movement. We can understand if we appreciate how the legs are attached to the body and how they function. Each leg is comprised of a column of bones of irregular size attached to each other in the healthy animal by free joints. The legs are attached to the body by means of large muscles, which are themselves attached to the body and upper limbs by means of long tendons. In the method of attachment, nature has perfected the ideal combination for the functions the fore and hind limbs are required to serve.

The forelimbs or the forepart of the body are supported in a sling made of the large muscles of the body connected to the extremities. Thus, the scapula or shoulder blade moves freely over the surface of the ribs, with which it is in loose contact. On the other hand, the rear limbs have a ball and socket joint. The top of the thigh bone is confined by strong ligaments to the socket (cup-like cavity) of the pelvis, thus forming the hip joint. It is through this joint that the hind limbs transmit their propulsive action and move the body forward.

It is in the act of travelling over rough country or in jumping from a height that the function of the forelimbs comes into play. The fact that the body is slung between the forelegs has a cushion effect when landing. Although they are organs of support, the forelimbs are specially designed to break and disperse the concussion of the weight of the body as it lands on the ground.

If the fore-end were constructed similarly to the hindquarter with a ball and socket joint, one can imagine the effect on the animal and the jarring on landing. A horse jumping a fence is a good example of how nature has protected the animal from injury by construction of the fore-end.

The Shoulder: again the Standard does not say what type of shoulder we should be trying to breed in our Border. However, we have a guide in the fact that the Standard does say "must be capable of following a horse and must combine activity with gameness". In all varieties of horses, from the heavy draught horse to the child's pony, ample inclination of the shoulder blade is of primary importance. If the shoulder is well laid on, good withers and a deep chest with good muscular attachment usually follows.

The well-laid on shoulder allows for great range and liberty of movement. On the other hand, when the shoulder blade is lacking in correct obliquity and is too upright, it usually lacks the desired length and therefore muscle attachment. The movement is therefore contracted, and the action short, cramped and lacking in the elasticity that is desired to enable the dog to follow a horse with ease and least effort.

In my opinion, it is unfortunate that many of those who are judging dogs have never had the opportunity to judge any other type of stock. Because of the lack of height in the Border, the points I have tried to draw attention to are probably not easily noticed by those

(Left) Crufts winners 1985. Mr. Ron Hillcoat with Ch. John Boy of Todgrove. Br. Mrs. Halley. b. 16/4/83. s. Tyneclyde Kruive. d. Todgrove Tanner. Dog CC & Res BOB. (Centre) Judge, author. (Right) Mr Nevile Hackett with Ch. Thistycroft Candlelight. Br Mr. N. Jamieson. b. 19/12/79. s. Maxton Murgatroyd. d. Edenbridge Moon Maiden. CC & BOB.

unaccustomed to judging horses, where the size of the animal is help-ful. Those who are interested in judging would be well advised to make the acquaintance of a good breeder of, preferably, heavy horses. If one examines the best specimens of either the Shire or the Clydes-dale horse, for instance, a good sloping shoulder is a feature of their makeup, of the last breed in particular. It is illuminating to observe the action of these heavy horses, their great stride, elasticity of move-ment and recoil, the important part the hind legs contribute to the propulsion of the great weight of the animal forward and the obliquity of the hind limb when extended backwards in this pro-pulsion. The points made in this discussion are more noticeable if the horse is in work, e.g. drawing a load. If the observer watches closely, it is very noticeable where the real point of impact with the ground is made. The traction forward is only made when the foot directed backward is firmly in contact with the surface of the ground. (This is more noticeable if the ground is soft.) If one observes the horse in work under a load, one will see how all the bones and muscles come into play. It will also be observed how important a well-laid-on shoulder is to the working horse. Only if the shoulder is correctly laid at the right angle can the collar linked to the load, which is fitted over its head and laid against the shoulder, fit properly.

The Standard of the breed does not at any point state how a Border should move. A considerable amount of emphasis has been placed on movement in recent years. Although in judging I am required to fol-low the general pattern as laid down, I have often wondered whether the respective Breed Clubs would not be better to advise that judges pay more attention to TYPE in the exhibit and forget about move-ment until they have established the correct type of Border. Type has been in my opinion sacrificed in many modern Borders for so-called soundness. (In expressing my views on this subject I am not advocat-ing, of course, that unsound dogs should not be penalised.)

Good movement is, in work, very significant. It is understandable how this interest in movement came into being in the judging of, e.g., heavy horses, hunters, or riding ponies. In the case of the heavy horse, the animal is required to work in crops growing in drills prob-ably 22″ or even 18″ apart. In order that a four-footed animal can walk down such a small width it must be sound, i.e., its front feet require to follow the direction of the fore end. There is no room in this type of work for the wide in front or behind movement so noticeable in dogs or in the wild animals in documentary films. In the hunter or the riding horse it is also important that the horse should move soundly as the rider's neck is at risk. A hunter or riding pony can trip and fall on other things on the course. The object of trying to breed a sound horse is to reduce the probability that it will trip over its own feet because of unsound movement. This need for soundness is more important in the work of horses than in the work of dogs.

The Foot: it is a well known saying by all breeders of heavy or light horses "no foot, no horse"; this could equally well be applied to the dog. The faddist in judging faults a dog for having one irregular tooth on the grounds that this is an inherited fault, but on the other hand he/she does not hesitate to put up a dog with bad feet, a far more significant fault in the Border and just as much inherited as a crooked tooth. Anyone who requires to use his/her feet and legs to do his/her job fully appreciates the value of the feet should anything befall them. A well known breeder of stock said to me on one occasion when we were discussing the merits of judging stock, "the first thing to look for in any animal when you are judging, or in particular say a stud animal, is its feet; if they please you then look upwards. If they don't, you need look no further."

The Standard says the Border foot should be "small with thick pads". The foot of the dog should look natural and be attached to the leg in a natural way. It should not look as if it has been attached to the leg as an afterthought. It should be small and rounded, extending into the pastern and then into the leg. Although the Standard requires the foot to be small, it is also understood, of course, that it must be large enough to be serviceable to the dog and to support its weight. The correct foot has been referred to as "catlike" but personally I am not too keen to accept this terminology as being correct for the feet. There should certainly be no resemblance to harefoot; neither should there be any tendency to be flat-footed. Probably the feet are best described as being close and compact with good pads.

The legs and feet when viewed from any position should be straight, with the leg bone carried down to the foot so that the finish of the leg and the start of the foot is hardly noticeable. The foot should not be spread out so that the toes can be seen, neither should they point inwards ("pigeon toe") nor be pointed outward, giving a splayed foot.

Sometimes the novice will be advised when buying a dog or when they attempt to judge for the first time, to look at the dog's head or coat. When I am judging an animal, however, as the stocksman advised, I look at the feet first and foremost. If the feet please me then I am interested in the rest of the animal. In the absence of good feet and legs to follow, the animal is not worth considering as a breed specimen. It is prudent to note also that breeders of many different animal breeds accept that feet are an important part of the animal, and that bad feet are easier to come by than good ones.

Tail: the Standard requires that the tail be "moderately short and fairly thick at the base then tapering, set on high and carried gaily but not curled over the back". There are too many spindle tails among the present day Borders; they lack the thickness at the base, being about the same thickness all the way from base to top. Tail position, too, is often incorrect.

If the tail is set too high, we lose the gentle slope over the croup. Moreover, the high set tail tends to be carried gaily. A tail curling over the back, although not a major fault, does take away from the general good appearance of the dog.

The racy hindquarters that the older breeders thought so desirable in the Border are due to the slight slope on the dog's croup and the well-set-on tail.

Borders that get their tail well up in some cases are also aggressive. They are often acceptable to the all-rounder judge in a variety class in particular, but the older breeders would not have them in preference to a Border with a well set on tail carried at a lower angle to the body. The more upright tail also gives the dog a shorter-coupled appearance. The Standard requires a dog "deep and narrow and fairly long"; one cannot have these requirements if the back is short, and it seems wrong to put up an animal who by reason of his tail set appears uncharacteristic, even if he is in actuality "fairly long".

Coat: "harsh and dense with close undercoat; the skin must be thick". This is one of the most important traits of the Border. A dog without a good harsh dense coat on a very cold day, if out on a hill working, is similar to the owner being there who left his jacket at home. The harsh coat on top is necessary to shed the rain; the dense close undercoat is necessary to keep the dog warm, as is the thick skin. The importance of a good coat on any animal that is out of doors for some period of time, summer and winter, is characterised in Galloway cattle. Their breeders speak of "good skins"; this terminology includes the dense harsh coat, the fine undercoat, and the thick skin that their Standard requires. (It struck me, on many occasions when I was inspecting this breed, how close the breeders' aims often were to what we, as Border breeders, were trying to achieve.) This breed of cattle spend their life outside on some of the higher hills. It is noticeable in the same environment that a thin skinned animal going with the Galloways on a cold day quite obviously shows signs of the cold, as the Galloways do not. Saying that such an animal looks miserable will explain the position to the reader.

As one of the few older breeders left in the breed today whose period in the breed has spanned the last of the older breeders of a generation ago, I cannot emphasise enough the importance of a good coat to a Border. Yet it is difficult to judge Border coats today because so often the dogs are stripped, well nigh skinned. This fashion is contrary to the rules of, in particular, the Southern Border Terrier Club, whose members at one of their meetings passed the following resolution:

> Exhibitors and judges should be reminded that it is not in keeping with the sporting traditions of the breed to have the coat trimmed or to have the head and tail supported by the handler in the ring. Borders should be shown on a loose lead. The coat should be of a natural weather resisting character. Old dead coat may be stripped off by hand where necessary.

The current habit of showing the Border in very tight coat is potentially dangerous to the breed. As the older breeders always maintained, when the stripping craze becomes popular, the coats will go. (Perhaps it would be a good idea, before a Border obtains its final certificate, that it be put in quarantine until the coat grows and can be judged by a panel of working terrier people to ascertain if it is the correct texture.) It is also of interest, with regard to the coat question, to note the decline in entries of the terrier breeds where stripping is the order of the day. It seems likely that these breeds have declined in numbers because the public, who are the people who create demand for the surplus stock, appear to have become tired of the need to have the dogs stripped and have switched to breeds that do not require stripping.

Colour: red, wheaten, grizzle and tan or blue and tan. It is often said by stocksmen that a good animal is never a bad colour, but there are many breeders and judges who become colour conscious. The inheritance of coat colour is not clearly understood and those of us who are breeders have not always the ability to interpret the coat shades in a young puppy in the nest at the date of registration as being colour X, Y, or Z.

Sometimes it is surprising when one looks back at the date of the registration to note the colour one registered the Border as a pup. The puppies that are red (that is, a solid red) are easily identified and they do not change. It is the dark grizzle colour that causes the problem, particularly if the legs show a lighter colouring; when these puppies become adults they are invariably nearer to a dark grizzle than to a so-called blue and tan, although many at nest age might be registered as blue and tan.

The red colour of the older breeders has to a great degree been lost; this in my own view has been due to the breeders selecting against the white gene. If you come across a real red dog today (that is, bodily solid red), there will probably be a white mark on it, on the chest or below on his belly. If you enquire further, it is likely you will find the dog is not registered and was bred in a hunt kennel where there is a mixture of terrier types as well as blood lines.

It appears that there is a considerable confusion among some of the breeders of Borders regarding colour inheritance. This is particularly so in relation to the so called blue and tan. There is no doubt that the greater proportion of these dogs today are BLACK not BLUE.

The blue aimed for by the older breeders was the smoky blue of the Kerry Blue, but with more white hairs through the body. In all the years of breeding I have only seen one real natural blue; it was a pup by Champion Maxton Matchless. Through the body it has an equal proportion of white hairs to the blue-not-black.

Champion Bargower Silver Dollar was another approaching the correct blue colour, although he did not have the abundance of white hairs that the other dog had in his body frame. Although I made Silver Dollar a Champion in a period of six weeks from the start of his show career, and he was as near to the colour as could be expected, there was a definite prejudice against this rare colour by judges.

There was also at that time (early 1950's), some correspondence and prejudice against the red Borders, as this colour, it was said, could be mistaken by hounds for a fox. It did not appear to occur to the same people that a pure white terrier working in a red coloured earth might also be mistaken for Reynard leaving the earth.

Judging your Border Terrier

It may be of interest to present here the method of stock judging I was taught, in the first stages by my father on heavy horses and later as a student at the West of Scotland College of Agriculture, where I was a member of the A team of stock judging for three years. (This team successfully competed in the National Stock Judging Competitions at the national Shows on all classes of stock.)

As students, our tutors of judging were all stocksmen of the highest calibre in their respective breeds, so we lacked nothing in tuition. The major teaching method used was the elimination competition. Your marks in the long series of competitions were added up, and the top students formed the A team, followed by a reserve (B team) or you fell by the wayside.

Let me try to demonstrate to the reader, in particular the novice, how to judge a dog (or a horse) as I was taught. Let us use an outline of a dog to illustrate the points I wish to draw attention to. let us imagine the dog is standing on the table in the normal accepted position in judging dogs at shows (although I prefer to judge the dog on the floor). Before you start to examine the dog, see that you are able to move round the table in all directions, so that you are able to observe the points without moving the dog.

The View from the Side

Stand well back so that you can take in an overall view of the dog. Your eye is the guide in this exercise, so take plenty of time. The dog should so stand that its weight is evenly balanced on all its legs and feet. If the conformation is unsound, the expert handler will no doubt try and put the dog in a correct standing position he would not normally assume. The dog will be uncomfortable in this position and will revert back to his accustomed position. Take time in your observations and watch carefully the actions of the handler and the dog. You can learn from both.

The dog is standing in a natural position. The weight should be

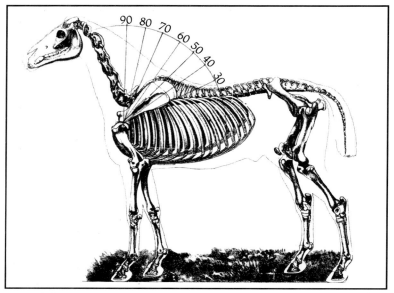

Skeletal rendering of a hunting horse showing shoulder layback.

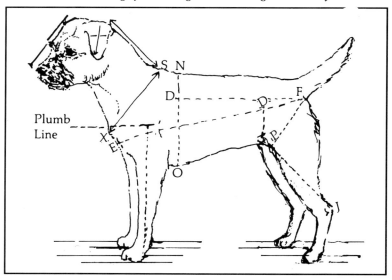

Conformation outline of a Border Terrier.

equally distributed on all its legs and feet. A vertical plumb line let fall to the floor from the shoulder joint (the lower part of the scapula meets the upper part of the humerus to form the shoulder joint) should divide the foreleg into two equal parts, and meet the ground a little behind the heel of the foot.

Similarly a vertical line let fall from the point of the shoulder to the floor should nearly meet the point of the toe. If the foot is much behind this point, the dog's equilibrium is imperfect. On the other hand if the line falls much behind the foot, the fetlock is probably wrong, with a tendency to have a low heel. The consequence of this is a weakness in the ligaments of the fetlock, and liability to sprain. If the line falls within the heel of the foot, the pastern must be too upright. If it falls a considerable distance behind this point, the pastern is too long.

The side of the dog having been examined and the points memorised, you must now move round to the front. A vertical line let fall from the middle of the forearm should equally divide the lower parts of the limb. There should be a reasonable space between the forelegs so that the dog has a good base of support. This is also necessary to accommodate the large muscles of the chest. It is also necessary to allow free movement. The older breeders considered about four fingers' space between the feet to be correct. The hind limbs should be directly placed behind the fore limbs.

If the line let fall from the middle of the forearm falls exteriorly, the legs are too close.

If the line falls within the legs they are too wide.

If the line divides equally the knee and the leg as far as the fetlock, and then falls in the inside, the toes will be unduly turned out.

If the line falls on the outside of the feet the dog is pigeon toed.

The View from the Rear

The conformation of the hind quarter viewed from the side should be considered at the same time as you are viewing the fore end. This is of course automatic in the case of the experienced judge. The hock should give the viewer the appearance of some strength as there are contained within it some large bones and muscles. It is this part of the body that propels the body forward.

There are two long bones in the upper part of the hind limb. The femur (upper part) forms a ball-and-socket joint with the pelvic girdle. The lower part of this bone meets the upper part of the tibia with other smaller ones to form the stifle joint. If the angulation between these two bones deviates from the normal, then there are two types of hock.

If the angle is too steep, then the hock is too straight.

If the angle is too great, then the hock becomes bent.

In the case of the plumb line, with the straight hock there is little distance between the line and the formation of the hock. In the case of the bent hock, there is considerable distance between the line and the hock.

The side view of the animal's rear conformation having been memorised, you now move to the rear. The hind limbs are normal when the plumb line let fall from the point of the hip (ischium bone) divides the limbs into two equal parts.

The hocks should be directly below the centre of gravity. Any lateral deviation from the perpendicular line, as when inclined too much in or too much out, is regarded as a source of weakness.

Having satisfied the question of general conformation by the means used by the stocksman, we turn to the distinctive character of the Border Terrier as laid down by the breed's Standard.

The Mouth

As required by the Standard, note whether the top teeth are slightly in front of the bottom incisor teeth, and whether the upper and lower canine teeth are properly locked in position.

The Head

Consider the Border Terrier's head with the head of an otter in mind. Look for a short broad muzzle with practically no stop, a low set eye, a very small ear, and a moderately broad skull, with overall a clean-cut head with little furnishing.

Balance

To judge this factor, begin by examining the exhibit for height, an important factor in a Border.

Basically, the balanced Border's proportions would appear to be similar to those of the horse. In the horse it is accepted by the best of the judges that a balanced horse stands about $2\frac{1}{2}$ times the length of his head (i.e., if the Border's head is 6 inches, his height should be about 15 inches).

The older breeders considered also that a good Border should be about $7\frac{1}{2}$–8 inches from the ground to the brisket.

The distance from the point of the shoulder to the point of the buttock should be about equal to the animal's height.

The length of the head is also equal to: the distance from the point of the withers to the point of the shoulder; the point of the buttock to the stifle joint; the distance from the stifle to the hock joint; and the length of the neck.

There are other qualities in the Border to consider, such as coat, feet and movement. These matters have been commented on in the course of discussing the Standard of the breed.

4

Breeding Border Terriers: A Geneticist's View

Breeding with Genetics in Mind

All who breed livestock whether they do so as a hobby or as a commercial enterprise, and whether they breed dogs, cattle, pigeons or the rabbit, practise some sort of breeding system. In using any system, moreover, a certain degree of luck is involved. Some have practised an inbreeding or line breeding system with considerable success, for instance, while others, using the same system, have had a disaster.

This difference in outcome is more noticeable in the commercial breeding of farm livestock than in dog breeding because in the breeding of farm animals, the surplus stock is sold on the open market, where all who are interested can express for themselves their opinion of the results of the breeder's skill. One can regularly witness from the gallery of the livestock market a strong competition among several breeders as they bid to obtain a particular stock bull or ram which in their opinion will breed the type of animal they have decided is correct.

It is on type that so much depends; type determines whether the breeder has been successful or not. Hence, the breeder must from the beginning resolve to breed a particular type of animal that he considers his ideal of the breed.

In dog breeding, where the luck comes into the game is, having purchased the foundation bitch or bitches, whether one is successful in the quest to select correct mates for them. In other words will the animals you breed together "nick", or produce the desired progeny?

The nicking of the two depends on the animals' genetic inheritance, only part of which is visible in their appearance, or phenotype. If the females have the genes which yield the same type as her mate, then the progeny will express that type. They will perhaps turn out to be Champions, or at least be better than their dams for the traits sought. On the other hand, if the genetic factors for type are not inherited by the resulting progeny, then the breeding is a loss—one has not advanced towards one's ideal type. The degree by which we are able to measure such a disaster depends on the final quality of the progeny.

In dog breeding one is concerned with the conformation, temperament, and coat of the animal in relation to the breed Standard. Of these, temperament must be considered before the animal's phenotype; there is no point in having an excellent phenotype with a vicious temper.

The profit aim of the commercial breeder can have significant effects on a breed. A commercial livestock farmer, who breeds animals for slaughter, may go to the sale and purchase any bull to put his cows in calf. He is not interested in the improvement of the country's livestock; he is only interested in the sale of his surplus stock. A similar type in dog breeding is the breeder who as soon as his dog becomes a Champion willingly breeds him to any bitch of the breed though she has no relationship to the dog and regardless of her phenotype and that of her relations. The resulting litter may or may not be of a high standard in relation to the breed as a whole. The breeder may be fortunate in that the genetic material contributed by the mates nicks, and lo and behold a winner is produced, by good fortune rather than good judgement.

This type of breeding (that is, the continued use of unrelated mates to the females of the kennel) at the best is little better than mongrel breeding. The resulting stock will be about average for the breed population as a whole. Such breeding does not bring about any improvement; in fact the stock, to use a genetic term, tends to regress: points of superiority possessed by one or another individual animals disappear.

The improvement in a stock has to be seen to be believed when the rightly bred male is introduced into a group of nondescript females of his breed. This improvement occurs because the well-bred animal is more often prepotent (homozygous) for his outstanding traits than are the nondescript (heterozygous) females for their traits. Thus he is able to pass his traits on to their progeny.

Crossbreeding

Crossbreeding should not be confused with mongrel breeding; in crossbreeding it is usual for the male to be of a high standard of the particular breed he represents and to be well-bred, i.e., homozygous for many traits. Thus his genes can dominate some of those of the females he is to be mated to, who are usually the progeny of a high quality animal of a different breed from the sire to be used.

The crossbreed known as a lurcher is a good example of cross-breeding in dogs. When I was at school there were many of these dogs following the covered gypsy caravans that travelled around the area, walking imediately behind or below the caravan. They were by a Greyhound *ex* a good Border Collie bitch. It was said the gypsies used the Greyhound for speed and the Border Collie for brains to get the lurchers, who in those days were the means of the gypsy family getting their dinners. In the late 1920's and 30's, many miners also had a lurcher to obtain the family's dinner. I understand there are Lurcher Shows held today which are quite popular events. All lurchers shown, however, are not of the traditional Greyhound/Collie cross.

Inbreeding and Selection

This system of breeding closely related animals together causes great controversy among breeders. It is blamed for all the evils that ever have befallen any stock. In fact, inbreeding, or close-relative mating—even the mating of father to daughter—does not of itself cause the progeny of the inbreeding to be defective. What happens is that progressive inbreeding causes to come to light any hidden (recessive) defects that are present in the genes of the breeding stock. These may have existed for some time, having been introduced into a stock quite unknowingly by the breeder, and may express themselves only generations after their introduction when two inbred animals, both having inherited the same recessive gene for the hidden trait, are mated. (Of course, mating two unrelated animals who are carrying the same recessive gene can also cause the same result.)

Inbreeding and selection is a long-term breeding system. Over several generations it reduces the heterozygosity of the original strain of foundation animals. In this way superior traits sought in the progeny, as successive related parents become homozygous for the trait, appear reliably. The closer the relationship of the animals mated, the faster heterozygosity is reduced in all traits, good and bad.

The one fact that should be remembered by the breeder who is going to pursue a policy of inbreeding is that inbreeding does not create anything that is not already there; and it is likely to cause recessive genes in the strain to come to the surface.

The basic concept of an inbreeding-and-selection system of breeding can be explained in the following way. Assuming that the breeders of your foundation dogs did not practise a close system of breeding, your foundation stock is a cross-section of the breed as a whole. Thus genetically they carry all the factors of the breed, good and bad alike. Your aim as a breeder is to improve the breed by strengthening in your foundation animals' progeny the good traits of the breed and eliminating weaker variants. Let us say a team of horses, some black and some white, represent that cross-section of the breed as a whole, your foundation stock. The black and white horses are yoked to the plough in no fixed system, the black and the white being equally dispersed throughout the team. Each horse represents a set of chromosomes with its gene complex. The horses are yoked in pairs, so that we have on the left of the ploughman the land horses, i.e., the horses that travel in the unploughed part of the field, representing the visible traits of the pups bred. On the right are the furrow horses, representing the pups' hidden or unexpressed traits. Our ploughman, the breeder, has at the back of his mind the type of dog he wishes to produce. This is achieved by sorting out the good genes from the undesirable ones by selection. In other words, our ploughman wishes to select out the black horses from his mixed black and white team so that the black are on the landward (visible) side of the team and the white are on the furrow (hidden) side. At the end of a bout (one length of the field being ploughed, or one generation of dogs) the ploughman selects a black horse from the furrow side and exchanges it with a white horse from the land side. Every time he goes to the end of a bout, he does the same thing, until he finishes up with all the black horses on the land side and the white horses on the furrow. This process represents the selections made by the breeder, generation by generation, of the desirable phenotype to carry on to the next generation.

The final result of your inbreeding programme is that by selection you have reduced the variability of your strain. It should be remembered of course that no matter how long an inbreeding system is used, the breeder will still get variations in traits, because one is dealing with many multiple groups of genes whose action is not fully understood and which can be influenced to some degree by environment. It should also be remembered that along with your selection for certain genes may come a number of unwanted recessive genes which will come to light if both partners in a mating are carriers of the factor. Clearly, in working to achieve one's ideal type through an inbreeding programme, one must be very careful indeed in selecting the animals to be mated. Dogs in particular should not be bred if they show questionable temperament.

Line Breeding

This breeding system also involves the breeding together of related animals. The animals are bred in such a way that the resulting progeny have a strong relationship to a particular excellent ancestor or line of ancestors. The degree of relationship of the mated animals is more distant than in inbreeding.

Inbreeding	Linebreeding
Sire to daughter	Half brother to half sister
Son to dam	Cousin to cousin
Full brother to sister	etc.

Note the diagram below:

	parents	grandparents	g. grandparents
			Sire H
		Sire D	Dam I
	Sire B		Sire H
		Dam E	Dam I
DOG A			Sire J
		Sire F	Dam K
	Dam C		Sire L
		Dam G	Dam M

The diagram represents a pedigreed animal with some repeats in its pedigree. The animal is not inbred because it has no common ancestor on both sides of its pedigree. (The sire of A above is not related to A's dam.)

The sire B *is* inbred, because he is a product of a full brother-to-sister mating. He is more homozygous for all his traits than his immediate ancestors were. The dog A inherits one half of B's genetic material (one member of each pair of genes that B has). There is nothing to indicate from the pedigree, however, that C will pass to A any genes identical to those passed to A by B. Homozygotism will not be likely.

To illustrate this further, if we mate two highly pedigreed animals of two different breeds (for example, a highly bred Ayrshire bull to a similarly highly bred Jersey cow) the fact that both parents are inbred in their respective breeds does not make their resulting progeny inbred. The crossbred progeny resulting from this mating would be likely to be heterozygous for a great number of traits, since it is unlikely that the Ayrshire bull and the Jersey cow would transmit many identical genes to the offspring.

On the other hand all dogs at some point have parents in common since they are members of the same species; so too the Ayrshire and Jersey belong to the same species. Thus they have some genes in common, however different from each other they seem to be.

In the history of the Border Terrier breed, for instance, it has been accepted from one generation to another that the Border Terrier is descended from the old Dandie Dinmonts and Bedlingtons; thus there must be some genes in common among the modern examples of these breeds. One indication of these common genes is that from time to time we see in some untrimmed Borders a tuft of soft hair on the crown of the head, referred to by the older breeders as a Dandie top knot.

The Recessive Gene and its Control

Often recessive genes express traits not wanted in the breed. Such a trait may be, for example, a red coat colour in a normally black breed or, if it is a lethal recessive, it may be one of many genetic defects which cause the deformity or death of the animal.

There has not been a lot of research done on these lethal or semi-lethal recessive genetic traits in animals, because when they occur they tend to be accepted by the breeder as "one of those things that can happen" within a breed.

Breeders should be on the alert for every genetic defect because if it is expressed in one animal, it lurks unexpressed in that animal's ancestors. Should there be a deformed pup in a litter, the breeder should consult his veterinary surgeon about the implications for his breeding programme of this event.

An Example of a Lethal Recessive and its Reduction

In the period of my service as the Department of Agriculture Livestock Improvements Officer, a farmer who wished to change his farming practice from dairying to beef production came into the office to discuss the pros and the cons of the government scheme which gave financial aid to such a change.

In view of the type of farm he had, we suggested he use a Galloway bull on his Ayrshire cows. The reason for the selection of the Galloway bull was the hope that the resulting crossbred progeny would have some of the hardy characteristics of the Galloway, e.g. good weatherproof coats and skins. It was also hoped the crossbred females would have inherited some of the milking ability of the Ayrshire, so that the farmer would have milk to sell for the period of the changeover. The proposal was that he retain the crossbred heifers and in time mate them to another Galloway bull. The heifers of this cross would have more milk than a Galloway female because of their Ayrshire ancestry, so there would be no problem rearing the calves.

Some three years after the discussion I called to see how the farmer was progressing and to find out if he was satisfied with the type of animal he was getting. He assured me he was delighted with the results of the change, but there was one factor he was unable to understand: he had had several deformed calves. His description of these was, "they have short hind legs and their guts hang out". Moreover, because of the short, tucked-up hind legs, in the cases where the calves were born breech first, his cows had great difficulty in calving. His veterinary surgeon had not seen such deformed calves before, nor had I.

As there were many Galloway herds in the area under my supervision, I started to query if any of the other Galloway breeders had had a similar experience with calves. To my surprise I found that there were several who had and who were prepared to discuss this matter.

All the herds were pedigreed, so any information I obtained could be analysed. If the deformity was the expression of a recessive gene, the pedigree would show a common sire or dam. In order to be sure no aspect of the environment was causing the deformity, I also gathered information regarding various aspects of husbandry. I was of course thinking about the thalidomide children, born with gross deformities after their mothers had taken the drug. No information supplied suggested environment was the cause of the defective calves.

The study had been in progress for some time when an article written by an Australian farmer who had a Galloway herd appeared in the *Galloway Journal*. He had had several calves born deformed but as he had been spraying the area, which had a lot of brambles, he had concluded the spray was the cause of the trouble. As our subsequent experience proved, however, the cause of the congenital defect was a recessive gene.

Quite a large number of congenital defects met in livestock breeding are caused by recessive genes, and the larger the number of similarly bred animals, the greater the possibility of the recessive gene defect coming to light. If normal animals are bred to a carrier, fifty per cent of the resulting progeny will be carriers; if these in turn are also bred to a carrier, 50% of the third-generation animals will be carriers, 12.5% will be defective, and only 32.5% will be normal. If carriers are mated, 25% of the progeny will be defective, 50% will also be carriers, and 25% will be normal.

The pattern of the breeding programme of the Galloway breeders who experienced the defect in their herds will be familiar to breeders of dogs. We can readily imagine a person who has been breeding purebred dogs for a number of years without any abnormal progeny being born. He or she then introduces a new stud dog into the kennel who is linebred to the established kennel of bitches. He has great hopes that the future pups will be the answer to his dreams. All goes well, and out of the mating several bitches are retained. The breeder then looks around for a new sire to mate to the retained progeny and obtains a son of the first dog (or another near relative) so that the line is kept intact. And with this mating comes a disaster, because both the new sire and the retained bitches carry a defective recessive gene.

The Galloway breeders had been breeding without any difficulties for many years. Then, it seemed, out of the blue came a deformed calf. It is not easy to accept that the problem has been hidden in a herd (or kennel) perhaps for generations. That is why breeders tend to think that the problem is from some other source—to them it is "one of those things one meets with in breeding"; there is no cure for the problem, and no profit in discussing it with others.

This philosophy does a great deal of harm to a breed. The importance of noting and discussing the event of defective progeny with your veterinary advisor or animal research centre personnel cannot be overemphasized. The general principle is that when a defect reaches the proportion of ten per cent in a breed or group, the defect is getting out of control. Since superior animals who are also carriers may be used widely in breeding, it may soon become impossible to prevent the defect from affecting the whole group or breed.

What had happened with the Galloways is that a breeder sold a bull to another breeder and the animal produced a number of deformed calves. The owner of the stock did not bother to notify the breeder of the bull, because it was "one of those things that happened in breeding" and just his bad luck that it had happened to him.

The first step toward eliminating an unwanted genetic trait is pedigree analysis. In the case of the Galloways, we examined the pedigrees of some 45 bulls and 117 cows that had either sired or borne abnormal calves. (There were some 126 such animals born on the farms.) We did so because the recessive trait becoming expressed meant both the sire and the dam of the affected animal were carriers. They in turn inherited the defective gene from their parents, who inherited it from their parents, and so on. In our pedigree analysis, the pattern of the defective recessive gene inheritance became quite clear—all the lines led to the same line of breeding.

The problem was how to identify and eliminate the carriers from the breeding population. (The affected animal is not a problem, since it dies or is destroyed soon after birth). Members of the Galloway Breed Council were contacted and the problem explained to them. A number of actions were taken.

First, the Chairman of the Breed Council persuaded the East of Scotland College of Agriculture (Genetics Division) to establish a herd of known carrier cows (i.e., cows who had had a deformed calf). The object of this was to test-mate several promising young bulls each year, the bulls being selected from the progeny of animals not known to be carriers. Each bull was test-mated to some twelve to fifteen cows. If all the resulting calves were normal, then a warranty was given that the bull was 95–98 per cent certain of being clear of the gene—i.e., he was a non-carrier. If on the other hand a defective calf was born, the bull was slaughtered.

The spread of a recessive gene can be rapid. If eight normal (AA) cows are mated to a carrier bull (Aa), four of the eight progeny will be carriers. In the next generation, after again using a carrier male, four of the eight progeny will be carriers, three will be normal, and one will be defective. The proportions remain steady in subsequent generations even if carrier males continue.

This trial, conducted by independent personnel, brought to light the difficulties the breeders were up against. It also showed in some cases how long it was before a defective calf turned up and bulls could be shown to be carriers. One bull brought in for use in the A-I Centre was first routinely test-mated and was found to be a carrier only from the last calf born in the test. Records obtained from breeders demonstrated that a cow could have some eleven or twelve calves and perhaps only the last calf would be defective and demonstrate she was a carrier. (The danger in such a case is that the dam could well be the dam of a good bull calf born earlier in her breeding life who was retained as a stock bull. He would have a fifty per cent chance of being a carrier; if so, he would be contributing his share of genes to continue the spread of the defect.)

On the other hand, one breeder informed me that, out of 28 cows, he had in one breeding season 14 deformed calves. He said he was in a state of such nervous tension that he was afraid to go to the hill to look at the herd.

A statistician will tell you that this latter occurrence of the one-in-eight proportion will happen only once in a hundred years, but it is too bad if you are the one to experience the once. The problem is that the proportion of one out of eight born deformed is true only when large numbers are the basis for the average.

A second step in our efforts to eliminate abnormal calves also concerned the removal of carrier sires. The Galloway Council introduced a rule that all defective calves had to be reported to the Council Secretary. Simultaneously an insurance scheme was introduced so that the breeders could insure their bulls against the chance of siring a defective animal; thus the loss of the bull would not defeat the farmer. Any bull that sired a deformed calf had to be slaughtered before compensation was paid.

As a result of this policy, breeders notified the Council Secretary of all the defective calves born in a particular breeding season. Thus the gene frequency within the Galloway population could be estimated and the extent of the problem clarified. If the frequency of the gene at the start of the project was, say, 20%, if non-carrier sires are used, the gene frequency can be reduced in four generations to two per cent. More important, *the number of abnormal offspring can be reduced to none in one generation.*

Recessive gene defects in dogs can also be eliminated and the presence of the recessive gene very much reduced by removal of carrier sires. Dogs that have produced defective progeny should be withdrawn from any breeding programme regardless of their other attributes. Similarly, the dams known to have produced aberrant offspring should be withdrawn from the breeding programme or grouped into a nucleus so that stud dogs can be tested for the genetic defect. Through the Breed Club it should be possible to organize a scheme of cooperation between breeders to test-mate males with carrier females.

Since the individual sire has a greater genetic influence on the breed than any particular female, the maximum effort in any breeding scheme should be concentrated on the screening of the males for any defective recessive genes. Warranties of different degrees can be assigned to particular sires on the outcome of test-mating according to the following table. (The higher the warranty, the more satisfaction.)

Number of normal offspring born to one male mated to carrier females	Chances out of 100 of a carrier male being detected
1	25
5	76
10	94
15	99
20	99.7
30	99.8
50	100

The aim in such a scheme should be to obtain for a potential sire a warranty of between 95% and 99% of being a non-carrier of the recessive gene being tested for.

Because of the demand for the test-mating of good stock sires and the limited number of carrier dams available to test them, Galloway breeders who had a very good bull with strong potential for future use by the national herd as a whole were advised that these bulls could be test-mated to their own daughters. The criteria that was the governing factor in this matter was the quality of the daughters available. Only if they were of a sufficiently high standard and to a degree free of other noticeable defects was this type of test-mating agreed to, particularly so if the bulls' pedigree was examined and found by the governing board to contain no known carriers, especially in the first three generations.

The result of the Galloway project was the sharp reduction in the frequency of the recessive gene, for by the use of a sire known to be clear the frequency can be reduced by 50% every generation.

The Galloway project was run for some ten years and resulted in what we set out to achieve—the elimination of abnormal calves. The project was finally wound up in autumn 1981, not only because of the lack of government money but also because, as there were no abnormal calves being born in any of the herds, we were no longer able to determine the carrier population. (At present there is no known test outside of test-mating to tell carriers from the normals.) Further, there will not be any abnormal calves born in the Galloway herds unless by some chance there should be a gene mutation. Over the years, the Galloway breeders have been alerted to this possibility.

Cryptorchidism, Monorchidism, Defective Genital Organs

In the early days of my introduction to the exhibition of dogs, the Kennel Club ruled that all dogs were to be examined for health by a team of qualified veterinary surgeons. In the case of males they were also examined to confirm the presence of two apparently normal testicles in the scrotal sac. The words "apparently normal" were used as there was some discussion as to what was in fact normal.

One of the amusing features of this exercise was to see a friend in the group of people who exhibited Toys grimly walking his dog outside the entrance to the arena in the hope that the dog would drop an updrawn testicle. On a previous occasion he had informed me the dog was normal at home but when he got excited he drew up his testicle into the abdominal cavity. The walking was done in hopes the dog would relax and drop the testicle and thus pass the veterinary surgeon. In the course of my duties under the Livestock Improvement Acts, I was required to examine various male animals in different breeds in order to confirm that they had two "apparently normal" testicles. On many occasions I came across animals with a considerable variation in the size of the testicles in the scrotal sac. I have also come across animals with two very small testicles or two very large ones.

Considerable variation in the size of the testicles was classified as Defective Genital Organs (D.G.O.) (Animals that are able to draw up one of the testicles must have a smaller testicle which can get through the canal into the abdomen.) Another condition found is an absence of testicles in the scrotal sac. This condition is called Cryptorchidism, and because the sperm within the testicles require to be kept at a lower temperature than inner body temperature, cryptorchid animals are sterile.

The most common type of abnormality I found among animals was having only one testicle in the scrotal sac. It was accepted that the other was still in the abdominal cavity. Such animals, commonly known among the farming community as "Rigs", are quite fertile. This condition is formally known as monorchidism, although purists in the science of genetics will say in debate that as there is a second testicle in the abdominal cavity, it is not a monorchid animal. Previous to the introduction of the Licensing Act, such animals were used in livestock breeding if they were particularly good examples of their breed.

The Livestock Improvement Act did not cover sheep breeding and the regular use of monorchids in this field of animal husbandry. They were called "Chasers". This term was used because they were put out after the normal tup (sire) had been out for his allotted time with a harness strapped round his withers holding a coloured block in a pouch below the brisket. In this way, the ewes mated are marked on the buttock with the colour block. The block is changed to a different colour for the "Chaser" tup. If the ewe does not settle to the first tup, she will return in season approximately sixteen days after her mating.

Therefore, any ewes that are not in lamb and return in season and are mated to the Chaser are marked with the different colour of the Chaser tup. The shepherd records the date of the change of tup and therefore knows when the ewe will lamb and to which tup she had bred.

The novice breeder will no doubt wish to know if monorchidism is hereditary and, if it is, what is the mode of inheritance. The geneticists have different thoughts on the mode of inheritance. Some believe it is due to a simple autosomal recessive gene. Other thoughts are that it is due to some type of familial trait. There is no clear pattern as yet established. If it is a simple hereditary factor due to a single recessive gene, the sire and the dam of the monorchid animal have the factor in a single dose and each has transmitted it to the male get, who is homozygous for the trait. If he is homozygous for the factor and is mated to a number of females, he passes the factor on to all his sons and daughters. This is where the laws of chance enter into the breeding system. The females remain an unknown quantity as we do not see their breeding organs.

If you request the advice of a geneticist who believes in the theory that monorchidism is due to a single autosomal recessive gene, his advice would be to discard the parents who by leaving a monorchid son have been proved to be carriers of the factor. But then the parents have received the factor from their parents, so where do you go from this point?

On the other side of the coin, you may be advised not to breed from a monorchid, as by doing so you are increasing your chance of breeding abnormal progeny. This type of genetic problem is sex limited and only visible in the male. The female may be homozygous or heterozygous for the factor. It is only after she has been the dam of a progeny displaying the condition that she can be regarded as a carrier of the factor. To test-mate, as was done in the case of the Galloway Breed, is in dogs much more difficult. The condition being displayed only in the male, a large number of pups would need to be born to give the required number of males to each female to prove whether she was carrying the factor. In such a test-mating programme, should the bitch be the dam of a normal male to a monorchid sire, then she is heterozygous and is no use for further test-mating.

On the other hand, if the bitch has produced a monorchid son and, if mated again to a monorchid sire produces a number of males all monorchids, then she is homozygous for the factor. This type of bitch could be used to test-mate a normal dog to determine if he is carrying the factor. The reader will realize that this will take time and money and thus be costly to the individual breeder. Such a test-mating, to be of any use to the breed, would require a number of bitches homozygous for the factor. To obtain them you would again have to test-mate, and if you obtained a number of bitches hetero-zygous for the factor you are back at square one.

In the game of livestock breeding in any class of stock, the theory of genetics and the practical results of that theory must be accepted by the breeder, and he/she must weigh up the pros and the cons in the light of what genetic knowledge is available. The breeder must then determine in his/her opinion whether or not to use a good monorchid dog.

The Results of Using a Monorchid Dog in our Experience

Let us look at the results of using a monorchid dog in a small kennel of closely bred bitches, where one would expect the results of a simple autosomal gene to surface in a characteristic genetic pattern, if the factor causing the condition is due to a simple recessive autosomal gene. The dog Millbank Tarka was a monorchid dog, sired by Ch. Maxton Matchless *ex* Triesta, bred by Mr. D. Cross, Knockdon, Maybole, Ayrshire. Mr. Cross was not interested in the exhibition side of dog showing. He was a member of the Dumfriesshire Otter Hunt. He gave the dog to the hunt. On seeing Tarka I realized his potential both from the exhibition side and as a sire on his breeding. The dog was by this time a well known worker with the hunt. On examination I realized that the dog was a monorchid.

If monorchidism is due to a simple autosomal recessive gene, then both the sire and the dam were carriers of the trait. All the male lines in the pedigree had been exhibited during the Kennel Club Rule confirming whether the animal was entire or not, and all had passed the test. In addition Ch. Maxton Matchless had a full brother normal and entire, much too dark in colour for me to retain. The remainder of the litter were females.

After the loss of M. Red Princess and Ch. M. Mannequin I asked Mrs. McKnight to allow a mating of Matchless to Ch. Marrburn

Morag so that I could get back into our established strain. Ch. Maxton Matchless was mated to his daughter Ch. Marrburn Morag, a litter sister to Tarka. The resulting litter was Ch. Maxton Monarch, Maxton Mhairi (two Res C.C.s) and Ch. Starrburn Sultan; the two other bitch pups were retained by the breeder, Mrs. McKnight.

The dam Ch. Marrburn Morag must have been heterozygous for the factor, as she was the dam of two entire dogs. (Both had been exhibited under the K.C. rule and gained their titles so there can be no doubt about the fact that they were entire.) Her daughter, Maxton Mhairi, was mated to the monorchid dog Millbank Tarka, her uncle and half brother (through the common sire Ch. M. Matchless). The resulting litter was three bitches and a dog. The bitch retained was Ch. Maxton Marla; a bitch was given to Mrs. McKnight; the other bitch pup, booked before it was born, was given to the people who had waited so patiently for it. The dog pup had only one testicle descended into the scrotal sac at the age of five months and two weeks. With only one testicle descended at that age and the K.C. Rule regarding monorchid dogs, he was no use to me for exhibition, so he left here for a good home in Dumfries. A few weeks later, a friend informed me that an experienced exhibitor in Smooth Fox Terriers had examined the dog and he was entire. This dog was exhibited by his owner Mr. W. Gordon and soon gained his title as Ch. Maxton Makrino.

The reader can debate the above experience I had in the use of a monorchid dog, and I can say that if the opportunity arose again under the same set of circumstances, I would not hesitate to use such a dog at stud. The results obtained were well worth the risk. In breeding you are just as liable to get a monorchid pup from an entire dog. In discussion with breeders of livestock in general, all have stated that in their view they have had no more abnormalities from the use of a monorchid sire than from the use of a normal entire stud.

I wish to note that in writing about the experience I had in the use of a monorchid dog, I am not advocating to the novice breeder to *look* for such a dog. The breeder must weigh up the merits of the case and, having studied all the information available to him/her, decide whether or not they are going to take the plunge.

On reflection, and with hindsight over a long number of years, I consider monorchidism is probably due to a familial trait in which delayed development has some role; possibly it is due to some aspect of environment. The evidence appears to be against it being due to a single autosomal recessive gene. However, before any theory could be accepted, a considerable amount of research and data would have to be generated to prove one theory against another.

The Breed clubs might undertake to do a breed survey of the condition, to get an overall picture of gene frequency and find out if some families are more prone to the condition than others. It might also be possible to compare this data with data in other dog breeds.

It may be possible that in some research centre unknown to me some work has been done on the occurrence of this abnormality in other breeds of animals.

Establishing a Strain of Border Terriers
Selecting the Foundation Bitch

The initial success or failure of anyone entering into livestock breeding will be determined by the selection of the foundation females. This applies to dogs in particular for the simple reason that at least initially the greater probability will be that you will be purchasing only one or two females. In the purchase of the brood bitch there are one or two things to go by. The most important is the temperament. A bitch of dicy temperament is of no use to anyone, either from a pet point of view or as a prospective brood to start your foundation breeding programme. I personally would not have either a dog or bitch unless they had a good temperament.

In writing this I assume that the prospective purchaser has a limited amount of cash available to invest in the enterprise. The buyer with the open cash book will find plenty of advisors and offers of bitches. There is, of course, the other type of breeder who will not part with his bitch for all the money available. These are to be respected, as really good bitches are hard to come by. If you see a good bitch suited to your needs and you are able to locate the breeder, it would be worthwhile to enquire if the dam of the bitch you like is still alive, whether she is still fit enough to be bred from, and if she is likely to be mated in the near future. This may appear to put your purchase a long way off, but if she is capable of breeding one good one, then she has every chance of breeding another, if she is well bred herself.

One often hears a breeder say about a good show bitch, "I would like a pup out of her." They seem to forget that she had a dam who by being the dam of a good bitch has proved she has inherited the essential genes to provide another of the same type. The better bet might be a pup out the dam rather than out the daughter, as the daughter is herself not proved. It is one of those unpredictable things in breeding, and seen in all breeding stock, that the dam might produce many good progeny, and the daughters be a dead loss as far as breeding is concerned. Through all livestock breeding, all top class winning females do not all turn out to be top class breeding prospects. On the other hand, in the same context there have been many examples of females who did not take the judge's eye who proved to be top quality breeding prospects. It all depends on the genetic make-up of the female and whether she meets up with the right male carrying the correct genetic make up. It is also a fact that there are many females who have the capabilities to produce good stock, but the right mate has not been selected for her by the owner-breeder at the time. The same female on being passed on to a breeder who selects another line of breeding may produce winning progeny.

If the bitch on offer has been bred from at some time, then one should go and see the progeny from the mating, and any by the same sire (i.e., see full brothers and sisters or, if by a different sire, half sibs). It is well to remember that any progeny being exhibited, particularly by a breeder, will be selected for exhibition. It is unlikely that the breeder will have been carefully exhibiting the mediocrity of the litter.

In the event of the bitch being by a popular stud dog, then one should have a look at the overall quality of his gets. Again, bearing in mind that it is unlikely that his worst progeny are on exhibition. (Although on occasion someone purchases a pet and then takes a notion to exhibit. In such cases those who have some knowledge of the breeding game see beneath the veil the probable value of the popular stud as a breeding animal.) The novice breeder should not forget if there is one being exhibited, one should ask oneself where have all the others gone, as there is likely to be more than one in any litter. If there should be only one, then all the more reason for inquiries into the cause, as infertility can be due to inheritance. At the time that A.I. was becoming popular in this country, a farmer in discussion about the merits of the use of A.I. bulls said to me, "What a great breeding bull (a certain sire) is proving to be!" This judgement was based on the fact that a son of the bull in question had had a certain amount of success in the show ring. I was aware that at that time the bull in question had sired some 600 calves. I replied that it was a poor sire, if he could only sire one good one in 600 matings.

If one is fortunate enough to find a bitch that has had a number of progeny, then the traits they show in their phenotype should be recorded, so that a close study can be made of them before finalising the deal. A bitch that throws good pups to different dogs is worth a lot to anyone starting a breeding kennel. This proves she has the wherewithal, and is capable of transmitting it to her progeny.

The genetic inheritance one is looking for in the foundation bitch is likely to be shown in her skeletal faults. These faults are relative in importance. The bitch may for example have too long a nose, from the point of her nose to the eye, than one would wish, or be doggy headed (i.e., have too coarse or strong a head for a bitch). Lack of femininity is not a good thing in a female of any breed. The bitch may have a soft coat, or she may have a wrong mouth. The faddists (fault finders) will reject her on these grounds alone, without further consideration. Yet a wrong mouth is the same as the other factors mentioned as faults.

The question one must then ask is, should one breed from a bitch with a wrong mouth? If this were her only outstanding fault and she had many outstanding virtues, then such a bitch should be preferred to one with a correct mouth and a soft coat. There are too many breeders who believe a soft coat is due to a single recessive gene, but to date research has not proved that this is a fact.

Again the faddist will tell you that as a result of breeding from such a wrong of mouth female, you will get wrong mouth pups. This is probably true, but on the other hand you have quite a high risk of getting defective mouths from a dog or bitch that is correct of the mouth according to the Standard. The best stocksmen I have discussed these matters with have not been breeders of dogs. (The latter have not had the wide experience of other livestock breeders in such matters, and in my view tend to look at such faults in a much too restricted field. In taking so narrow a view it is surprising that anyone takes up breeding at all.) Faults of any kind should be looked at in relation to the overall virtues of the particular animal. Keep in mind that faults due to a recessive gene or combination of genes are as liable to be transmitted as the virtues making up the top quality animal.

Assume you have been dissuaded from purchasing a bitch for some reason, e.g., for the sake of discussion her defective mouth. Then by chance (one of the great words of livestock breeding) the breeder offers you a full sister, correct in her mouth. Are you going to purchase either of them, bearing in mind you have refused the first bitch on the grounds that she has a defective mouth? If you are prepared to settle for the second alternative, then you should remember that it is not an unknown, in the breeding of Border Terriers, for those with correct mouths to throw defective progeny. It is a common happening in all breeds where the breeder is aiming for a short face with a moderately broad skull. Those who have been engaged in research into this field have come to the conclusion that the defective mouths that arise are due to a set of multiple genes rather than to any single recessive gene. It would seem that if you aim to breed for the characteristic head, then difficulty with the mouth is a problem you will require to live with, as it is associated with all stock where the Standard requires a short face and a broad skull.

This leaves you with another problem. If you accept that the defective mouth is an hereditary condition, then all the progeny of the brood bitch, the stud dog that sired the defective animal and any progeny of the brood bitch, the dam of the defective pup, are liable to be carriers. In such cases one unfortunately cannot tell which of the progeny are the carriers. Do you, therefore, discard all the progeny of the stud dog and the brood bitch, if any are available for sale? The problem can be put to the reader in another way. The government under the Licensing of Bulls (Breeding) Act made it a condition that any farm animal showing a mouth defect was to be refused a licence and required, if a male, to be castrated. (There was no control over the females.) At that time objections were being raised by the breeders because of this restriction. A conference was held so that the Professional Officers could meet the administrators. After a lot of discussion I thought I would put the cat up with the pigeons, so I said, "I do not see any useful purpose in refusing a licence for a bull that shows the defect, and have the bull slaughtered or castrated, and still allow the sire of the animal to continue to be used for breeding. Or for that matter, continue to allow the dam to be kept as a dam for further stock bulls. Therefore, the sire should be dealt with the same way as the bull with the fault. Otherwise, this problem will always be with the breeders." I realized of course that such a suggestion was too drastic to become a government policy. The discussion itself shows the nature of the problem in all breeds of livestock. There is a gamble in all livestock breeding.

The newcomer to the breed in looking for a foundation bitch would be well advised to contact a small breeder who has only a few dogs and has not the room for or the desire to have many dogs. The late Dr. Lilico and Neil McEwen M.R.C.V.S. said to me when I started breeding, "Do not get too many, and achieve as high a standard as you can with those you have. Avoid a bitch or dog that is plain." (This terminology used by stocksmen means that the animal has not visible character especially in head. The animal does not attract one's attention.) Some advise one to secure an older bitch that has proved her worth as a breeder as a foundation bitch. This I consider would be difficult, as few breeders are willing to part with such a bitch if for no other reason than sentiment. In sum, top quality bitches are difficult to come by unless there is some very good reason that makes the owner part with the bitch.

I can give an example of trying to purchase such a quality bitch. When I was stationed in Hawick, I used to pass the kennels of the late Tom and Jim Crozier on my way to the Department Office each morning. They had a very good young bitch at that time. I tried to purchase her but as they were breeder exhibitors I was informed she was not for sale; they required her as a stock bitch. However, some time later Mr. Tom Crozier died and I heard that as a result the dogs were to be reduced, as Jim did not have the room for them. I again tried to purchase the bitch. But this time I heard that John Renton had acquired her, as there had been some agreement between Tom and him at the time the dam was mated to Renton's dog. This bitch later became Ch. Vic Merry and was sold to Miss Vaux. So I had the near miss of purchasing a Champion as our foundation bitch.

On another occasion I had to visit the late Neil McEwen M.R.C.V.S. about some department business. In the course of our discussion a young bitch came into the room. She took my fancy so I tried to purchase her, but was again informed she was not for sale. Again I was dealing with a seasoned breeder exhibitor. Later she became Ch. Lucy Ryan. So, I had a further miss in purchasing a Champion.

Another lesson we can learn from the stocksman farmer is to avoid the female with the masculine appearance. This is the type I have often referred to when judging, and in discussion. This type is much too common among Border bitches of today. In head they are much too doggy in appearance. These comments do not mean that your foundation bitch should lack bone. Bitches very light in bone are at a disadvantage as brood bitches. The Standard says, "not too heavy in bone." There is a difference between the two extremes. Adam Forster put it to me in the following way about a light-boned bitch: "The dog is expected to do a lot with one like that."

Although I mentioned a number of matters to be considered in the selection of the foundation bitch, the newcomer to the breed should be aware that the final selection will prove to be one of the great gambles that the newcomer must face. If fortunate enough to find the right type of bitch which has in addition the correct genetic makeup, such a bitch mated to the right dog will give the newcomer the start of his/her kennel. The genuine breeder will take note of his breeding efforts, as will the genuine judge. If the newcomer is a genuine and dedicated breeder-exhibitor, defeats in the show ring will not upset carefully laid breeding plans.

Selecting the Foundation Sire

Having purchased a brood bitch, the newcomer to the breed will no doubt wish to start a breeding programme. It appears that in very few cases do they look to the future. Yet a breeding programme should be based on subsequent generations, not on the particular one resulting from the immediate mating.

The genuine breeder should be thinking about the female pups that will, it is hoped, result from the first mating. The object in mating your foundation bitch is to establish a line for the future, and you cannot do that without first of all thinking about the next generation. This applies all the time in breeding of all livestock. In making this assertion I am, of course, thinking about the dedicated breeder, who has in mind the future of the breed. In my opinion we all too often find in the world of dogs more of the other kind of breeder described by an important breeder friend as "so-called breeders who only appear to have the ability to open the gate and let the bull out among the coo's". Another of his comments was, "Dina talk to me aboo't genes and chromosomes. That talk is only fer they boffin's that ye fin' in aboot research places. They have never milked a coo in their life. A' sometimes wunner if they whad ken wit end tae sit at tae milk her."

On the other hand he was at all times a great advocate of family breeding. In his established herd, he had developed several families, and his system was to use a bull of one family to mate to the cows of another family. He was in fact crossing out and crossing in so that he had a considerable gene pool to work on without going out of his own herd. On many occasions I would say to him, "You keep telling me you do not know anything about genes and chromosomes but in fact you are doing exactly what any geneticist would probably advise you to do."

The success or otherwise of any selected mating is in the choice of the stud dog. The progeny resulting from the mating will answer whether the stud dog has the genetic makeup to transmit to his progeny the characteristics you are hoping to attain in your future stock. Bearing in mind the points already made you are in a quandary in the selection of your stud dog as to what he will sire if you do not have information that he is prepotent for the traits you seek. In other words, what is important is not so much what the dog looks like (i.e., his ability to win Challenge Certificates), but his ability to transmit to his progeny the desired characteristics of the breed. A dog that is a consistent sire of good stock is of much greater value to the breed as a whole than one that has won numerous certificates but has out of all the bitches mated to him sired relatively nothing worth considering.

Newcomers to the breed should look hard at dogs that do a good deal of winning in the show ring and ask themselves the following questions: does the particular dog in all respects comply with the Standard of breed? Is the dog capable of being spanned at the heart by the owner of the brood bitch? Is his head like that of an otter? Has he a good top coat and undercoat? Has he a good temperament? The owner of the brood bitch should in my view take the opportunity to study the head of an otter. By so doing the newcomer will be in the position to consider the points to be aimed for in the selection of the stud dog with a reasonable otter type head. There are plenty of dogs that qualify as champions who feature in my opinion overly strong coarse heads. The otter does not have a strong coarse head but one that is clean-cut, with no suggestion of coarseness. If the stud dog you are considering has a strong head, you will probably find if you examine him more closely that in addition he is of strong bone, with a heavy body. Nature has deemed it that any animal with a coarse head requires a strong neck and body to balance the head. Remember the head is at the extremity of the neck, thus acting as a fulcrum. If you put a weight on the end of stick, the same weight is more easily held if the stick is short and thick if the weight is heavy. The same weight balanced on the end of a thin stick, if long enough and capable of supporting the weight, will bend. In nature if the animal is heavy headed and for some reason the neck is inadequate the animal raises its head to support the weight. The animal, in other words, has a tendency to be what is known among stocksmen as "ewe necked". In extreme cases it has as well a characteristic weak gait when walking.

If the dog you are considering has been siring good progeny in relation to the Standard, is of a good type, and you find on careful examination that he is a good representative of his breed, you will probably find on examination of his pedigree that he is descended from some of the best breeding lines.

As with the foundation bitch, one should also consider any relatives that may be available to see. Has he full brothers, sisters or half-sibs? Is his sire still alive, and if so, did he breed well? What faults do his families show in their phenotype? If they are not Champions, is there a reason for this omission? One should not forget that a dog in the hands of a comparatively unknown exhibitor could well be of Championship Standard, but did not make the grade because he was not exhibited frequently enough. There have also been some mediocre Champions made up by those who show very often.

One must also keep in mind that there are some dogs who have had a reputation as being good sires who have been mated to some of the best bred and best appearing bitches in the breed. There are other dogs perhaps of equal or better merit who have had to establish their reputation as breeders on fewer numbers of lesser quality bitches. Another factor to consider is the age of the dogs being considered as possible studs. If for example one of the dogs is older, then he probably has sired more progeny to examine. Also his progeny will probably be older and therefore more of them will be mature enough to exhibit.

In considering the dogs as potential studs, you should ask yourself several other questions. Does the potential sire have a good coat as required by the Standard, or does he have a coat that is in need of constant stripping to keep in trim? A more fundamental question is whether he has sired any aberrant progeny due to lethal or semi-lethal genes. Remember, if he has, half of his sperm is worthless, as half of his progeny will be carriers for the defect. The risk of progeny from this type of dog is that in line or inbreeding systems the carriers may meet up with other carriers in subsequent mating and the defect may be expressed.

There is, of course, the commercial type breeder who has several stud dogs, probably of different type and pedigree. That being so, they usually attract numerous bitches, also of different types and pedigree. It would be against the law of chance if one of the dogs did not produce winning progeny to one of the bitches. This, of course, does not make such a dog a great sire. One must ask oneself if the type progeny being produced is the type that one wishes to breed.

The genuine dedicated breeder of dogs has many factors to consider in trying to establish a strain and getting information is often difficult. It is unfortunate that for example we do not have reliable statistics about the number of bitches mated to a particular dog, and the number of progeny born from the particular mating. We read all about the number of Challenge Certificates won by breeders or exhibitors, but against this type of information we do not know how many pups were born and discarded to obtain those capable of winning Challenge Certificates, nor have we ready information about the number of times that the particular dog was exhibited and went cardless under competent judges.

The ideal mate for the bitch is the prepotent sire, if one can find him. He will be the dog that carries homozygous genes for all the factors we want in our future stock. Such dogs are few and far between.

We will assume that the bitch selected for the foundation of the kennel, the best that could be obtained at the price, has several faults. Perhaps she has a longer nose (end of nose to eye) than you wish; then the stud dog should have a short face and if possible be descended from a short-faced family. If she is low to ground (i.e., short on the leg), the stud dog should be on the leg. If she shows a tendency to dip in the back, then the stud dog should have a level back. The object of the exercise is to try and balance the defects of one against the other.

*Walter and Joy Gardner with five generations of Maxton breeding. L-r: Ch.
Marrburn Morag; her daughter, Maxton Mhairi; her daughter, Ch. Maxton
Marla (full sister to Ch. Maxton Makrino); her daughter Maxton Marsala
and her pups.*

Another saying of my pedigree breeder friend is "Breed strength to
strength, the best points of the one to the best points of the other." By
so doing you hope that in the resulting litter there are some pups
homozygous for attributes that you wish to see in your resulting
Champions.

However, you must also remember that your ideal will, when you
come to breed from it, in all probability throw some of the defects
that you have tried to breed out. Thus you may find that you have
some pups with the long nose of the dam or the low to ground type of
her ancestors. Again the Mendelian principle has come into play. This
will continue to happen in your future generations unless you have
been successful in establishing a prepotent strain of dog or bitch. It is

Ch/Future Fame b. 10th August 1948. Br Mr. Whitelaw (1051 AG). S. Fearsome Fellow (1440 VV). D. Tombo Squeak.

in trying to attain this object that the system of breeding and inbreeding is so beneficial, if wisely used and with the object of improving the strain.

One may be lucky in using an outcross in breeding. (That is, in the use of a strain that has no relationship to the strain you have.) If so, then the results if good are the result of good luck rather than good breeding judgement. The resulting champions from such a mating have arrived because it so happened that the dog and the bitch happened to be carrying the required complement of the genes in their genetic make up, and by sheer accident in the segregation of the genes these combined at the time of fertilization. The breeder (i.e., the person that owns the bitch at the time the pups are born as defined by the K.C.) has hit the jackpot. The breeder of such a Champion will receive from some the accolades of success. But such an outbred Champion may not have inherited the genetic make-up to establish a *strain* of Champions.

On the other hand the dedicated breeder who may have the right ideas about his/her breeding plans, who has selected the right lines as the foundation of the strain, is capable of regularly producing pups

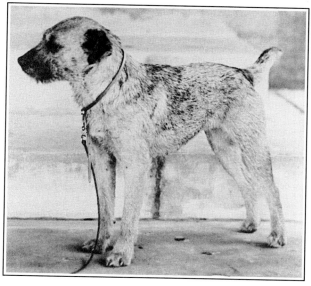

*His daughter Maxton Red Princess (829 AN) b. September
1952. By Ch/Future Fame ex M. Red Hazel. Brs Mr & Mrs
W. J. F. Gardner.*

above the average of the breed as a whole. (The reader should bear in
mind that the average of any breed takes in all pups born and alive.
The average of the breed is not the ups and downs of those that are
selected for exhibition.) The progeny from a linebred or inbred strain
of stud dog will all be similar in phenotype, and if the foundation has
been laid on sound lines, there should be no really inferior pups.
Despite his merits, perhaps, such a well-bred good dog may not for
some reason catch the eye of the judges. Maybe he was not exhibited
enough, or was in the wrong hands, or was not presented well. If his
faults, whatever they may be, are not of a serious hereditary type, his
linebred spermatozoa have greater potential than that of the outcross
dog to sire pups of the type the breeder wishes to produce. This is due
to the selection process over the period of years it has taken to build
up the strain, and the elimination of the unwanted characters, found
initially in the foundation strain of a strain. The well bred dog, given
the same number of well bred bitches as the outcross champion, will
breed a greater number of potential champions.

Maxton May Queen (664 AP) b. 6th May 1964. By Ch/Future Fame ex M. Red Princess. Brs Mr & Mrs W. J. F. Gardner.

Breeding merit and how well bred prepotent sires can sire good stock can be illustrated by looking at another breed of livestock, as the principle is the same for any breed. It all depends on obtaining the correct genetic material in the sire.

At the time when the Clydesdale horse was the main source of power on farms, particularly in Scotland, the coveted award for both males and females was the Cawdor Cup, which is still the blue ribbon of the Clydesdale World. There is one awarded for females and one for males. This trophy was first presented in 1892.

The Clydesdale stallion Baron's Pride was the most successful sire of winners of this trophy, having sired some eleven winners, two males and nine females. But he himself never won the trophy. In other words, he never caught the judge's eye. He also sired seven mares who produced Cawdor Cup winners. His record for Cawdor Cup winners covers some eighteen animals. However, this record was eclipsed by the prepotent sire father-to-daughter bred Dunure Footprint. This stallion was probably the greatest breeding horse of any breed. His prize-winning progeny were the most numerous of any

Ch/Maxton Matchless (2312 AQ) b. 6th July 1956. Maxton May Queen's son by Ch/Future Fame. Brs Mr & Mrs W. J. F. Gardner.

breeding stallion. He won at all ages, from a yearling to a four-year-old, at which time he was withdrawn from the show ring. But it is as a sire he is most remembered. He sired five male and five female winners of the Cawdor Cup and the dams of twelve winners of that trophy. He was therefore the sire, or the sire of the dam, of no fewer than twenty-two Cawdor Cup winners. The nearest rival to this great record is his own grandsire, Baron's Pride, the sire of Footprint's father, Baron of Buchlyvie. Dunure Footprint eclipsed all his fore-fathers by the fact that he also won the Cawdor Cup, as a two-year-old.

Mr. W. Dunlop, the breeder of Dunure Footprint, in a lecture on Clydesdales in 1936, emphasized the role of the female in breeding. He drew attention to the fact that Dunure Footprint was his dam's first foal, and that by the same sire she produced later four other winners of the highest honours. This demonstrates that within the field of Clydesdale breeding there has been a consistency of breeding results or accomplishments that has not yet been attained in dog breeding, even though in dogs there are multiple births (litters of up

Ch/Marrburn Morag. Br Mr. D. Cross & owned by Mrs. McKnight, a daughter of Ch/Maxton Matchless ex Triesta, and full sister to Millbank Tarka of Dumfriesshire Otter Hound fame.

to eleven have been recorded in Borders). There should therefore be quite a number of specimens to select from. With wise and patient breeding efforts, we breeders of dogs should be able to achieve the breeding accomplishment of the Clydesdale breeders.

Why we Chose Champion Future Fame as our Foundation Sire

I have been asked on occasion why I chose Future Fame as our foundation sire and in particular why I inbred into that line. (On occasion, of course, I have been asked why I inbreed dogs at all. I have tried to make that clear in this chapter.)

When we established our kennel and I started to attend shows and meet the breeders, I thought all the advice I was given was sound. I acted on that advice, and I was not at all pleased with the first pups I bred. I remember a well known breeder of beef cattle saying to me on one occasion, "If you ever breed a very good animal by a certain mating, then next time round change the sire. To repeat the mating will only lead to a disappointment." (This statement of course showed that he was dealing with a heterozygous strain. A prepotent sire will contribute superior stock to good females at each mating.) In any case, I thought that as I was not pleased with the matings there would be no harm in a change.

To understand how I then arrived at the choice of Ch. Future Fame, one must know something of our foundation bitch. I was quite pleased with her on type. She was a solid red with dark points. In critiquing her one might consider her to be slightly long from the end of her nose to her eye, but she had plenty of strength, and noses can be too short and weak, which is probably a more serious fault. She had a good breadth of skull, well balanced ear placement, and maybe more than enough ear, good reach of neck into a well placed shoulder. She tended to move slightly wide in front, but had good body length, with good depth. She was easily spanned at the shoulder.

She was bred by a Mrs. Scot, whose husband was a shepherd on a high hill farm in Roxburghshire. We met Mrs. Scot first at the S.K.C. show in Edinburgh and learned that she had at home a bitch for sale. The reason she gave for selling her was that as her husband was a shepherd and had several Border Collies, and with the winter approaching she felt they had plenty of dogs to look after. The Collies were essential to her husband's work, so they came first in the priorities of kennels and rations.

I was informed the bitch had won a first or two at the local show under the late J. Renton. I asked her to let me have the bitch on 14 days approval, since I had not seen her. Hazel duly arrived. When we let her out of the box we saw she was as lean as the proverbial crow, but we were so impressed with her it was decided then and there to dispatch the cheque in payment. We certainly never regretted the purchase of Hazel. No one could have wished for a more loveable companion.

I liked Future Fame the first time I saw him at the S.K.C. show in Edinburgh although Mrs. Pacey, who was a well known allrounder judge, did not place him. The late Jim Crozier was at the ringside and we had a discussion of the dogs exhibited. His opinion agreed with my own. I had a discussion with the late Adam Forster about his dogs and the breed in general. As a result he sent me the pedigree of the dog. He had marked with an asterisk all the dogs in the pedigree of his own breeding. It was obvious he had a good strain of dogs that had done a lot of winning, if not in his hands then in the hands of others who could exhibit them more than he could, at championship shows in particular.

Ch. Future Fame was by a dog called Fearsome Fellow, owned by his daughter, Miss E. Forster. Fearsome Fellow was born 11th April 1938, and he was 13 years of age when he died. I had heard many good reports about him as a Border. Montagu Horn, who was the column writer for *Our Dogs* at the time, wrote on the occasion of his death:

> I have heard this week of the loss to the Breed of Fearsome Fellow, who was 13 years old. If memory serves me correct he appeared at two Ch. Shows when he was a youngster, taking the reserve C.C.s on each occasion. But he had been best in show at open events before the War. By Furious Fighter *ex* Finery, he was a popular sire in the North if not in the country over some ten year period. His litters have produced many Champions and there are few kennels in the country that do not have his blood in their stock. I have had the pleasure of association with Jock (he later became known as old Jock) on several occasions far removed from any show ring and knew him to be all a Border should be.

It is of interest to note that in the year 1950, counting first prize winners at championship shows only, the following dogs sired the following number of first prize winners:

Ch. Future Fame	25 (by Fearsome Fellow *ex* Tombo Squeak)
Ch. Aldham Joker	19 (by Ch. Barb Wire *ex* Country Girl)
Callum	19 (by Ch. Fox Lair *ex* Dipley Dinah)
Fearsome Fellow	16 (by Furious Fighter *ex* Finery
Swallowfield Salvo	15 (by Callum *ex* Skirden Sen)
Ribbleside Rodger	15 (by Deerstone Defender *ex* Ribbleside Rusk)

The following bitches were the dams of the following number of first prize winners:

Fully Fashioned	14 (by Fearsome Fellow *ex* Flamingo)
Nettle Tip	12 (by Portholme Rob *ex* Raisgill Ribbon)
Raisgill Ribbon	11(by Callum *ex* Raisgill Radiant)
Orenza	10 (by Robin Hood *ex* Madas)
Hornbeam Heathbell	9 (by Aldham Joker *ex* Swallowfield Sadie)
Bladnock Tinkerbell	6 (by Dipley Dusty *ex* Bladnock May Mischief)

It will be seen from the list that Ch. Future Fame was the sire of the largest number of winners, and that his sire had also a good number to his credit. Also in bitches the same line of breeding was again top of the list. This appeared to me to be a very good indication of the sire's potential, although I accept that a prepotent sire would not probably have been so successful had a sire such as Fearsome Fellow not laid the foundations for him. In other words the genetic material to produce the winning dogs was carried by both Future Fame and Fearsome Fellow, who had inherited these through his sire and his dam. The bitches that were being mated to him then were carrying the type of genes to give the winners. This can be demonstrated if the reader studies the pedigree of Ch. Future Fame in Appendix B. The reader should also bear in mind that in the late A. Forster the breed had one who even at the date I am referring to (around 1950) had been in the Breed some 50-odd years. So in that period he must have seen the best and the worst of the dogs. In fact he more or less grew up with the breed. In discussions with him about the better dogs and bitches that he could remember his thoughts always turned to such names as Fearsome Fellow, a great favourite of his. "The best of the lot" was how he described him to me.

Furious Fighter was well named. He was a tremendous worker but was badly mauled by a fox. He won the certificate at Richmond Championship Show in 1935 under Mr. W. F. Morris, a well-known judge in those days. He was later sold to Sir J. Renwick and was worked with his hounds.

Finery was another favourite. This bitch was also a great favourite of the late J. Renton. She won the premier show for Border Terriers (Bellingham) in 1938 and the following year the Certificate at Harrogate. Sir John Renwick was the judge. Later she was owned by Capt. M. C. Hamilton.

A comment of John Renton's comes to mind. When we discussed these dogs of the past he said, "We are losing the good solid red colour of Finery and Romance." The latter was the dam of Furious Fighter.

The Sire of Finery, Gem of Gold, was another dog that was thought a lot of by both Forster and Renton. There is a degree of inbreeding in Ch. Future Fame, as Finery's sire Gem of Gold is a half brother to the sire of Furious Fighter, Ch. Ranter. Both are sired by Rival. Gold Tip, the sire of Romance, is also by Rival. Finery's dam is Stung Again who is by Ch. Blister, who is by Revenge and Finery's paternal grandam Ch. Benton Biddy, also by Revenge.

The two dogs Rival and Revenge feature very much in the history of establishing the Border Terrier as we know it today. These two dogs also bring us to the period where in pedigrees we meet up with those dogs that were unregistered, although the breeding would no doubt be known to the owners of the dogs. The breeding system then used, if one can call it that, would no doubt be to breed to the type of dog fit to perform the work required from the Border. The reader must remember that these breeders of workers were the men who drew up the Standard of the Breed in the first instance. The Standard was not drawn up for the show ring, but was designed to breed a working terrier capable of going to ground. Old photographs show that all the older type dogs are on the leg, narrowly built with a fairly long length of body.

It is notable that Rival is himself an inbred dog, as he was by Rab of Redesdale *ex* Tibby (unr). Tibby was also by Flint *ex* Border Dream (unr) so that Rival is the result of a half brother to half sister mating. Flint is by Ch. Ivo Roisterer born in 1915 *ex* the famous bitch bred and owned by the late A. Forster, Coquetdale Vic. This bitch was not only a good type—three years in succession she won the first cup put up for competition for Borders when the original Northumberland Border Terrier Club was formed—but as I have pointed out earlier she was also a very good worker.

Let us now consider the female side of this pedigree.

Romance, the dam of Furious Fighter, was sired by a dog registered as Gold Tip, who was by Rival. His dam was Harbottle Vic by Rocket *ex* Coquetdale Vic, who was sired by Barrow Jock. This dog Adam described as "a good local dog". Her dam was Nailer II.

The female side of Romance's pedigree takes us back into similar lines. Her dam was a bitch called Miss Tut bred by Adam Forster in 1922. She is by Flint *ex* Coquetdale Reward. Reward was by Tug who was by Ch. Ivo Roisterer *ex* Oxnam Vic. Coquetdale Reward's dam was Little Midget, by Titlington Jock *ex* Coquetdale Vic.

The female side of Finery takes the reader back into the same lines of breeding, as her dam, Stung Again, is by Ch. Blister by Revenge. Her dam is Liddesdale Nettle, bred by the late W. Barton.

The dam of Ch. F. Fame, Tombo Squeak, bred by Mr. and Mrs. Eccles, was by the biggish sound dog called Ch. Boxer Boy, who was sired by Ch. Aldham Joker. The male line of this dog traces back

Maxton Mac centre and his dam foreground. Left Maxton Marza. Top left of the three Mahanain (who was lost). Madalene Mindy's rear above Marza.

Miss Tut   Rocket   Coquetdale Vic   Coquetdale Reward
Coquetdale Vic was Little Midget's dam.
Coquetdale Reward was Little Midget's daughter.

Ch Maxton Makrino full brother to Ch Maxton Marla

Kate Murphy (left) and Ruth Ann Naun with Ch Maxton Merry
Mac in January 1985 (Massachusetts, USA).

Author with Mrs Barbara Kemp, Robert Naun.

Showing white on chest of border terrier puppy.

through his sire Ch. Barb Wire sired by Ch. Dinger. This dog was by Gem of Gold *ex* Beeswing. Ch. Barb Wire's dam, Ch. Tod Hunter, is by Revenge *ex* Causey Bridget.

The dam of Ch. Boxer Boy was Daphne's Dream, who was by Ch. Wedale Jock. Jock was by Ch. Heronslea *ex* Shaw's Lady, by Ch. Blister *ex* Patchwork. Daphne's Dream's dam was Delight, owned by Sir John Renwick. She was sired by Ch. Grakle by Ch. Ranter *ex* Queen of the Hunt, a very much admired bitch owned by Dodd and Carruthers, both of whom were keen hunting men. In fact Mr. Dodd was the Master of the local pack of hounds. Tombo Squeak's dam, Cheviot Penny Plain, was sired by a dog called Reedswire who was owned by Mrs. Dodd. His sire is Carousel and his dam is Catcleugh Bess. Both of these were unregistered and untraced. They would no doubt be working Borders.

The dam of Cheviot Penny Plain was Coronation Queen of the Mist and she was out of Shaw's Lady, sired by Ch. Dinger. The pedigrees of both have been commented upon under the sire's line of breeding.

If we now look at the breeding of our foundation bitch Red Hazel we will see how she fitted into the breeding of Ch. Future Fame. (See appendix B.)

Red Hazel was by one of the late David Black's dogs, Tweedside Red Playboy, who was by the famous Aldham Joker who has been mentioned in the pedigree of Ch. Future Fame, and is the great grandsire of F.F.'s dam Tombo Squeak.

Tweedside Red Playboy's dam Felton Gem is sired by one of A. Forster's dogs, Terry, who was sired by one of A. Forster's dogs called Coquetdale Sandy. Sandy's dam is the renowned Finery, again owned by A. Forster, and Finery was the dam of Fearsome Fellow. Felton Gem traces through the female line, her dam Felton Patsy, to Forster's old bitch Gippy, a full sister to Coquetdale Vic. Gippy was the dam of Ch. Titlington Tatler.

Cherry Pie, the dam of Hazel, was *ex* Judy who was by a dog called High Jinks, sired by the famous Ch. Grakle *ex* a bitch called Happy Valley. She was *ex* Queen of the Hunt and was owned by Dodd and Carruthers. She had two C.C.s and was a well known bitch of her day as a worker. She was by a dog called Tally Ho *ex* Foxie and was grizzle in colour. A line from Briery Lass I have been unable to trace.

Siobhan with Marcia (Merry). Siobhan aged 2 yrs—Merry aged 17 yrs.
"Papa, me good baby me luv melly."

It is a remarkable thing in livestock breeding that the breeder does not look into these matters in the critical way that one should. A number of times in discussion even the top breeders in all the breeds I have been associated with admit that in their breeding programme Bull X or Y should have been retained longer in the herd and that Bull/Stallion Z should have had its throat cut at a much earlier date. Critical consideration of pedigrees would help us here, though all breeders make their predictions and at the end of the trial come to the conclusion that there is nothing more unpredictable than breeding.

As I have indicated earlier in connection with this matter, I pursued the wrong course for some time until it dawned on me that I was on the wrong lines. It is for this reason I suggest to the newcomer to the breed to study the type of dog you are going to use. Be quite clear in your views what your aim is to be and do not be deterred by the advice you are given about the dogs you have in mind. God gave all people two ears so that you can listen with one and let the material you do not wish to retain pass through and out the other.

Selecting a Puppy from your Litter for Exhibition and Breeding

You are at a considerable disadvantage in choosing a puppy for the exhibition side of dog breeding if you are a novice in the breed, particularly if you do not have the advantage of knowing the near relations of the parents of your litter. It is one thing in stock breeding to have seen the sire and the dam, and taken note of their general conformation, their weaknesses and their strengths. It is a good deal more to have been fortunate enough to see the grandsires and granddams. Then at least you have some idea how big some of your pups may grow to when mature (or how small).

Let us for the sake of discussion consider that the sire is on the big side by the Standard, and the dam is a little type, short on the leg and thickset of body. The progeny of such a mating, if there were sufficient numbers, would follow Mendel's Law of Genetic Segregation. In other words when your pups mature, how big they will be or how little depends on the mate selection made in the previous generations, and whether at that time there were big or small dogs introduced.

The advantage the experienced breeder has in this respect is that if he/she has over the years been linebreeding and to a degree inbreeding and selecting homebred bitches and dogs for future stock, he/she has a considerable knowledge of what the pups are going to look like on maturity. In one stock there will not be the degree of variation which exists in the breed in several.

There are certain guidelines the novice breeder can bear in mind in choosing a pup for exhibition and breeding. The late A. Forster told me when I started to breed Borders, "Always select the puppy with the greatest breadth between the eyes, as the Border's head grows from there, and if in the first instance you get the best headed pup, all you can hope for thereafter is that the other parts will be equally good." The late Hugh Pybus, one of the older breeders when I came into the breed, having never been without a Border since his boyhood, said that the time to select a Border puppy is at eight weeks of age, that they will no doubt change during the later periods of growth but they will in time return to the one you considered to be the best puppy at eight weeks.

You will need to study your litter at length.

When you feed the bitch with the puppies, you should sit down and study them individually. The more you study them, the more each one becomes an individual to you. As they grow older, watch how they move across the nest. There may be one you can exclude because it is wide in front, or one that for some reason does not please you behind.

Then there is the question of colour. The pup that is widest between the eyes may not be the colour you wished, it is too dark. But the lovely red pup has a soft coat, and you wish to avoid this because you have memorized what the Standard requires. It also has another fault, a white foot. The extent to which the white extends on the foot determines whether the puppy should be considered further in your selection. If only the tips of the foot show some white hairs, these usually disappear as the puppy ages. White on the chest, if only a small mark, also usually fills in when the coat grows. This is particularly true if there are also dark hairs on the chest as well as white. The puppy on maturity will have an area on the chest approaching a grizzle colour, and the area that was white will not be noticeable.

What are their ears like? Are they nice small ears in proportion to the size of the head at this age? Are the ears V shaped or do they have a tendency to be rounded, and of more generous proportion than one would wish?

The puppies having reached the age of around six to eight weeks, you will be able to examine them on a table, supporting them by hand. At this stage you should be trying to imagine what they will look like when mature. (Care is required to prevent any accidents such as a puppy falling off the table. A little tidbit encourages and gives the pup confidence at this stage.)

In standing, do they give you the impression that in height and body length they represent what you wish in the finished article? The height the puppy is going to be is probably best determined at the age of six months. If you are frightened at that age that the pup is going to be too tall, the chances are that it will finish up on the leg and on maturity will be balanced. The body on maturing takes away from the height. On the other hand, if the puppy lacks height at six months, on maturity, as the body develops, it will appear short on the leg, that is, it will seem low to ground.

The conformation aspects of the exercise in selecting a puppy having been completed, there are still two important matters to attend to in the selection. You have at some stage to examine their mouths, and this should be done at as early an age as possible. Although at first they will have no teeth, if you are gentle you may be able to see if both jaws are more or less level. If you are unable to do this visibly when they are so small, gently draw one of your fingers across the jaws while closed. In so doing you can determine if the two jaws are together at the front of the mouth. If one feels further back than the other, then you will require to keep a watchful eye as the puppy matures. As the puppy teeth come into place, if the lower teeth are behind the top teeth, the chances are that the mouth will be correct on maturity. (Although the second teeth are larger than the temporary teeth, the growth of the mouth parts is such that the second teeth take over the same position as the first teeth.)

On the other hand if there is any deviation of the two jaws from the normal, particularly if the lower jaw teeth are slightly in front of the upper, such a mouth has a considerable chance of not being within the requirements of the Standard. In a puppy, this type of mouth can best be described as having a roughness: when you draw your finger down from the upper teeth, you feel the edges of the lower teeth. It can happen in the growth of the head and the jaw bones that because of the action of the multiple genes, one or other of the jaws develops more rapidly. This results in the jaw being overshot or undershot.

If the pup you have selected is a male, then you have an additional hazard. Has he any, or one, or two testicles? The testicles descend into the scrotal sac at a much earlier age than most dog breeders realize. (This probably is earlier in some breeds than in others but it is the one thing I examine all the dogs in the litter for as soon as possible. If I find a dog with one testicle descended and the other still retained, I keep a careful watch on him until the testicle descends.)

Although I advise the early examination of your male pups to find out whether the testicles have descended or not, I also advise this to be done with considerable care, and very gently. It should be remembered that a puppy at this age could be injured quite easily. If the puppy has not two normal (for age) testicles in the scrotal sac at six months of age, then the chances of the other testicle descending become very doubtful indeed. This does not mean that it may not descend at a later date; indeed I have known this to happen—no doubt Nature's way of proving humans wrong.

At the final stage for decision, if it is a bitch pup you require then see that it has feminine characteristics and is not "doggy headed"; in the case of the dog, it should be like a dog in head, not a bitch.

Coat Colour Inheritance in Border Terriers

The newcomer to the breed may be wondering where the so-called "blue" (really black) in modern blue-and-tan Borders comes from. In the 1950s there was some controversy in the dog papers about the colour black, so-called blue.

For example, a breeder/judge was judging a Championship Show and in his report he gave the dog the C.C. and Best of Breed but made the following comment in the critique—"A saddleback, I like his racy outlook, able to run with hounds, hard coat and pelt, a wonderful mover, his general outline and expression were all Border, though his colour is too black like several others present. This in my opinion is wrong; it should be steel blue colour. Has Welsh Terrier been introduced in some of our Border forebears?"

Well, the judges of those days stated their views. The owner of the dog, Miss May Long, one of the most respected and at that time one of the older breeders, having owned Borders for some 25 years (Miss Long had her first Border in the early thirties) replied:

It was of great surprise to me to read the remarks made by

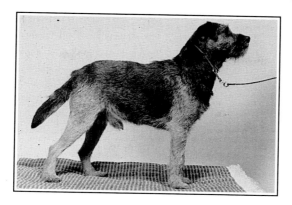

Ch/Bargower Silver Dollar owned by Bert Drummond Bargower, famous Ayrshire breeder.

	Ginger	Minatam
Ch/Bargower Silver Dollar		Braw Lass
	Dusty Maid	Tweedside Red Silver Brach

two judges regarding the colour of Winstonhall Wiseman. With 25 years' experience in the breed, to me he is a true blue and tan with tan head and legs with the silver (or whatever colour you like to call it) and tan hairs on his coat. My second Border bitch was given to me by the late Mr. W. Welton, who at one time was in partnership with the late Mr. J. Dodd when living in Northumberland. He said she was a blue and tan. Her back was quite black (head and legs tan) the same as some that are being shown today. He also told me she was bred from the very best old Border blood. Anyhow she had a Champion in her very first litter over twenty years ago. As you say, there were always Borders of this colour.

(Our Dogs 2/12/1953.)

Subsequently the late J. J. Pawson of the Dipley prefix made the following comment on colour:

Miss Long writes she had a black and tan over 20 years ago but I had more than one black-backed one long before that and so have many other people. But the point is that it doesn't make them right or included in the Standard of the breed as recognized by the Clubs. I am not referring to the dogs with the dark grizzle backs but ones that are dead black without any light hairs mixed in. There used to be some Borders called "bare skinned" in the north, in other words smooth coated, but that does not make them correct according to the Standard. Mr. Welton of course had many dogs through his hands and even if he was a Northumbrian it does not necessarily follow that he knew them from a show point of view. We must not get away from the show Standard of the Clubs.

About the same time as this correspondence was taking place, Mr. Montagu Horn, the breed note contributor for *Our Dogs,* wrote in his column:

There were black and tan Borders being shown and winning long before 1930, amongst them being Allen Piper, whelped 20/5/21, br. Mr. G. Wearmouth, s. Gyp (North Tyne Gyp) d. Jean of Tynesdale c. black and tan, 1 C.C. Owner J. Dodds.

The late George Thompson's dog Terrific, whelped 1924, was a son of Allen Piper. [Although I was able to trace the pedigree of Allen Piper, I have no information on the dam of Terrific to date. *W. J. F. G.*]

Later there was Mr. J. J Pawson's Dipley Dave b. 10/9/29 s. Arton Billy d. Dipley Darna c. black and tan, 1 C.C.

[Some other black and tans were] Sambo, owner J. Dodds, br. Mrs. Armstrong, b. April 1921, s. Gyp (i.e. North Tyne Gyp) d. Midge (unr), c. black and tan; Sir John Renwick's Newminster Radiant, br. Sir J. Renwick, b. April 1944, s. Newminster Jimmy, d. Newminster Ranee, c. black and tan.

A black and tan that gained his title was Champion Mac-Merry, though I think his owner once said he could be best described as a dark grizzle and tan. [If I had been asked to describe the colour of this dog I would agree that he was a dark grizzle and tan. I knew this dog well, as I saw him many times in Hawick and at the Shows at that time. *W. J. F. G.*]

The bitch Champion Station Masher br. Mr. A. Fox, b. 11/4/24 s. Oxnam Pincher d. Jed (unr) is described as "grizzle, dark back" in *Border Terrier Champions and Certificate Winners* by Miss Orme.

The late Wattie Irving in the many discussions I had with him on the topic of colour always referred to Station Masher as a "saddle back". This terminology was used by the older breeders to describe a dog with the dark patch of hair extending from the withers along the back to the loins. In many dogs, the area covered by this patch of hair resembled a saddle on a horse—hence the name "saddle back". I have not seen a true saddle back for many years.

Mr. Horn quotes, from Rawdon Lee's *Modern Terriers* (1902), from a letter received from Mr. Jacob Robson, Byrness, Northumberland, written some sixty odd years ago. Mr. Robson stated his family had long bred the terriers known as Border Terriers and on their colours wrote, "the favourite colour is red or mustard although there are plenty of the variety pepper coloured and others *black* and tan." In his own description in the same article, Rawdon Lee states that:

The colours are mostly red or wheaten, or what I should call a yellow in varying shades; others are pepper and salt, more or less light or dark, the latter almost approaching black. White is usually found on the chest; a white foot; occasionally they have a white streak up the face. Black and tan is not often found and entirely black and white and tan as in the modern Fox Terrier are never found in the pure strain. It has been kept pure now for fifty years or more whatever might have been the case earlier.

[Note: this letter would have been written around 1850.]

Rawdon Lee was in his day a prominent Fox Terrier and Irish Terrier breeder/exhibitor/judge and personally knew the terriers in the different parts of Northumberland, Cumberland and Westmorland. It should be noted that neither Mr. Jacob Robson nor Rawdon Lee ever mentioned the colour blue and tan, in connection with the Border Terrier they knew some sixty years ago, i.e. around 1850.

Accompanying the chapter in Rawdon Lee's book is an excellent illustration of five of the early Borders, this being a copy from a photograph belonging to Mr. J. Robson. Describing them, Rawdon Lee writes of "the three being yellow and two being black and tan." Many years later and nearer the time of many present day Border breeders (i.e. around 1950 era), black and tan was still given as a recognized colour.

About the same time or probably a year or so later, the late Miss H. G. Orme wrote to the same paper about coat colour inheritance:

Is it not possible that the strains of Border Terriers now being bred for show purposes carry a liver gene for coat colour derived from their co-origin with the terriers from which the Bedlingtons were derived? We used to have the liver nosed yellow coated ones. Borders carrying a liver factor when mated to an agouti (grizzle and tan) will, I think, produce a solid black back. I have never bred a black back from the mating of two grizzles but have done so with a grizzle and red. Any crosses hinted at by some correspondents might account for the terrier action we sometimes see but not I think for the coat colour. Certain strains carry the blue grizzle colour and I believe this line came from the late George Thompson's otter hunt terriers, which in turn came from the Pringles. Many of the latter were light wheaten. With the present trend of breeding, an albino litter seems remote!

It seems clear then that as far back as 1850 there were black Border Terriers belonging to the Robson family. The late Captain Sir John Renwick's (Bart) Newminster strain also carried the genes for the black factor. The late Sir John was very keen on coats, and emphatic in telling breeders to pay attention to them. In his opinion there were too many with soft coats. In addition some had white feet, which he felt was a sign of a near cross of the Fox Terrier blood. The late Wattie Irving said to me on several occasions that you never find a blue and tan with a soft coat.

In a discussion I had with the late John Renton about this black colour and its origin in Borders, he was quite sure that a cross of the Welsh or Manchester Terrier had been introduced at some time in the past. It was his opinion that this had been done to improve the fronts and to give them more height in the leg. This of course was in the very early days of the breed and even at that time there would be no breeder living who could for certain state the facts.

The late Adam Forster on one occasion in discussion about colour thought a cross of the Border Collie had got into them and in his view this accounted for the black and in addition the white.

This latter theory should not be discounted without some thought, for the following reason. The farms of the original Border Terrier breeders were outlying places well off the beaten track. The other breed of dogs likely to be associated with the type of farm they had would be a Collie, essential for the herding of the sheep. Is it not likely that on the same farm there was a terrier bitch then called a Border, and a male Border Collie? It does not take much imagination to understand how this cross could arise: the terrier comes in season and is mated to the Collie by accident; there is a bitch puppy in the litter who is found a good home. In phenotype she is more like the terrier mother, and in time is mated back to a terrier dog. Someone likes the terrier type pups and another bitch is kept by someone who again mates the bitch to a terrier dog. As the matings progress, the terrier-type is retained, as there is no backcross to the Collie again. The terrier-type will have inherited its colour from the original bitch and the black from the Collie. The successive generations will carry the factor for black. There is no record of such a breeding, but surely it seems likely to have happened in the sort of environment we found the Border Terrier in originally.

Should one require a particular coat colour in a Border, the difficulty about the inheritance of coat colour in dogs in general and Border Terriers in particular is that there is insufficient information on the ways in which the various colours become expressed. It is well known amongst Border Terrier breeders, for instance, that in most cases Borders are very dark at birth and get lighter in quite varying degrees as they get older.

In cattle because of the numerous experiments done and the consistent records kept, the colour inheritance picture is much clearer. In Shorthorns, for instance, it is well known that if a white bull is bred to red cows, the red is dominant to white, though the dominance is incomplete and intermediate roans and white-and-reds occur.

The frequent dominance of the darker colours in other livestock species may be significant to Borders. Although there is little knowledge on the inheritance of the coat colour in our breed, in recent years there has been an upsurge of blacks-not-blues. If they are continuously used at stud, the breed will in a matter of a few years become one of predominantly dark dogs, for the gene for this colour may soon dominate the others. The dark grizzles will then be lost to the breed as it appears to me we have already lost to a degree the genetic material for the good reds that I knew when I came into the breed thirty-odd years ago. Today we never see the wheatens that were in vogue many years ago.

Border Terrier Size

In conversation with Border Terrier breeders the question of size usually comes up for debate. On one such occasion it was said that a Border Terrier standing about 14 inches from the ground was too small to follow a horse and hounds. The Standard of course states that the Border must be capable of doing this. Some people trying to defend this requirement have stated that the horse in question must be a small pony.

Let us have this question answered by facts from men who have experience following the hounds on a horse. It is their opinion that matters.

The late Jacob Robson, M.F.H. Border Hunt, one of the founders of the Border Terrier breed, kept a diary of the hunts in his area. Extracts from his diary have been published in a book by C. M. Fergusson, *Border Sports and Sportsmen* (J. Catherall & Co., Printers, 1932). In some of these diary entries, mention is made of the Border Terrier, and although these terriers are not named on all occasions, I am sure they would be with the hunt at all times. A hunt is described in the year 1875, on February 3rd, which mentions the weight of the Border Terrier at the time. Robson notes that Flint, the famous terrier, weighed about 14 pounds, and could bolt foxes out of holes which had hitherto been considered impossible places.

Robson also describes a hunt run in the year 1883, which indicates that the Border followed the hounds. He notes that the hounds found on an area called Kielder Nick and the hunt lasted from 8.30 a.m. till 4 p.m. Robson described this run as the longest he ever had. Some of the runs described lasted some 28 to 30 miles. The one from Kielder Nick must have been even longer. It appears that on this particular day the ground was frozen and they were therefore able to follow the fox over some very bad ground that would have been impossible otherwise. The run went as follows: "From Kielder Nick run by Emblehope, Blackburnhead, Rooking Kiln, Windburn through the Reel to Stobbs and recrossing by Evenstones, Cleugbrae, Ashtrees, Rattenraw, Piedon, Highgreen, Blackburnhead, then very fast to Rooking Kiln, Reedswood, Yearning, Kielder Nick, Oh Me Edge, White Crag, Crowsen, Concern and to ground at Carry Burn."

Robson adds that the terriers Flint and Jack were put in but the fox would not bolt and as darkness had set in they had to make the best

way they could down Scalp Burn to Kielder, where they stayed over-
night. The following morning they returned to the earth armed with a
spade, where they got the fox and Flint out dead and Jack alive. The
note finishes with the comment that "Flint was a very bonny Border
Terrier and belonged to David Hall of Ingram". It is of interest to
note that it also appears that only two followers finished the hunt that
day.

Another hunt Robson described took place in the year 1883; it
found fox on Emblewood and ran Oh Me Edge, Kielder, Gunsleugh,
Girdlestone, Coomsden, Bating Hope, Carter Fell, Whitelee, and
Lumsden Law before killing an old fox in Ramshope Hill. Robson
concludes, "Bess, a ten months old Border Terrier, followed after
hounds all the way and got forward after they killed."

The horses ridden to the hunt as far as I can gather were not
ponies—they were around 14 hands high, usually sired by a
thoroughbred stallion, the resulting female (filly) put back to a
thoroughbred stallion. These horses were good enough to be raced in
the steeplechases held at that time. Considering the distances and the
type of ground covered, they must have had good constitutions and
have been sure footed, as must have been the dogs following.

In the above, relative to size, we have examined the recorded views
of one of the original breeders who was hunting and using Borders in
1875 and afterwards. Let us now have a look at someone of a later
date.

The late Sir John Buchanan-Jardine, B. T., M. F. H., in his excellent
book *Hounds of the World* makes the point about height of the leg in
Beagles. He mentions that there are a great many different opinions
as to what should be the best height for a pack of Beagles:

It depends to a certain extent on the individual taste and also of
course on the nature of the country to be hunted, but taken as a
whole I am inclined to think that about 14 to 14½ inches is about
the right size for Beagles in most countries. I once had a pack of
Beagles largely composed of hounds that were too big for other
people. They were sixteen inches high and *no living man could
have kept near them on a straight running hare* as they would
have made a good well bred hunter gallop, but by knowing the
country and cutting the corners, though by no means a good
runner, I managed to see a lot of sport with them, about eight

times out of ten. On the other two times they would get on a travelling jack hare and I used to have to go and look for them in a motor car.

The same author gives good advice to breeders of Beagles that can be applied to Border Terriers, and breeders would be well advised to note what he says. "The main points to aim at in breeding Beagles, after nose of course which is the absolute first consideration, are good backs, loins and a good depth of body, for without those points such small hounds cannot have the necessary stamina and may tire before the hare."

Further evidence of the ability of the Border to follow a good horse comes from Mrs. J. Talbot, who with her husband farms in the Norfolk area. Her grandparents were Dr. and Mrs. Geikie, who had Border Terriers in the early 1920's. Mrs. Talbot informed me on one occasion she was here whilst discussing the height of leg in a Border that as a point of interest she tried her Border while exercising her Arab bred horse. Selecting the longest field on the farm, she set off at a fast gallop keeping her eye on the Border who (10 months old at the time) was up alongside the horse and ready for another go. Mrs. Talbot said the bitch was not even out of breath. The reader can take it from these examples that a Border on the leg can follow and keep up with a horse and need only stand 14″ at the withers. A balanced dog overall will also have no difficulty in meeting the Standard's requirement of going to ground if of course the dog has the nose and the working instinct.

As a final note on terrier size and conformation, Mr. R. Clapham in his interesting book *Fox Hunting on the Lakeland Fells* (1932) confirms the views expressed by J. Robson on the essential requirements of the working terrier. He states that the terriers are the most important part of the hunt, and without them it would be impossible to locate the fox when he has gone to ground.

He also confirms that most of the terriers are crossbred and have Bedlington blood. The evidence of this, he notes, is light silky hair on their heads. He adds that silky hair body covering is not wanted on a Fell terrier, for the coats are too fine and the dog is unable to withstand the cold properly.

Clapham then compares the terrier on the leg to the short legged type, stating that a short legged dog is handicapped on rough ground or in snow. A biggish terrier he feels is decidedly useful in places he can work up to his fox, but in the majority of Lakeland borrans or earths the smaller dog is to be preferred. He adds that for work on the Fells a terrier must be able to squeeze through very narrow places, be active, and be sufficiently high on the leg to enable him to follow the huntsman through snow or rough ground without tiring. He ends by going on to explode a fallacy that has gained popular ground in recent years. Some people seem to think that a terrier when creeping into a narrow place works himself along on its chest, and they conclude that a wide chested, short legged dog is best for this purpose. As a matter of fact, the dog lies on his side and works himself ahead with his legs.

Limitations of the Pedigree and the Working Certificate

How much is a pedigree worth? A first point to remember is that the accuracy of any pedigree is dependent on the honesty of the breeder of the dog in question.

In the period of time before the establishment of Breed Societies and (in the case of Borders), recognition by the Kennel Club, the respective breeds were in comparatively few hands and the breeds had a local reputation as did the breeders. Everyone in the village knew one another. The local blacksmith, the stone mason and the wheelwright would all have their own cows (usually seen grazing the roadside) and their own type of dog. The early show catalogues of the societies that catered for the respective breeds show by the lack of information about the animals' breeding the complete indifference of the breeders to the records of the ancestry of their dogs. The breeder stood by his name and his reputation.

Many stories have been told of the importance breeders placed on their reputations. One is that a buyer purchased a bull from a breeder and then sent his son to the breeder requesting a pedigree. The reply was, "Go tell your father I bred the bull." Another story often told in pedigree circles is of a pair of established breeders who very much wanted a bull calf sired by a particular bull out of a very good cow. Payment had already been arranged should the cow have a bull calf. They both took turns at watching the cow in a small field near the farm steading, much to the amusement of the owner of the cow. In due course a bull calf was born. The two buyers wished without further delay to take the calf to its new home, fearful that the breeder might substitute another for it in their absence. As they put the calf into their car and were about to leave, the breeder said, "Aye, ye ken its mither but ye hae tae accept my word about its faither."

Another story tells us that the youngest son of a breeder was walking along the road leading a young bull when two well known breeders came along in their car. Both had heard about this excellent young bull so they stopped the car to have a look at the animal. One of the breeders said to the young man, "How is the bull bred?"

The youngster replied "Go down to the ferm and oor Jock ale gae it a pedigree as lang as yer arm."

What the stories point out is that it is the integrity of the breeder that matters and on this integrity depends whether or not the written word is worth more than the paper it is written on. There have been cases of pedigrees being in doubt, and their claims are difficult to check. (A considerable amount of work has been done on blood grouping in the larger breeds of livestock, but as yet I have not heard of this in dogs.)

At the time of the foundation of the Breed, pedigrees were unimportant. The dogs were kept with the hounds. They followed the hunt all day and went to ground. If they did not, they were no use to the hunt and no doubt found a suitable home. The Master knew every dog and its ancestry, his terriers as well as his hounds. He no doubt felt as A. Forster said, that the marks on the dog's face were a better testimony of the dog's ability to do the job than any pedigree. In a similar way, in gundogs, a dog with a classic pedigree who is a show champion on conformation is not as valuable to the real gundog breeder as the dog with a reasonable conformation who has proved his worth in the field trials.

Moreover, typical modern pedigrees do not reveal information crucial to the breeder. For instance, has the sire produced abnormal progeny of a recessive type? In Galloway cattle has the sire produced the defect known as Tibial Heminal? In the dog, has the sire produced the recessive condition called Retinal Atrophy? If he has, no matter how classic the pedigree, such a sire is useless to breed from. To do so would only result in the spread of the gene.

The serious breeder of the future should be more selective in examining the pedigree of the possible stud dog. There are more important matters in breeding than the winning of Challenge Certificates. As a guide in such matters, the newcomer should enquire if the stud dog has been examined for such defects as Retinal Atrophy, Hip Dysplasia and heart defects. Is the stud owner prepared to certify that the dog has not to his knowledge sired any abnormal progeny? After all, in using the dog you are in fact purchasing for a fee the dog's semen, in the hope that you will get a litter of puppies. As a purchaser you are entitled to know that what you are purchasing is free of known defects. Naturally, no stud owner can guarantee that the results of the mating will produce Champions. But the stud owner should endeavour to find out if his stud dog is in fact free of invisible deformities likely to be of an hereditary nature. There are tests available to determine such matters and it is up to the breeder to find out that his stud dog is free from them.

In the future the discerning breeder will show in his pedigree all the necessary information that someone interested in the improvement of the breed will need to have at his/her disposal. He will not confine himself to a list of the names of the ancestors of the animal in question but will provide interesting facts about whether the sire is free of the hereditary defects common in all breeds of livestock since pedigree records have been maintained.

Pedigrees are sometimes shown in which the Champions are emphasized in a different coloured ink. The newcomers to the dog game should bear in mind that whether a dog becomes a Champion or not depends on the available competition at the time the dog was being exhibited, on how many good Champions were in the ring at the same time, and on the number of championship shows given with C.C.s for the breed. In the early days there were some nine shows with certificates. This made for keen competition between the breeders of the time. (The breed was also confined to fewer individuals who had agreed on a particular type. Their views did not conflict as much as opinions do today.)

The Working Certificate

In farm livestock, the breeding pedigree is associated with production. In the dairy industry, for example, the dam of a sire is recorded as having given X gallons of milk in so many days of production. The daughters of the sire are recorded as having produced X gallons in a similar period of time. A system of contemporary comparisons is worked out, and these are published for the interested potential purchaser to study. In the beef industry a similar type of information is given in relation to the ability of the sire during a period of growth to put on weight (i.e., live weight gain over so many days). The sons and daughters of the sire in turn are officially recorded so that the breeders are aware of the ability of the strain to do the job it was intended to do. This work is done on an official basis so that the tests are governed by the same conditions.

In Border Terriers the only criteria of the worth of the dog to do the job it was intended to do is the Working Certificate. This type of certificate was introduced by the Club so that the member could have his dog or bitch tried for working ability. The certificate is issued by the clubs, and is signed by the Master of the Hunt where the dog was tried at, e.g., fox. I do not recollect that the certificate states that the Master of the Hunt was in fact present when the dog was tried, or that the Master in fact identified the dog at work as the one represented by the pedigree registered with the K.C.

The older breeders did not hold such certificates in very high esteem. In fact they were in agreement that in some cases these had been issued by over-generous huntsmen to dogs they had never seen. This practice resulted in the genuine certificate not being accepted at its real worth. The older breeders would often comment on the dealings in working certificates that occurred in the pubs. Unscrupulous gamekeepers and huntsmen would produce scraps of paper with the name of a dog written on it, alleging that it had been entered and was a good worker. Such scraps of paper, it was alleged, even had the blood of the fox (or was it the dog's blood?) on them to prove their authenticity.

The original idea of the Working Certificate was a good one for those who were unable to have their dogs entered, probably because they did not have the facilities to do so in their neighbourhood. But when the clubs became involved, the officers should have taken control and been present when the dog was being tried, and some system of identification should have been developed.

5

Some Aspects of Animal Nutrition

The nutrition of the dog is no different from that of other farm animals in that they require a balanced diet. The one factor that is different in the case of the dog or the horse is that we are dealing with an animal with a simple stomach. Ruminants have a more complex digestive system, and are able to utilise the more fibrous food stuff. As a result, they are able to establish within the digestive tract an enormous number of bacteria and other types of organisms associated with digestion. In some cases, should a particular substance be missing, the bacteria in the rumen can manufacture the protein or the vitamin from the raw material by a simple chemical process. Ruminants are entirely independent of the Vitamin B complex in their food, for instance. (The absence of this complex vitamin in the diet of those of us who were P.O.W.s with the Japanese caused havoc and the death of many soldiers.) On the other hand, ruminants are dependent on such trace elements as cobalt. In the absence of this trace element, ruminants, e.g., sheep, can suffer from a nutritional disease called "pine", of sporadic distribution. It was discovered that impure iron was more effective in the prevention of the disease than any other substance. On investigation it became clear that the iron was not important; the element cobalt and cobalt alone was the preventive agent. In some way this element is necessary for the essential building up of the vitamin B12 in ruminants. In areas of Scotland and New Zealand where this nutritional disease is prevalent, the pasture is dressed with cobaltised superphosphate.

Copper is another trace element that is sometimes associated with nutrient deficiency. In Southern Australia there is a deficiency of copper in some of the pastures, particularly in sandy soil. Merino sheep grazing there gave evidence of a copper deficiency. Their wool lost the "crimp" so characteristic of Merino wool. Some of the sheep developed a progressive anemia, and the black sheep grazing the area lost the pigmentation of their wool as well as the crimp. When the deficiency was corrected, the symptoms disappeared.

In Britain among sheep stock there is a deficiency disease called "Swayback" in newborn lambs. It is a form of paralysis caused by degenerative changes in the lamb's nervous system occurring before birth. The lambs suffering from this deficiency lack the ability to use their hind legs, and when moving they drag them. Agricultural research into this deficiency has not proved conclusively that the deficiency of copper is the actual cause of this disease, but the fact remains that the dosing of the ewes with copper drenches or providing a mineralised salt lick prevents its occurrence. It is thought that some form of blockage of normal nutrition occurs in the absence of the element copper.

The need for an adequate supply of both minerals and vitamins in the diet of animals dependent on man for their needs cannot be emphasized too much.

The Constituents of the ration

Those of us who were P.O.W.s with the Japanese are probably more food conscious than others, particularly about vitamins. To deal briefly with some aspects of an adequate ration for the dog we can note that food constituents can be divided into six main groups: protein, carbohydrates, fat, minerals, vitamins and water.

Protein

Protein is made up and on digestion breaks down into amino acids, and different proteins contain different amino acids. While wheat, barley and rice appear to be adequate sources of protein for animals, maize does not. The reason for this is that on digestion the maize protein does not yield one of the amino acids (called trypophane), which is an essential constituent of animal body protein. For this reason dog foodstuff should contain several of the known cereals in addition to maize.

Carbohydrates

As the term suggests, the carbohydrates are composed of the three elements carbon, hydrogen and oxygen. These elements are the main sources of energy to the animal body. On digestion small quantities are stored in the liver. The rest is immediately available, as sugar and as muscle builders in the form of glycogen, or animal starch. The carbohydrates should form the greater part of the animal's ration. All sugars, starches, cellulose, and fibre are carbohydrates.

Fat

The fat in the body is composed of the same three elements as the carbohydrates (carbon, hydrogen, oxygen) but in different proportions. It is an important source of energy when the body is not obtaining an adequate supply of food or is under unusual demands, such as active work. Stored fat is a concentrated energy. (In the early days of our P.O.W. life, the big fat fellow had a greater chance of survival than the very thin fellow because the former could draw on his stored fat reserves.)

Minerals

If you put on the dogs' meat to cook and forget about it, it is completely burned to ash, the mineral matter of the body tissue. Ninety per cent of the ash is composed of two elements, calcium and phosphorous, which make up the hard constituents of bone.

In the early days of research into animal nutrition much attention was paid to the need for calcium and phosphorus, these being the main elements studied, no doubt because they were present in such large amounts. The need for other essential elements was discovered in a rather spectacular way, by a scientist named Theiler and his colleagues working in South Africa. He was investigating the high mortality among cattle grazing the South African Veldt, who were eating decayed bones and dying from infections obtained. (The cattle whose remains they had eaten would no doubt have died from some disease.) The blood of the affected cattle was found on analysis to be low in phosphorous. Supplementary feeding of bone-meal restored the blood phosphorous to normal, and the cattle stopped eating the bones.

The research work in this field done in this country has drawn attention to the fact that the plants eaten by the grazing animal have a higher mineral content than those uneaten or rejected by them. It is obvious that minerals are essential to the animal and if the diet is lacking in any of them or they are not present in adequate amounts, no animal can thrive. Lack of them, in fact, can lead to the animal's death.

Vitamin B Complex

The study of vitamins is still in its infancy though research is progressing. An adequate supply of vitamins is required by all living animals. Some ruminants appear to have the ability to synthesise them, because of the type of bacteria in their rumen. It is known that at least six vitamins of the complex vitamin B (and also vitamin K) are synthesised by the rumen bacteria. The dog, however, having like the human a simple digestive system, is unable to synthesise these vitamins and is dependent on an adequate supply in the diet.

The carnivora living in the wild would supplement the diet by eating the remains of animals that had died. The mineral-rich bones as well as the muscles, the livers, and the meat of the animals they caught in hunting, with the additional fruit and berries and green leaves, would no doubt keep them in a healthy state.

A diet deficient in vitamins leads to certain diseases and can cause death. In the case of the P.O.W.s, we developed Pellagra and Beri Beri because of the lack of the Vitamin B complex in our diet. The most immediate symptom of Beri Beri was lack of co-ordinated movement because of degeneration of the nerve endings. In attempting to walk in a straight line you found you deviated between the two points, unable to keep to it. Thiamin also appears to be important to carbohydrate digestion. In this connection it was of interest that those P.O.W.s who were sweet toothed, and who traded anything for extra sugar, suffered earlier from the deficiency than those who did not take the sugar when it was available.

The vitamin B2 (riboflavin) deficiency causes a dermatitis of the skin. With P.O.W.s the dermatitis appeared first as a reddening of the skin, on the chest, abdomen, and the inner surface of the legs, involving the scrotum in the male.

Riboflavin is widely distributed. It is contained in milk, eggs, yeast (Vetzymes), fruits and vegetables, and especially liver and kidneys. It is worth noting, in considering an animal's ration, that the Riboflavin value of food decreases when it is heat treated.

Farm and shepherd Collies have a much better nutritional diet now than they did at the end of the last War. At that time shepherds in particular were reluctant to feed meat to their dogs in the belief that this would encourage them to worry sheep. The consequent lack of the Vitamin B complex affected many animals.

It is remarkable how soon animals suffering from a vitamin deficiency recover after the vitamin is given to them, even in small quantities. On one occasion I visited a hill farm where the owner was a keen sheep dog trial enthusiast. He informed me his good young dog was suffering some ailment. I had a look at the dog with him, and it was obvious to me it was suffering from "Black Tongue" due to the lack of the Vitamin B complex. I told him to give the dog some raw eggs, milk, and meat, and to obtain some Vetzymes and give the dog these as a regular part of the diet. He phoned the next day to say there was already a big improvement in the dog's condition. The next time I was at the farm it was a beautifully conditioned dog that met me. I was pleased to think I had helped to save its life.

The result of the vitamin deficiency in our P.O.W. diet was so disabling that the Japanese insisted that a poultry farm be started, the capital to purchase the hens to come from the pay of the officers. Chinese hens were obtained, but they were still unimproved from an egg laying point of view; they were a broody type and did not lay many eggs at a time. Fortunately we were able to purchase a few White Leghorn hens and cockerels. As the Technical Advisor to the project I crossed the White Leghorn cockerels on to the native hens. In due course, the eggs from this cross were hatched out to give a less broody pullet with an increased egg production.

A number of the personnel in the camp were gradually going blind due to lack of vitamins. It was only natural that the worst cases were prescribed one of our scarce and much-needed raw eggs. On this information becoming general knowledge, the number of bad eyes in the camp increased. To distinguish the genuine sufferers from the egg seekers with the limited equipment we had, a doctor was placed in charge of the eggs and the eye patients had to report to him after they had had their eyes tested. If the patient was considered an egg case, the doctor (who had a tray of eggs on a table) told him that his name was on an egg. If the patient found the right egg, the doctor took charge of it, telling the patient that having found the correct egg his eyes could not be that bad and there were others in a much worse state than he and more in need of it.

Another experience of how little and how quickly a subject suffering from a deficiency in vitamins responds to the restoration of the deficiency in the diet concerned some young chickens on our poultry farm, which we were permitted to work at only for whatever period the Guard Commander allowed.

A batch of young chickens about six weeks old appeared one

morning to be off colour. On this particular morning our visit was a hurried one, as the Guard Commander was not in a good mood. The following morning we noticed that some of the chickens had drooping heads; they appeared to have lost control of the muscles of their necks. I decided they were suffering from a vitamin deficiency. By chance our hosts had that day brought in some fresh fish. In relation to some 4,000 P.O.W.s the amount was negligible, but to our chickens that fish was worth its weight in gold. All the livers and other innards were cut into very small pieces and fed to the chicks with the aid of a pin. Those that could not swallow received crushed liver juice. It was indeed remarkable the difference this made to them. In a day or two they were quite healthy.

Vitamin C

Scientists endeavouring to produce Scurvy in dogs by feeding rations deficient in Vitamin C have been relatively unsuccessful and there is some evidence to indicate that the dog is capable of synthesising its own vitamin C. However, sometimes there are reports that symptoms of a Vitamin C deficiency have been observed, and this has been relieved by the addition of lemon juice to the diet. Lemon juice is rich in ascorbic acid, the factor for vitamin C. Animals that are entirely dependent on cooked foods could be liable to suffer from this deficiency if they do not have access to uncooked green food or a source of something containing ascorbic acid.

Vitamin D

When the nutritional mineral metabolism is upset in the growing animal or the human, bone deformities in the long bones of the legs occur (Rickets). The teeth can also be defective. Although the problem in humans is seldom seen now because of the advance in the standard of living, it was a common factor in growing children in large cities like Glasgow between World Wars I and II. This was due primarily to the low nutritional diet, with the lack of adequate sources of calcium and phosphorous in the food. It was also due to the lack of sunlight and sufficient vitamin D to regulate the absorption of these minerals into the bone structure.

To try to alleviate the condition the authorities purchased two large houses, with grounds attached, in a country district of Ayrshire.

Children suffering from this condition were sent to these houses for some 14 days in the summer months each year.

Veterinary surgeons in country practices during the same period were well aware of the same problem among the farmers' and the shepherds' dogs. At that time, the Collies' diet was mostly composed of porridge and maize. On these farms fresh milk was a scarce commodity until the spring of the year. The dogs' diet was low in protein and the minerals calcium and phosphorous. It also lacked Vitamin D. Bone deformities were common in young growing dogs, and in particular, in puppies born on the farm in winter.

The best sources of Vitamin D are fish liver oils and irradiated foods. With the action of the sunlight on the skin, the animal is able to manufacture its own Vitamin D. The result of a deficiency in the level of calcium and Vitamin D in animals, in addition to long bone and teeth problems, is eclampsia (called milk fever in cattle).

One final note to keep in mind when considering animal nutrition is that in addition to an adequacy in the components of the food supply, it is also necessary to have a healthy digestive system so that the food can be broken down into its digestible form. This processing is a complex factory organisation involving enzymes contained in the digestive juices, and some forms of bacteria. Animals suffering deficiency problems may have a problem properly absorbing certain nutrients they have been fed.

Some Practical Advice for the Border Terrier Breeder

- In order to keep the whelps reasonably small and thus make whelping easier for the bitch, it is best not to give her any additional food at all during pregnancy, especially in the last few weeks when the whelps are growing rapidly. The protein part of her diet should be increased, but no additional bulk food given.

- Do not allow strangers to handle your pups or your nursing bitch, as they could quite easily carry disease to the pups in the nest. Do not allow the nursing bitch outside your own garden for the same reason.

- Though she seems ready to be bred, a bitch may refuse a dog for any of the following reasons: (a) she is earlier or later in the oestrous cycle than you suppose; (b) she may have strictures, persistent hymen or a growth within the vagina; (c) she may be responding to the loved owner's presence. In the latter case, the owner should leave and the breeder should try again.)

- Some time before a bitch who is to be bred is due in season, add wheat germ meal and a brew of raspberry leaf to her food. The latter serves to make whelping easier and the wheat germ meal contains vitamin E, which is certainly required for fertility in both the male and the female. The bitch to be bred should also be wormed if worms are present. It is well to keep in mind that hookworms do not always show up, even in a blood sample.

- A good way to determine whether you are feeding the pregnant bitch properly is to feel along her backbone. If as the pregnancy goes on the backbone is getting less covered with flesh, perhaps diet should be increased. If on the other hand flesh on the back bone is increasing, you are giving her too much. Lean bitches will whelp more easily and do their pups better than fat ones.

- Maiden bitches or bitches carrying large litters tend to whelp a day or two earlier than the 63 days commonly noted as the term of pregnancy in dogs.

- You should ensure that your bitch obtains a supply of Vitamin D and soluble calcium in her diet, in order to prevent milk eclampsia (sometimes called parturition fever or, in cows, milk fever). Cod liver oil or halibut liver oil capsules are a readily available source of vitamin D. Soluble calcium is available in calcium gluconate (two teaspoons daily).

- The cheapest form of calcium one can obtain is egg shells. All the egg shells here are put in a slow oven and after drying are ground to a fine powder, using a bottle as a pestle. In-whelp bitches get a teaspoonful sprinkled on their food every other day; they get a teaspoonful of cod liver oil on their food daily. (The Vitamin D in the oil is essential in the absorbence of calcium.)

- Some scientists believe that some animals are unable to mobilize the calcium and magnesium necessary to prevent eclampsia despite being given vitamin D and absorbable calcium, perhaps because of a parathyroid gland deficiency. If a bitch has this problem it may be best not to breed her.

- The important factor in the whelping is not how long the bitch takes to start actual labour but, after sustained labour is started, how long it takes for a pup to be born.

- The whelping bitch should be allowed to eat the placenta since it contains numerous antibodies useful to her and also has a laxative effect.
- To remove any placenta still adhering to the newborn pup's nose, I rub the pup's nose along the dam's coat against the direction of the hair growth.
- It is reckoned that normal pups at birth are about 1/50 of the dam's body weight.
- In the event you have forgotten to obtain milk substitute and need to supplement the diet of weak newborn pups, the nearest diet to bitch's milk is fresh raw eggs, reduced with equal parts of fresh cow's milk.
- I start our pups to lap at about three weeks on a mixture of two parts fresh cow's milk to one part raw eggs for a week or so; I add finely minced meat with a little water to make a gravy consistency or a gruel of both foods about the fourth week. Roughage is avoided for young pups.
- If you must bottle-feed pups, a strong cardboard disc fitted around the neck of the bottle gives the pup something to push against, as he would against the dam's teat. It is remarkable the difference this makes in the pup's taking food.
- The best method I have found to start young pups feeding is to form your hand into a cup, with a drop or two of the egg and milk mixture in the centre. This method prevents getting any liquid in the nose and the warm hand and probably the odour of the mixture encourages each pup to lick.
- Innoculations should be started around 10-11 weeks. The pups carry their mother's immunity up to that point. For good effect innoculations should be carried out previous to the pups reaching 16 weeks of age.

6

Some Breed Club History

In all breeds of livestock, after a few breeders get together and some interest is shown in the breed, it follows that a club is formed. The Border Terrier breed is no exception. I felt it would be of interest to summarise the early Breed Club record where possible.

Although the earliest records of the Club have been lost, data is available onwards from the October 1, 1930 meeting of the Club, held in Edinburgh some 10 years after the breed was recognised by the Kennel Club.

The members present at that 1930 meeting were: Mr. J. Wallace (Chairman), Dr. Fullerton, Messrs J. J. Pawson, J. W. Bonsor, G. Sordy, J. Smart, W. Irving and Mr. J. Dodd (Treasurer). The Secretary was Mr. G. Thompson. Evidently a previous meeting had been held on August 4, 1930.

The Secretary read a letter from Mr. Holland Buckley, the Secretary of The K.C. This letter intimated that Mr. J. D. Bonsor was unable to judge at the National Terrier Show and the Secretary requested the Committee to furnish a list of names so that a judge could be selected from the list. The Secretary of the K.C. also informed the Club that C.C.'s were not required for Border Terriers at the Birmingham Dog Show. He also noted that a spare set of C.C.'s had been offered to the Metropolitan & Essex Show and declined. This matter was remitted to Mr. J. J. Pawson and the Secretary to arrange for the reallocation of the certificates.

It is interesting to note that in those days the Club Committee had a say in the reallocation of certificates.

Another interesting reflection of breed history is contained in the last paragraph of this minute. The Secretary announced that since the Mifield Silver Challenge Trophy had been won three times and therefore fulfilled the conditions under which the Trophy had been presented by Mrs. Kavanagh Bone, the cup now became the property of the winner, Mrs. A. Forster. He also announced that Mrs. Forster had expressed her willingness to replace the cup she had won.

It also appears that in the early days there was no permanent Committee Chairman; the Committee elected the Chairman at the meeting. By way of example, at the Annual General Meeting on October 1, 1930, on the motion of Mr. J. J. Pawson, seconded by Mr. George Sordy, Mr. J. Wallace was voted to the chair. At this meeting the Chairman announced the election of the undernoted persons to serve on the committee for the following year:

Appleyard, K. C. (Major)	Hamilton-Adams, J.
Barton, Wm.	Fullerton, Dr.
Bonsor, J. D.	Knight-Bruce, J. W. (Major)
Irving, W.	Sordy, George
Pawson, J. J.	Renton, J.
Wilson, Wm.	Smart, J.
Rankine, Mrs.	Wallace, J.
Carruthers, John	Watson, W.
Drurie, James	Wilson, J. Muir
Forster, Adam	Vaux, Miss H.
Hardie, Evelyn	Renwick, Sir John
Farmer, Douglas	

The above list more or less comprises the major breeders of Border Terriers at that time. Apart from a few losses, these people continued to breed and exhibit Border Terriers at the main shows up to the 1950's and 1960's.

At the same meeting the following members were elected to serve on the breed's panel of judges:

Pawson, W.	Wallace, J.
Appelyard, K.C. (Major)	Forster, A.
Barton, W.	Forster, Mrs.
Bonsor, J. D.	Fullerton, D. C.
Carruthers, J. R.	Hamilton-Adams, J.
Dodd, J.	Sordy, Geo.
Irving, W.	Renwick, Sir John R.
Pawson, C. R.	Smart, J.
Pattison, W.	Thompson, G.
Renton, J. T.	Watson, W.

Again apart from loss through natural causes, many of the above individuals were active in the breed after World War Two.

It appears, also, the Committee moved its meetings from place to place. The 1931 meeting was held in Hexham, for instance. It was announced at that meeting that Mr. J. Smart would judge the Edinburgh Show and Mr. J. Thompson would judge the English Kennel Club Show in October 1932.

The committee also agreed that the following shows should be supported:

Richmond	25%
Darlington	Two Special Prizes
Harrogate	Two Special Prizes
Paisley	25%
Consett	25%
Bellingham	Two Special Prizes
Hexham	Two Special Prizes
Scottish Kennel Club	Two Special Prizes

The Secretary intimated that the Club's annual meeting and show could be held in conjunction with the Kennel Club Show in London on October 7-8, 1931. This was agreed to, provided two Novice classes and a class for dogs or bitches holding a working certificate could be added:

Puppy Dog	Puppy Bitch
Novice Dog	Novice Bitch
Limit Dog	Limit Bitch
Open Dog	Open Bitch

A letter was read from the Ladies Kennel Association regarding its Championship show to be held in May 1932. The Committee agreed to guarantee 25% provided the judge was from the Club's panel of judges.

But a letter from the Royal College of Veterinary surgeons in respect of rebuilding the College and Endowment Fund was laid on the table.

A letter from Mr. J. J. Pawson, Hon. Secretary of the Southern Club, was read, suggesting that the Working Certificates issued by the two Clubs be interchangeable. It was agreed that the suggestion be adopted.

The Committee held their meeting as arranged at the Kennel Club show in London, October 7-8, 1931. The members of the Committee at that time were Mr. J. Wallace (Chairman), Messrs. J. D. Bonsor, J. J. Pawson, Douglas Farmer, J. Hamilton-Adams, J. H. W. Knight-Bruce (Major). There were several new names for membership: Lady Hamilton, Mr. R. G. Morrison, Mrs. E. Baughey, Mr. Calvert Butler (a well known allrounder) and Terrier Judge Mr. R. B. Mayor.

A letter from the Secretary of Crufts Dog Show was submitted appealing for support in respect of the Crufts Show to be held on February 10-11, 1932. It was agreed that the letter be laid on the table. (This decision demonstrates the older breeders' attitude to Crufts. They did not attach to it the glamour it is accorded today. In fact some of the older breeders never judged Crufts. J. Renton and Wattie Irving were both up in years before they judged that show.)

At the same committee meeting they agreed to support the following shows: Ayr Show, 1932 50%, Novice (D) or (B), Limit and Open (D) and (B) classes. Carlisle Show, two Special Prizes. They also agreed that the deficiency reported on the Durham County Show (twelve shillings and sixpence) and Paisley (four shillings) should be paid. The Club's Annual General Meeting was held at the Crystal Palace, London, October 7, 1931. Mr. J. Wallace was in the chair. Other than approving the Club's financial position and confirming the approved judges, there was nothing new in the minutes.

In 1932, the Committee of the Club met in Edinburgh on Wednesday, September 28. The Chairman was again Mr. J. Wallace and present were Messrs. J. D. Bonsor, W. Drurie, W. Irving, J. T. Renton, Sir J. R. Renwick, J. Smart, J. J. Pawson and George Thompson (Secretary). The committee agreed that the club's liabilities in respect of the following shows should be approved for payment.

Newcastle	January 1, 1932	1 pd., 5 s.
L. K. Association	May 11, 1932	1 pd., 5 s., 7 d.
Leeds	June 25, 1932	2 pds., 5 s.
Richmond	July 5, 1932	1 pd., 7 s., 6 d.
Darlington	July 25, 1932	2 pds., 3 s., 9 d.

Appeals for support were submitted and it was agreed to support classes for Border Terriers at the following shows: National Terrier Club, Olympia, June 3, 1933, Judge Mr. Hamilton-Adams; Ladies Kennel Club, May 1933, Judge Mr. W. Watson, 25%.

An appeal to support Crufts of February 1933 was declined.

The Border Terrier Club's A.G.M. for 1932 was held in the North British Hotel, Edinburgh, on the same day as the Committee meeting (Wednesday, September 28).

The same members were present and remained on the club's Committee. At this meeting the Chairman (Mr. Wallace) referred to the loss the Border Terrier Club had sustained by the untimely death of Mrs. A. Forster. (It was many years later that I learned about the tragic circumstances of how this happened from both Wattie Irving and John Renton. Mrs. Forster was visiting her brother in Newcastle and was waiting for a bus. The bus to avoid a car veered on to the pavement and Mrs. Forster was killed, on 23 July 1932.)

At this meeting a letter was read from Mr. J. Dodd, announcing his resignation from his position as Hon. Treasurer. Appreciation of his services to the club over the period he held office (some 10 years) were recorded with the best thanks of the members. It was proposed by Mr. J. Bonsor, seconded by Miss Hardie, and resolved that Mr. J. Renton be elected to be the club's Hon. Treasurer. This office John held until his death in 1970, some 40 years.

At a meeting of the Club Committee the day previous to the A.G.M., a letter was read from a Mr. J. Drymen, Newton Stewart, Wigtownshire, intimating his inability to obtain working certificates signed by a Master of Hounds. It was agreed because of the type of country in which his terriers were worked to accept a certificate signed by a gamekeeper or some other reliable person. At the same meeting it was reported that Mr. J. Smart had presented a Silver Challenge Cup to be known as the Twenpie Cup to replace the Tweedside Cup which had been won outright. The Committee's thanks were recorded.

At the A.G.M. in Edinburgh in September 1933, the same Committee and panel of judges was approved but there was nothing further of interest in the minutes.

At the A.G.M. held in Edinburgh, September 26, 1934, a new name appears on the Committee. Miss Vaux was elected to the Committee and became Secretary in 1937. (This post she held until 1950, when she resigned due to ill health.)

The Club Committee also held a meeting on September 26, 1934, in Edinburgh. The same members were present and again Mr. Wallace was in the chair. The minutes of this meeting, although they contain nothing of any unusual content, indicate how the breed is expanding. This is shown by the fact that there are several new names added to the list of members:

Major H. S. Wolley	Cheltenham
Mrs. Wolley	Cheltenham
Mr. D. Chappe-Hall	Sussex
Dr. W. Lilico	Wigtown, Wigtownshire, Scotland
Major H. Jones	Suffolk
F. H. S. McDavid	Edinburgh
J. Smart	Tweedmouth
Jas. McLaren	Haddington

(Dr. Lilico was one of the veteran breeders when I came into the breed in the late 1940's. He later became Chairman of the Club.)

The death of Mr. Douglas Farmer, who had been a member of the club since the early days, was reported to the Committee. A letter from the Canadian Kennel Club was submitted to the Committee and the Secretary's action confirmed. It is unfortunate that the contents of the letter are not minuted, and no doubt this letter was lost along with the earlier records of the club. It would have been of interest to the historian to have had an insight into this letter. The fact that a letter was received from the Canadian Club indicates that someone abroad was interested in the breed. I wonder if the Canadian Kennel Club has a record of the letter?

It was reported that Capt. Hamilton and Miss D. M. Dobie had both given special prizes to the club. The following deficits were reported:

Harrogate (Championship)	4 pds., 16 s.
Darlington (Championship)	3 pds., 5 s.
Leeds (Championship)	2 pds., 2 s., 9 d.
Richmond (Championship)	1 pd., 7 s., 6 d.

Appeals for support of the under mentioned shows was agreed:

Northern Joint Terrier Show	November 24, 1934	25%
Glasgow Championship Show	February 27, 1935	25%
Ayr Championship Show	April, 1935	25%
Richmond Championship Show	July 9, 1935	25%

It will be seen from the forgoing that the members of the Committee by their guarantee of the classes at these shows was adding to the breed's general interest, and (from the fact that the membership of the club was expanding) their action was paying dividends. The present-day breeders owe a lot of thanks to these older breeders for their endeavours in this field. At the A.G.M. in 1934 some 23 members attended, drawn from all over the country.

In 1935 the Committee held a meeting at the Crystal Palace, London, on October 9. On a motion by Mr. J. Renton, seconded by Mr. W. Irving, Capt. M. C. Hamilton was voted to the chair. The Chairman referred to the death of Mr. J. Wallace, who had been Chairman by popular vote since 1930. The deaths of Dr. E. Tate and Mr. Watson were also recorded. There were four resignations and one new member recorded. It was reported that the club's deficit of 1 pound 10 shillings on the guarantee of the Glasgow Championship Show, on February 27, 1935, had been paid. It was agreed to offer two pieces of silver for the Novice Bitch and Novice Dog classes at Ayr Show on April 29, 1936, the prizes to be confined to members of the Club. Again an appeal in respect of Crufts Show was laid on the table.

On the same day (October 9, 1935), the Club's A.G.M. followed the Committee meeting at the Crystal Palace, London. Capt. M. C. Hamilton was elected to the Chair and the same members were elected to the Club Committee. The Club's judges list was confirmed. At this meeting Major J. H. W. Knight-Bruce submitted a letter to the Committee regarding a scheme for holding field trials for Border Terriers and after some discussion it was decided that Major Knight-Bruce be empowered to form a sub-committee of three members and submit a report to the next A.G.M. It is unfortunate that there are no details given regarding how this scheme was to be operated, and I cannot find any further reference to it in the minutes that follow. There is no reference to it in the minutes of the next year's A.G.M.

At their 1935 meeting the Committee discussed the appointment of judges for the 1936 Scottish Kennel Club Show in Glasgow and the Kennel Club show in London. It was decided to forward a Panel of Judges for the Glasgow Show and to request that the Kennel Club make a selection from the undermentioned list in respect to the shows in Edinburgh and London:

Edinburgh:	London:
Miss Vaux	Capt. M. C. Hamilton
Mr. A. Dunn	Major J. H. W. Knight-Bruce
Mr. G. Thompson	Mr. E. C. Spence

It was proposed by Mr. J. Renton and seconded by Miss Vaux that Capt. M. C. Hamilton be appointed Chairman of the Club to fill the vacancy caused by the death of Mr. J. Wallace.

It was so voted, in the minutes of the meeting of the Border Terrier Club Committee held after the judging at the Scottish Kennel Club Show in Edinburgh on September 30, 1936.

Meetings on all occasions started with a formal statement of approval of Club finance reports (usually as follows: "The notice of the meeting having been read, it was *proposed* by the Chairman, *seconded* by Dr. Lilico and *resolved* that the statement of Accounts for the year ended December 31, 1935, here presented be received and adopted"). The minutes at no time however give any indication of the Club's specific financial position at this time.

The minutes of this 1935 meeting contain a list of members to serve on the Club's panel of judges for the ensuing year. It also gives the addresses of the members of the panel. This is divided into a North Area and South Area.

Many of the members listed above were serving on the Club's Committee and did much to steer the breed's activities. It was these members who really laid the foundations for the breed.

At this 1936 meeting the Secretary was instructed to write to the Duchess of Gloucester to request her to accept the Presidency of the Club.

In 1937 the Border Terrier Club Committee held its next meeting at Olympia, London, on Wednesday, October 6, after the judging. The minutes followed their usual procedure (approving the statement of the accounts for the previous year ending December 31). The same members of the Committee were confirmed in office. Again the members' panel of judges was confirmed. Two new names were added to the members list:

Viscountess Portman	Staple Fitzdaniel Manor, Taunton, England
Mrs. S. Mulcaster	St. John's Cottage, Huntingdon, England

These names were added to the Southern list.

An interesting proposal was made from the Chair (Capt. M. C. Hamilton): *Proposed* by the Chairman, and *seconded* by Mr. J. Renton: "That all future meetings be held in Edinburgh". An amendment was: *Proposed* by Sir J. Renwick and *seconded* by B. R. Mayor, "That the meetings be held in London and Edinburgh alternatively as in the past". On being put to the meeting, the amendment carried. (Unfortunately, the number of votes recorded is not given in the records.)

In 1938 minutes of the proceedings of the A.G.M. held in Edinburgh at the Scottish Kennel Club Show after the judging in October

North Area:

Mr. W. Barton	Outer Huntly, Askirk, Selkirk
Mr. J. D. Bonsor	14 Buccleugh St., Hawick, Roxburghshire
Mr. J. R. Carruthers	High Lean, West Woodburn, Northumberland
Mr. A. Forster	Harbottle, Morpeth, Northumberland
Mr. W. Irving	Station House, Musselburgh, Scotland
Mjr. W. Paterson	Millfield House, Millfield Terrace, Hexham, Northumberland
Mr. J. Renton	Lanton Gardens, Duns, Berwickshire
Mr. G. Sordy	Heckley, High House, Alnwick, Northumberland
Mr. J. Smart	3 Grosvenor Place, Tweedmouth, Berwick-on-Tweed
Sir John Renwick	Riversdale, Bellingham, Northumberland
Miss H. Vaux	Low Straforth Hall, Barnard Castle, Co. Durham
Capt. M. C. Hamilton	Forest Cottage, Forrest Hall, Newcastle upon Tyne
Mr. A. Dunn (Major)	Redden Farm, Kelso, Roxburghshire, Scotland

South Area:

Mr. R. G. Morrison	Wayside, Hadleigh, Suffolk, England
Mr. B. R. Mayor	134 Milton Road, Cambridge, England
Mr. J. J. Pawson	Hartley Witney, Hants, England
Mr. C. R. Pawson	Longcott, Faringdon, Berks, England
Mr. W. Welton	Benton End, Hadleigh, Suffolk, England
Viscountess Portman	Staple Fitzdaniel Manor, Taunton
Mr. Calvert Butler	Dale House, Carnford, Lancashire, England
Major Knight-Bruce	Deans Hill, Harrietsham, Kent, England
Miss Richmond	Exford, Somerset, England
Mr. E. C. Spencer	The Park, Overstone, Northampton, England.

Mr. John Carruthers of Barrow Farm, Upper Coquetdale and Rock, renamed Mick, later purchased by Mr. Hamilton Adams, renamed Ivo Roisterer and became a champion.

165

show that the Chairman confirmed the names on the Club's Panel of Judges. This is the same list as previously, again divided into North and South. The name of Mr. D. Black (Tweedside Kennels) was added to the Northern list.

It may be of interest to the reader that Mr. Black had previously been in Bulldogs, but his wife had the Borders before he started showing them under the Tweedside Prefix (Tweedside Kennels, Berwick-upon-Tweed). I remember that at one of the first Championship shows I attended just after the War, D. Black appeared in the ring in a Special Beginners Class, much to the consternation of the other exhibitors. (The Tweedside dogs previous to the War had won many Certificates.) I believe from memory it was at the Crufts Show just after the War. This class then was confined to exhibitors who had not won a C.C. in the Breed. Wattie Irving said to me when the talk started, "What's all the fuss about? David has not won a certificate in his own right. All the Tweedside certificates were won by Mrs. Black."

The name of Dr. Lilico (Benvoir, Wigtownshire, Scotland) was added in this year to the judges list.

New names on the Southern list were those of

Mrs. K. Twist	Old Hall, Little Bourne, Canterbury, England.
Lady Russell	Swallowfield, Reading, Berks, England
Mr. R. Hall	Skipton, Nr. Leeds, Yorkshire, England

There again appears to have been some difference in opinion between the members of the Committee regarding where the meetings were to be held. At this meeting it was *proposed* by Dr. Lilico, *seconded* by Mr. J. D. Bonsor and *resolved*: "That the motion passed at the last Annual General Meeting that future meetings be held in London and Edinburgh alternatively, be rescinded, and that all future meetings be held in Edinburgh." Also, it was *proposed* by Mr. J. D. Bonsor, *seconded* by Dr. Lilico, and *resolved*, "that a meeting of the Committee could be held at any time without previous notice." It was also resolved that the annual subscription of 5 shillings per annum be continued.

Although this meeting was held on October 8, 1938, the minutes were not signed until August 9, 1946, World War Two interfering with the proceedings of the Club. The minutes of the meeting were then signed by W. Irving.

The recommencement of the Club's activities after the War was in the holding of a Championship Show at Workington on August 9, 1946, when the above minutes were signed. The Chairman was Mr. W. Irving; the Secretary Miss H. Vaux; the Treasurer was Mr. J. Renton.

The first meeting of the Club I attended was at the Edinburgh Championship Show in 1947. There were not many present at the meeting and the absence of the Secretary, Miss Vaux, due to illness, was explained by the Chairman, Mr. W. Irving. There was a suggestion made that the Committee might look into the feasibility of holding a Championship show at Berwick-upon-Tweed. Other than this item there was nothing of interest. The fact that the proposed show was never held to my knowledge must have been due to the lack of real interest in this place as a venue.

In 1950 an Annual General Meeting of the Club was held in the Kelvin Hall, Glasgow, on Friday, March 3, 1950. But again there was a poor attendance. Miss Vaux was still in ill health. It was agreed to postpone the meeting until the Carlisle Championship Show in August. The Chairman, Mr. W. Irving, was authorized to forward to the Kennel Club, the Club Constitution and the Breed Standard for ratification. The minute was signed on August 12, 1950.

The adjourned Annual General Meeting was held at Carlisle Championship Show after the judging. The minutes of the previous meeting were approved and a statement of the accounts for the year ending December 31, 1949, was adopted, showing a balance of 175 pounds, 9 shillings, 4 pence. At this meeting a letter was read from Miss Vaux announcing her resignation as Secretary due to her continued ill health. The Secretary was requested to write to her thanking her for her services to the Club. At this meeting after both Mr. Lazonby and Mr. J. Shiach, both being keen and enthusiastic for the breed, refused the post of Secretary, Mr. Mitchell proposed that Dr. Lilico be appointed Chairman, Mr. J. Renton to continue as Treasurer, and Mr. W. Irving be Secretary. This was agreed to by the members. There were some new members who joined the Committee, including myself.

There appears to be nothing in the minutes following the above until the Annual General Meeting held at the Carlisle Championship Show in 1952. The Club accounts up to December 31, 1951, showed a balance of 222 pounds, 10 shillings, 9 pence. At this meeting Dr. Lilico, who had been suffering from overwork and ill health, tendered his resignation as Chairman. This was reluctantly accepted and the hope was expressed that he would soon regain his usual good health. Several members paid tribute to his long association and the help he had given to the Club.

Mr. Mitchell proposed that Mr. A. Forster be elected Chairman. This was unanimously adopted. Mr. J. Renton continued as Treasurer, Mr. W. Irving continued as Secretary. In this trio we had in office the three breeders with the longest association with the breed. Adam Forster, through his association with the Carruthers family, had been involved practically since the very foundation of the breed, establishing his own kennel in 1916. Wattie Irving established his kennel late in the 1920's and John Renton his at about the same time.

Robert Hall was elected to the Committee in the place of A. Forster, and as an old breeder, John Copland, had died and Miss Richmond had resigned due to the distance she had to travel, Mrs. Holmes and Mrs. Fairley were elected to the vacancies caused.

Mr. Mitchell proposed that two silver trophies be purchased to be won outright at the 1953 show for the best bitch and best dog to commemorate the coronation of Queen Elizabeth.

At this point the club history has been traced from the early 1930's (the earliest period of recorded history of the Club) until the 1950's. The following period is more or less within the aspect of modern history and, apart from the routine procedure at the A.G.M. of confirming the office bearers and the financial position of the Club, there is little to report other than deaths of long-standing members. At the 1953 A.G.M., for instance, the chairman, Mr. A. Forster, reported to the members in sympathetic terms the sudden death of Mr. Fred Mitchell, who had been a enthusiastic member of the Club for a very long time. He had been a member of the Committee for a number of years. The members paid tribute to his passing. An Auctioneer by profession, Fred Mitchell had been associated with the livestock breeding industry during his lifetime. This close connection with the industry brought him into contact with the problems that Breed Societies had come up against. The knowledge he gained over the years in this field enabled him to be in a position to give good counsel to those who sought his advice. At a subsequent A.G.M., Mr. Forster announced that Mrs. Mitchell had donated to the Club a Silver Trophy to be called the Fred Mitchell Trophy, to be awarded to the winner of the most points at the Jedburgh and Kelso Club shows.

A further point of interest to the newcomer to the Breed was raised at one of the A.G.M.s year or so previous to Adam Forster's death. The question of mouths was raised and Adam Forster gave his view that a dog should not be severely penalized by the fact that it had an odd tooth irregular in the formation. He felt that this was not a bad mouth and the displacement of an odd tooth should not be too severely penalized. At the same meeting he also spoke about terriers being shown short of coat due to the excessive trimming that was becoming so evident. This in his opinion made it difficult to judge the type of coat of the animal.

It is a pity that some of the younger generation of my time in the breed have not had the opportunity to speak to such a breeder as Adam, with his wealth of experience of both the working and exhibition sides of the breed. He not only could speak from his own experience but also could draw on the experience of his family.

After Adam Forster's death in 1963 the Chair was held in an interim capacity by Mr. Jim Shiach, who had been in the breed for many years, but was not a dedicated shower. He liked a Border for its companionship and the breed for its working capabilities.

At the A.G.M. in Carlisle after the judging, I was voted to the Chair in the place of the late A. Forster. I accepted this honour with a feeling of some trepidation, at the thought of following in the footsteps of one of the great breeders, and one of the most experienced at that time. Although Joy and I had been in the breed almost 20 years then, in relation to some others it was not a long time. I held the Chair for some 10 years, and resigned to allow some of the younger people to have an opportunity to have a share of the honour. I have never regretted the decision.

In leaving the Chair I realized that the breed and the breeders were moving into a new era. There were at that point none active in the affairs of the Club that had known and enjoyed the friendship of the older breeders in the fortunate way I had, meeting them at shows, competing against them, and visiting them in their homes. I had

Revenge, b. 12/8/1922. Revenge was one of the great sires of the breed and along with Mr. W. Carruthers' Rival they laid the foundations of the breed. Revenge was sired by a dog called Buittie who was by Branton Mick ex Flossie. Flossie was the dam of Ch/Ivo Roisterer. Revenge's dam was Little Midget who was bred by A. Forster. Little Midget's was by a dog called Titlington Jock ex Coquetdale Vic. Coquetdale Vic's (1210 CC) b. 27th February 1916 sire was Barrow Jock (unr), d. Nailer II. And Barrow Jock, bred by Mr. J. Carruthers, b. 10th March 1913 Mack (unr unt) ex Nettle. Revenge sired: Ch/Todhunter, Ch/Benton Biddy, Ch/Happy Mood, Ch/Bladnock Raider, Ch/Blister, Ch/Not So Dusty by Ch/Blister, Ch/Sharepusher by Stingo by Ch/Blister, Ch/Finchdale Lass by Stingo by Ch/Blister, Ch/What Fettle by Ch/Bladnock Raider, Ch/Gay Fine by Ch/Bladnock Raider, Dipley Deans by Ch/Bladnock Raider, Puffin by Ch/Bladnock Raider, Speed of Wind by Ch/Blister.

listened to their views about most subjects concerning the breed and the dogs of the past. The great thing about these exhibitors was that when they were judging, they had no friends exhibiting the dogs. The type of dog in their opinion most according to the Standard won. As exhibitors they were the same: win or lose, no criticism nor complaints.

In leaving the Chair I felt that I had passed through the transitory period of yesterday, through today (my period in the Chair) and that we were now entering the realm of tomorrow. I wondered what the tomorrow would be. I wondered whether the breed would become dominated by showgoers, and the lust for Challenge Certificates. I had had the fortunate experience in my life of being able to look at the livestock industry as a whole, and I had seen the results of the show ring on a number of our breeds. The lesson to be taken from what I saw is that the show ring had done nothing for them. We can only hope that the caring Breed Club members can prevent the disastrous effect on the Border Terrier which has occurred in some other breeds.

Some Early Langholm and Ayr Agricultural Show Results

The Langholm Show of the Eskdale and District Agricultural Society was one of the first such exhibitions to be established (about 1833). Unfortunately, records relative to the dog section of the shows earlier than 1901 have been lost, so our tracing must begin with the latter date. While the tracing is incomplete, these signs of Border Terrier activity shed some light on the early days of the breed.

In 1901 the Eskdale and District show was held at Langholm on the grounds of the Buccleugh Estate by permission of the Duke of Buccleugh. Since that time, the show has been held in the same place by permission of successive Dukes, and a section for Borders has always been preserved. In the earliest catalogues the following condition is stated: "All dogs to be chained in their places by 10:00 A.M. and to remain there during the show." The above condition is still observed. Fencing stobs are driven into the ground in the area close to the dog ring and the number of the exhibit is nailed to the stob.

Langholm Show Results
1901   Langholm Show
      Border Terrier Dog or Bitch

	1st	W. Irving (Whitshields)	dog: Vic
	2nd	Tom Bell (Langholm)	dog: unspecified
	3rd	W. E. Graham Wilson (Wilton)	dog: Liddesdale Pepper 4 yrs
		J. G. Wilson (Wilton Green, Hawick)	dog: Kilder King, 6 mths

1902 pages lost out of the catalogue

1903

Border Terrier Dog or Bitch

1st	W. E. Annandale (Hopsrigg Farm, Langholm)	dog: Peter 2 yrs
2nd	J. T. Dodd (Riccarton)	dog: Flint
3rd	W. Bell (Langholm)	dog: Flint
	Miss M. Paterson (Terrona Farm, Langholm)	dog: Belle

1904

1st	W. Elliot (Kirndean Farm, Langholm)	dog: Tip
2nd	J. J. Paterson (Terrona Farm, Langholm)	dog: Nipper
3rd	W. Bell (Langholm)	dog: Gyp
	Miss May Paterson (Terrona Farm, Langholm)	dog: Belle
	W. E. Annandale (Hopsrigg Farm, Langholm)	dog: Peter
	Ralf Brown (Bruntshieldbog Farm, Langholm)	dog: Finery 6 mths.

1905 Placings are not recorded in the following years

J. R. Hall
J. J. Paterson (Terrona Farm, Langholm)

1912

W. Carruthers (Phaup, Teviothead, Hawick)	dog: Pepper
R. Wilson	dog: Floriday
T. Nichol (Cooms Farm)	dog: Vic
W. Barton (Whitrope Farm)	dog: Newton Rock
W. Barton	dog: Venus
J. Elliot Miller	dog: Enzieholm Rodger
J. J. Paterson (Terrona Farm)	dog: unspecified
Miss Jean Elliot (Blackburn)	dog: unspecified

1913

Victor Hall (Potsholm Farm, Langholm)	dog: Gilsland Rock
Miss Jean Elliot (Blackburn, Newcastleton)	dog: Bess
F. Graham (Bridgend, Langholm)	dog: Jimmy by Rock ex Venus
W. Barton (Whitrope Farm)	dog: Piper by Rock ex Venus
W. Barton (Whitrope Farm)	dog: Wasp by Rock ex Venus
W. Barton (Whitrope Farm)	dog: Nailer by Rock ex Venus
W. Barton (Whitrope Farm)	dog: Venus by Venture ex Bess
J. Telford (Blacksmith)	dog: Tib
Bella Scott (Phaupknowe, Riccarton)	dog: Teri
C. Murray (Douglen)	dog: unspecified

T. Nicol (Cooms)	dog: Vic
Jasper Dodd (Newcastleton)	dog: Sandy
Andrew Smith (Holmhood, Langholm)	dog: unspecified
J. Steel (Bridge St., Lockerbie)	dog: unspecified

The entry fee in these days was one shilling.

The Ayr Show

Another agricultural society that catered for the dog exhibitors in the early days was Ayrshire Agricultural Association. This society was established in 1835. There were classes for dogs at this show first about 1873. The classes in the early shows were mostly for Gundogs, Setters. Greyhounds, Dandie Dinmonts and Scottish Terriers. In addition to these there were classes for Smooth and Rough-haired Terriers. There were 16 entries in these classes in 1873, mostly Skyes and Dandies.

After the Border Terriers were recognized by the Kennel Club, this association was one of the first to cater for the breed. In 1920 the following exhibitors showed their dogs. This must have been the first show after the K.C. recognized the breed.

1920 Ayr
 Open Dog or Bitch
  1st Scott's Tinker, br. W. Barton, b. June 6, 1919 by N. T. Gyp *ex* Barton's Tibbie
  2nd D. Kerr's Bunty, br. Dumfries Otter Hunt Club, b. unknown, by Ginger
  3rd W. Scott's Rip, br. W. Barton, b. June 1919, by N. T. Gyp *ex* Barton's Tibbie
  4th J. Stevenson's Tib br. Dr. Hall, b. June 1919, by Hexham dog *ex* Moss

1921 Puppy Dog or Bitch
  1st W. Home, Chirnside Bounder br. Mrs. Jackson, b. May 20, 1920, by Jock *ex* Tib
  2nd D. Highet, Mossknowe Ginger, br. Mr. Graham, b. October 1, 1920 by Flint *ex* Sprue
  3rd J. Girdwood, Glenmuir Sage, br. Mr. Graham, by Flint *ex* Spice
  4th Miss Bell Irving, Millbank Beauty, by Flint *ex* Fury

 Novice Dog or Bitch
  1st Stevenson's Tib, br. Dr. Hall, b. June 1919, by Hexham dog *ex* Moss
  2nd Chirnside Bounder
  3rd Girdwood's Glenmuir Sage

 Open Dog
  1st T. Lawrence's Teri, br. Exh., b. April 21, 1916, by Jock *ex* Tib
  2nd Miss Bell Irving's Tinker, br. Mr. W. Harrison, b. June 16, 1919, by N. T. Gyp *ex* Tibbie

 Open Bitch
  1st Barton's Liddesdale Bess, br. J. Davidson, b. August 1917, by Nailer *ex* Pearl
  2nd D. S. Kerr's Bounty, br. Dumfrieshire Otter Hunt, b. unknown, by Ginger *ex* Unknown

[In this case the exhibitors who made the entry must have called the bitch Unknown, maybe because they did not know her parentage. One can hardly accept that the dam was unknown. — W.J.F.G.]

1922

Puppy Dog or Bitch
1st   Jackson's Daphne, br. Mrs. Armstrong, b. April 10, 1921, by N. T. Gyp *ex* Midge

Novice Dog or Bitch
1st   T. Girdwood's Glenmuir Sage, br. Mr. Graham, b. October 1, 1920, by Flint *ex* Sprue

Open Dog
1st   Adam Reid's Clincher, br. W. Harrison b. December 31, 1919, by Gyp *ex* Daisy

Open Bitch
1st   G. Thompson's Themis, br. Exh, b. December 31, 1920, by N. T. Gyp *ex* Tatters
2nd   Girdwood's Glenmuir Sage
3rd   Jackson's Daphne

A. Reid's address was given as Drumlanrig Sq., Hawick: D. Jackson's as 34 Ashleigh Grove, West Jesmond, Newcastle upon Tyne. The name of the judge is shown for the first time as a Mr. J. Maxwell.

1923

Novice Dog or Bitch
1st   Dodd & Carruthers, Allen Piper, br. Mr. Wearmouth, b. May 1921 by Gyp *ex* Jean

Open Dog or Bitch
1st   A. Reid's Clincher, b. December 31, 1919
2nd   Dodd & Carruthers' Grip of Tynedale, b. June 1920, by Gyp *ex* Nell
3rd   Allen Piper

1924   The 1924 Show was cancelled because of Foot and Mouth disease among cattle in the district of Ayrshire.

1925   Judge Miss Bell Irving

Open Dog
1st   Dodd's Ch. Dandy of Tynedale, br. Mr. Bryden, b. November 1, 1921, by Gyp *ex* Otterburn Lass

Puppy Dog or Bitch
1st   W. A. MacGregor (Jun), br. Exh, Robina b. June 1924, by Tinker *ex* Rona
2nd   W. Neilson's McMustard, br. W. Elliott, by Sniper *ex* Vic

Open Bitch
1st   Dodd & Carruthers' Foxie, br. Mr. Biggs, b. May 20, 1923, by Flint *ex* Thistle
2nd   W. Neilson's Muffin, br. Mr. F. Archer, b. September 16, 1923, by Mist *ex* Viper
3rd   Breckenbridge The Undiscovered, br. birth & pedigree unknown

Novice Dog or Bitch
1st   Robina
2nd   McMustard

174

3rd   The Undiscovered

Dog or Bitch holding a working certificate
1st   J. Dodd's Ch. Dandy of Tynedale
2nd   Carruther's & Dodd's Foxie

1927   Ayr, Judge T. Lawrence

Puppy Dog or Bitch
1st   Dodd & Carruthers' Forrit-On, br. Exh, b. May 10, 1926, by Tally Ho *ex* Dainty
2nd   M. Young's Rule, br. Dr. Geikie, b. June 12, 1926, by Terrific *ex* Till
3rd   W. MacGregor's Tibbie Shiels, br. Eks, b. July 20, 1926, by Tinker *ex* Rona

Novice Dog or Bitch
1st   M. Young's Coquet, b. August 17, 1924, by Casually Jimmy *ex* Reek

Limit Dog
1st   Irving's Arnton Billy, b. October 10, 1925, by Ch. Tinker *ex* Station Masher
2nd   A. Plunkett's Rufus O'Cree by Ch. Tinker *ex* Tody
3rd   T. B. Adamson's Ben of Tweedon, br. Exh, b. July 25, 1925, by Ch. Tinker *ex* Betty

Open Dog
1st   Arnton Billy
2nd   Ben of Tweeden
3rd   Forrit-On

R. Durie's McKill by Scaur *ex* Scarside

Limit Bitch
1st   Irving's Station Masher, br. A. Fox b. April 11, 1924, by Pincher *ex* Jed
2nd   Tait's Perk, br. Bristowe, b. March 27, 1924, by Ch. Tinker *ex* Tassie
3rd   Barton's Liddesdale Wasp, br. February 10, 1925, by Redden *ex* Betty

Open Bitch
Repeat

W. Barton was at the farm of Whitrope, Nr. Newcastleton, Roxburghshire.
W. Irving was at Riccarton, Nr. Newcastleton, Roxburghshire.

1928   Judge T. Bonsor

Puppy Dog or Bitch
1st   Irving's Winnie of Druffe, br. A. Reid, b. June 11, 1927, by Arton Billy *ex* My Own
2nd   Dodd & Carruthers' Wind'im, br. W. Irving by Forrit-On *ex* Station Masher
3rd   T. Crozier's Howdenburn Gem, br. Exh., b. September 19, 1927, by Flighty Rob *ex* Rose Marie
4th   Mrs. D. Armstrong's Hankam Grand Parade, br. J. Miller, b. April 28, 1927, by Perigord *ex* High Level Winnie

Novice Dog or Bitch
1st   Dodd & Carruthers' Wind'im
2nd   Hankam Grand Parade
3rd   Irving's Din Sheila by Perigord *ex* Parkhead Vic

Limit Dog

1st   Ben of Tweeden
2nd Dodd & Carruthers' Hankam Tinker, b. April 28, 1927, by Perigord *ex* High Level Canter
3rd Hankam Grand Parade
4th Adamson's Little Jock Elliot by Ben of Tweeden *ex* Jean O' The Side

Open Dog
  1st   Ben of Tweeden
  2nd Hankam Tinker
  3rd Hankam Grand Parade
  4th Arnton Billy

Limit Bitch
  1st   Reid's My Own, br. Exh, b. July 24, 1923, by Huntsman *ex* Parkhead Vic
  2nd Din Sheila
  3rd Adamson's Blink Bonny Bess, br. Exh, b. March 14, 1927, by Arnton Billy
  4th Tait's Perk, br. Bristowe, b. March 24, 1924, by Ch. Tinker *ex* Tassie

W. J. Foster, Warrick Road, Carlisle, exhibited a bitch called Jean O' The Side, b. July 28, 1926, br. Mr. Adamson, by Quick Work *ex* Spearo.

Open Bitch
Repeat

1929 Judge Major Hope

Novice Dog or Bitch
  1st   Whitrope Don, br. W. Barton, b. May 18, 1928, by Red Rock *ex* Liddesdale Nettle
  2nd Drurie's Biff Betts, br. Miss Clark, b. May 4, 1928, by Tweedside Red Topper *ex* Beauty
  3rd Adamson's Betty O' The Wall, br. M. J. Holmes, b. August 5, 1928, by Ch. Ben of Tweeden *ex* Popsea
  4th Dr. Lilico's Bladnock Twink b. October 25, 1928, by Ben of Tweeden *ex* Bladnock Gyp

Limit Dog or Bitch
  1st   Whitrope Don
  2nd Biff Betts
  3rd Betty O' The Wall
  4th Bladnock Betty

Open Dog or Bitch
  1st   Whitrope Don
  2nd J. H. Reid's Scott by Arnton Billy *ex* Floss

Dodd & Carruthers had one entry, Hike Halloa, by Sambo *ex* Dolly.

1930 Judge J. Millican

Novice Dog or Bitch
  1st   Adamson's Jack of Larrison, br. J. Turnbull, b. August 29, 1928, by Ben of Tweeden *ex* Compounder
  2nd Lilico's Betty O' The Wall, br. T. Holmes by Ben of Tweeden *ex* Popsea
  3rd Dr. Bryce's Twenpie Towser, br. J. Smart by Twenpie Tinker *ex* Twenpiel Nell.

Limit Dog or Bitch

1st   Jack of Larriston
2nd Lilico's Betty O' The Wall
3rd   Drurie's Nickum, b. April 12, 1929, by Dumfries Dainty *ex* Cutty Sark
4th   Dr. Bryce's Twenpie Towser

Open Dog or Bitch
Repeat

[Note: W. Irving had a dog entered called Rico by Arnton Billy *ex* Tibbie O' The Side for sale at 20 pounds, and that was in 1930. W.F.J.G.]

1931   Judge Mr. J. T. Bonsor

Puppy Dog
1st   A. Reid's Heronslea, br. W. Irving, b. June 26, 1930, by Stirrup *ex* Tiot Fancy Best dog
2nd Dodd and Carruthers' Grakle, br. Exh., by Ch. Ranter *ex* Queen of the Hunt
3rd   Durie's The Delver, br. Exh by Nickum *ex* The Megster [Nickum was by Dainty *ex* Cutty Sark]
4th   Irving's Rocky, b. May 16, 1930, by Whitrope Don *ex* Station Masher

Novice Dog
1st   Heronslea
2nd Grakle
3rd   The Delver
4th   Vaux's Dryburn Defaulter, b. April 5, 1930, by Rival *ex* Wasparnton

Limit Dog
1st   Heronslea
2nd Tarset Lad (Dodd & Carruthers)
3rd   Mrs. Telfer's The Nickum, b. February 5, 1930, by Worry'im *ex* Dainty
4th   Holmes Markum O' The Wall, b. July 12, 1929, br. Exh by Whinstone *ex* Popsea

Open Dog
1st   Heronslea
2nd Mrs. Black's Tweedside Red Trumpeter, br. Mr. T. Oliver, b. February 12, 1928, by Tweedside Red Topper *ex* Fly Topper
3rd   Tarset Lad

Puppy Bitch
1st   Dodd and Carruthers' Lady Ruby, br. Exh by Ch. Ranter *ex* Queen of the Hunt
2nd J. Renton's Tod Hunter, br. C. Renner by Revenge *ex* Causey Bridget
3rd   Muir Wilson's Sunnyside Scarum, br. Exh, b. July 27, 1930, by The Barber *ex* Tweedside Red Sensation [The Barber was by Dumfriesshire Dainty *ex* Cutty Sark]

Novice Bitch
1st   Dodd & Carruthers' Lady Ruby
2nd Stevenson's Traquair Gipsy, br. N. McEwen by Bladnock Twink *ex* Taynish
3rd   Dr. W. Henderson Bryce, Red Fizzer, br. J. Drurie by McKill *ex* Biff Betts

Limit Bitch
1st   Belle of the Hunt

2nd   Fairbairn's Jetherts Here, b. July 18, 1927, by Ch. Tweedside Red
Topper *ex* Trixie

3rd   Tod Hunter

Brace Class
  Drurie's
  Res Dodd & Carruthers

Team Class
  Dodd & Carruthers

Working Class

1st   Dodd & Carruthers' Belle of the Hunt

2nd Wilson's The Barber

3rd   Renton's Dandy Warrior

7

Some concluding remarks

This book was written in the hope that it might be of interest to the new Border Terrier owner, potential breeder, and eventual judge. After all it is the newcomers to the breed who will determine whether or not the Border Terrier will survive as a natural and unspoiled working terrier of the type that the original founders of the breed intended it to be. I hope I have succeeded at least in part in my effort to convey what I know of the breed. Some few last points:

- The sharply increasing number of people interested in the breed either as owners of companions or as possible founders of a breeding kennel is indicated in the increase in the number of registrations through the years (see Appendix C). This explosion of interest, if not handled with extreme care by the current breeders, in a short period of time can lead, as it has in other breeds affected by popularity, to a deterioration in the breed. In all livestock breeds no single factor has contributed more to the deterioration of the quality of a breed than popularity. When a breed becomes popular, commercially-minded people who do not have the breed's interest at heart become involved, and everything capable of being bred from, irrespective of its merit and the merit of the parents, is bred. Those who see the exhibition side of the dog game only as an arena for personal triumph also become involved.

  Already there are signs that all is not well within the breed. Those interested in the working side of the breed are writing to the dog journals and club magazines complaining about the deterioration of some Border Terrier traits, particularly of the growing loss of hard weatherproof coats.

- Since judges by their awards can directly affect whether or not a trait like hard coats will continue in the breed, we who are interested in the Border Terrier would do well to help actively to maintain a high standard of judging. Those interested in judging should be encouraged, for instance, to attend some of the agricultural shows where there are classes for Heavy Horses and Hunters in order to study the methods of these carefully-trained judges. Breed Club Committees could make efforts to encourage all members to attend these judging demonstrations where the various points in the animal's conformation, its good points as well as its faults, are drawn to the attention of the onlookers. Such an exercise would inform the breeder and owner as well as the judge, and would help to sustain breed quality.

- As I have mentioned before, I think it is unfortunate that in the world of dogs we do not have some rather reliable means of distinguishing the successful breeder or judge as do breeders in the field of livestock husbandry, who can express their views through their response in the open sale ring. Perhaps some clear means for breeders of dogs to respond to the judges' decisions can be developed by the Breed Clubs.

- It is also worth noting that in the livestock industry, great breeders are defined in the first instance not as show winners but as men and women who have established a quality strain or type of animal within their breed. The prepotency of their stud animals stamps their progeny. This is an ideal the breeder of dogs should strive for, for such striving will lead to breed improvement if the purpose and Standard of the breed is kept in mind.

- While inbreeding and close linebreeding are chief methods of establishing type, I do not advise anyone who is starting a breeding kennel immediately to inbreed. In all breeds of dogs there has already been too much indiscriminate and uninformed inbreeding, with dire results. If you believe that the best means to improve your existing foundation stock is to inbreed, before you do so you must take on the responsibility to make thorough and lengthy enquiries into the background of the stock you have, and, maybe more important, find out about the character and methods of those who were involved in the breeding of the stock. The breed's future depends on your care in this matter.

- The most important factor in the breeding of all dogs is to breed good dogs with good reliable temperaments, the sort of dog your children or grandchildren can love to their hearts' content. The quality dog with a good temperament is considerably more valuable to the owner/breeder than the champion, however good, with a questionable disposition.

- Finally, if you as a newcomer wish to breed a good line of dogs, by all means take an interest in the exhibition side of the game, and take advantage of the discussions of the breed that you may hear at these meetings. By all means seek advice. But in the end, remember you are responsible for developing your own well-thought-out-breeding policy. Having done so, stick to it through thick and thin with the breed's benefit in mind.

And may I wish all who care about the Border Terrier, whether as companions or as breeding stock, the best of luck with these remarkable animals.

APPENDIX A

Measurements of a Strain of Border Terriers

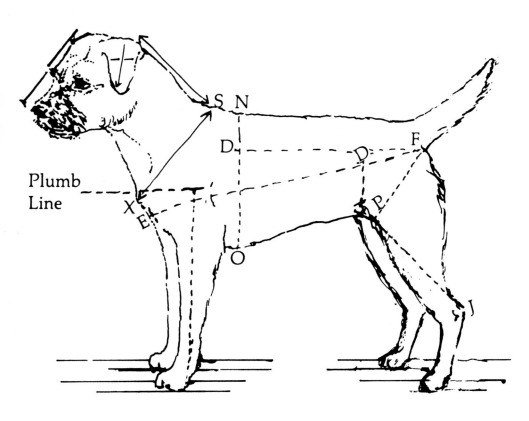

Name of Dog	Nose to Eye	Eye to Skull	Muzzle Thickness	Breadth of Skull	Skull to Withers	Withers to Tailhead	Tail	Height at Withers	Height to Brisket	Width of Ear	Length of Ear	Width around Girth
Maxton Bunty Lass	2"	4 3/16"	7 9/16"	3 12/16"	4 3/16"	13½"	6½"	14"	7¼"	2"	2⅜"	17"
Maxton Marguerite	1 9/16	4¼	7 6/16	3¼	4¾	13⅝	6¼	13	7	1¾	2¼	17 13/16
Ch. Maxton Monarch	1 14/16	3½	7 12/16	3½	5½	14½	7	15	7½	2	2¾	18½
Maxton Mhairi	2 3/16	4	7½	3⅜	6½	12¼	7½	14¾	7¾	2 3/16	3	17¾
Maxton Makimino	2 3/16	4	7¾	3⅝	5	14	7	14⅝	7	2¼	3 3/16	18½
Millbank Tarka	2¼	4½	7	4	4	13	7	14½	7½	2½	2½	18¾
Ch. Marrburn Morag	2	4½	7	3 3/16	5	13	6	14	7	1½	2½	17¾
Maxton Mouchi	2	4	7	3½	5	13	7	15	7½	2	3	18
Ch Maxton Marla	2	4	7½	3½	5	13	6	14	7½	1½	2	17
Maxton Matriona	2¼	4	7	4	6	13	7	15	7½	2	3	17
Maxton May Martinet	2⅛	4¼	7	4¼	6	13½	7	15¼	7½	2	3	17
Maxton Marsala	2	4	7	4	5½	12	6	14	6½	1½	2	17½
Maxton Marcia	2	4	6½	4	5	12	6	13½	7½	1½	2	18½
Mansergh Coat D'Azure	2	3½	6	4	6	12	5½	14¼	7¼	1¾	2	17
Maxton Melba	2	4	6	4	6	13	6	14	7	2	3	17½
Maxton Merryman	2	4	6½	4	6	13	7	14½	7¼	1½	3	18
Tickon Harpie	2	4	5½	3½	4	12	4½	14½	7	1½	3	15½
Felldyne Undine	2	4	7½	3½	6	13	7½	15	8	1½	3	18½
Maxton Murgatroyd	2	4	7¼	4	5	13	6½	14½	7½	1¾	2¾	18¼
Edenbrae Highland Prince	2½	4½	8	4¼	6	13	9	16	8	2½	3	18½
Edenbrae Moon Maiden	2¼	3¾	7	3½	6	12½	6	14	7			18
Maxton Madi	2	4	7	4	5	12	6	15	7	2	3	17
Maxton Marzine	2	3½	6	3½	4	13	6	14	6	2	3	18
Ch. Maxton Makrino	2¼	4½	7½	4	6	13	6½	14½	7	2	3	16
Maxton Malaga	2	4	7	4	5	13	6	14	7	2	2½	18
Maxton Mahanain	2	4	5½	4	5½	11½	6½	14½	7½	1½	2	17½
Maxton Marisa	2¼	3½	6¾	3½	5½	11	6	14	6½	1¾	2¼	17
Annanhill Mindy of Maxton	2	3½	7	4	6	13	6½	13¾	7½	1¾	2¾	16
Maxton Marza	2	3½	7	4	5½	12	5½	12½	6½	1¾	3	16½
Average	2.04	3.962	6.595	3.806	5.345	12.530	6.474	14.328	7	1.854	2.493	

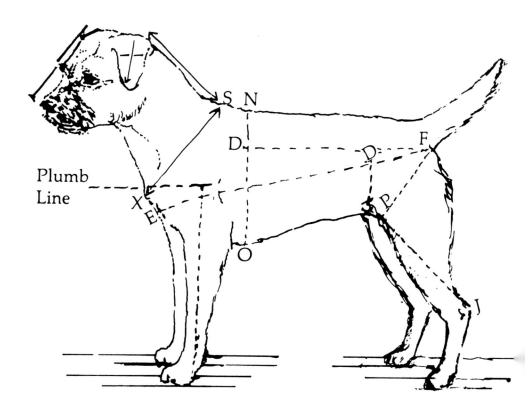

Plumb
Line

Name of Dog	X—S	D—D	D—F	P—F	E—F	N—O	P—J	D—J
Maxton Bunty Lass								
Maxton Marguerite						6″		
Ch. Maxton Monarch								
Maxton Mhairi	7″	9″	5″	6⅞″	15″	7½″	6¼″	6″
Maxton Makimino								
Millbank Tarka								
Ch. Marrburn Morag								
Maxton Mouchi	6	9	5½	7	15	8	6	6
Ch. Maxton Marla	6½	6	5	5	13½	6½	5½	6
Maxton Matriona	6	8	4	5½	14½	7½	6¼	6
Maxton May Martinet	6	7	5	5	15	7	6	6
Maxton Marsala	6	9	5	5	14½	8	5	4½
Maxton Marcia	6	9½	5	5½	15	6	5	5
Mansergh Coat D'Azure	5	7	5	5	13½	7	5½	6½
Maxton Melba	6	9	6	5	14	7	6	6
Maxton Merryman	6	9	4½	5	14½	7¼	5	5
Tickon Harpie	4	7	4	4	14	7	6	4
Felldyne Undine	6	7	5	6	15	7	5	6
Maxton Murgatroyd	5	9	4	4½	14	7	6	6
Edenbrae Highland Prince	6	9	5½	6	16	8	6½	6
Edenbrae Moon Maiden	6	8	4½	6½	15½	6¼	6½	5
Maxton Madi	5	8½	4½	5	14	7½	5	4½
Maxton Marzine	7	9	5	5	12	8	5	4
Ch. Maxton Makrino	6½	9	5½	5½	15	7½	6	6
Maxton Malaga	6	9	5½	5	14	7	5	6
Maxton Mahanain	6	8¼	4	5	13	7½	5	5
Maxton Marisa	5	8½	4	5½	13	7½	4½	5
Annanhill Mindy of Maxton	5	9	4¼	4½	14	6¼	4	5
Maxton Marza	5½	9	4	5	14	6	5	4½
Average	5.804	7.076	4.489	5.217	14.195	7.11	5.413	5.391

See Diagram above for indication of points measured.

APPENDIX B

Pedigrees of a Foundation Dog & Bitch

PEDIGREE: CH FUTURE FAME (Foundation Sire) born August 10, 1948. Breeder: Mr. Whitelaw. Colour: grizzle.

sire

parents	grandparents	gr. grandparents	gr. gr. grandparents	gr. gr. gr. grandparents
Fearsome Fellow *c. brindle*	Furious Fighter *c. brindle* 1 CC	Ch Ranter *c. brindle*	Rival *c. brindle*	Rab of Redesdale
				Tibby (unr)
			Coquetdale Reward	Tug
				Little Midget
		Romance *c. red*	Gold Tip	Rival
				Harbottle Vic
			Miss Tut *c. brindle*	Flint
				Coquetdale Reward
	Finery *c. red* 1 CC	Gem of Gold	Rival	Rab of Redesdale
				Tibby (unr)
			Ch Benton Biddy *c. red*	Revenge
				Molly Way
		Stung Again *c. red grizzle*	Ch Blister *c. red grizzle*	Revenge
				Causey Bridget
			Liddesdale Nettle	Whistler
				Liddesdale Wendy

dam

parents	grandparents	gr. grandparents	gr. gr. grandparents	gr. gr. gr. grandparents
Tombo Squeak	Ch Boxer Boy	Ch Aldham Joker *c. red*	Ch Barb Wire *c. red*	Ch Dinger
				Ch Tod Hunter (sire: Revenge)
			Country Girl	Randale
				Hunting Sally
		Daphne's Dream	Ch Wedale Jock *c. red grizzle (white foot)*	Ch Heronslea
				Shaw's Lady
			Delight	Ch Grakle (sire: Ch Ranter)
				Newminster Wisp
	Cheviot Penny Plain	Reedswire	Carousel (unt)	Rival
				Stately
			Catcleugh Bess (unr)	Flint
				Vic (unr)
		Coronation Queen of the Mist	Ch Dinger	Gem of Gold (sire: Rival)
				Beeswing
			Shaw's Lady	Ch Blister (sire: Revenge)
				Patchwork

parents	grandparents	gr. grandparents	gr. gr. grandparents	gr. gr. gr. grandparents
sire Tweedside Red Playboy	Ch Aldham Joker	Ch Barb Wire	Ch Dinger	Gem of Gold (sire: Rival)
				Beeswing
			Ch Tod Hunter	Revenge
				Causey Bridget
		Country Girl	Randale	Renton
				Bunty (unr)
			Hunting Sally	Whitrope Don
				Din Sheila
	Felton Gem	Terry	Coquetdale Sandy	Whita
				Bramble
			Finery	Gem of Gold (sire: Rival)
				Stung Again
		Felton Patsy	Towser	Remyard's Revival
				Fawdon Whin
			Pop	Vanquished
				Floss
dam Cherry Pie	School Boy	Epigram 2 CC's	Ch Dinger	Gem of Gold (sire: Rival)
				Beeswing
			Linshiel Rainbird	Ch Ben of Tweeden
				Foomert
		Ale Bunty	Snooker (unt)	Ch Dinger
				Miss Sheena
			Cheeky Betty	
	Judy	High Jinks	Ch Grakle	Ch Ranter (sire: Rival)
				Queen of the Hunt
			Happy Valley	Ch Dinger
				Ginger Nut
		Briery Lass	Whitrope Don	Rea Rock
				Liddesdale Nettle
			Biff Betts	Ch Tweedside Red Topper
				Beauty

APPENDIX C

Border Terrier Kennel Club Registrations
1913—1983

Year		No. Reg.	Year		No. Reg.
1913	....	1	1949	....	815
1914	....	14	1950	....	659
1915	....	2	1951	....	718
1916	....	11	1952	....	645
1917	....	—	1953	....	564
1918	....	—	1954	....	644
1919	....	13	1955	....	643
1920	....	111	1956	....	747
1921	....	202	1957	....	849
1922	....	208	1958	....	805
1923	....	203	1959	....	802
1924	....	235	1960	....	907
1925	....	262	1961	....	866
1926	....	237	1962	....	810
1927	....	187	1963	....	911
1928	....	178	1964	....	871
1929	....	182	1965	....	827
1930	....	207	1966	....	799
1931	....	178	1967	....	800
1932	....	196	1968	....	803
1933	....	231	1969	....	918
1934	....	232	1970	....	953
1935	....	253	1971	....	902
1936	....	260	1972	....	1026
1937	....	290	1973	....	1029
1938	....	365	1974	....	1051
1939	....	267	1975	....	1111*
1940	....	69	1976	....	477
1941	....	52	1977	....	340
1942	....	103	1978	....	868
1943	....	114	1979	....	1196
1944	....	260	1980	....	1227
1945	....	376	1981	....	1152
1946	....	571	1982	....	1219
1947	....	650	1983	....	1330
1948	....	674			

APPENDIX D

Some Notes on Diverse Subjects

On the Stamina of Horses, Dogs, and Men

A few quotations about hunting from Ferguson's *Border Sports and Sportsmen*:

In the season 1895-96 we were out 81 days, killed 105 foxes and ran 40 to ground. . . .

As an instance of what a wide country a fox may know, I may say that Robbie Potts once told me that when he lived at Singdean near Note of the Gate, he traced a fox in the snow all the way from there by Jedgeads Fell, etc., to Carter Bar, where the fox had risen. He heard later that someone on the same day had traced this fox from Whithaugh near Newcastleton, to Singdean. Robbie Potts also told me he once drew two foxes out of a hole (after they had dug all day near Bewshaugh) by the forefeet and he did not get bitten. I can vouch personally that he was the gamest taker out of a fox I ever saw. . . .

It has been the custom for many years for the pack to go over to Hindhope four times each season to hunt the Scotch side of the Border. They used to hunt three consecutive days, using the same horses and the same hounds. Had hounds and horses not been made of cast steel they could not have done it, not forgetting the terriers who followed all day. . . .

I have mentioned the Border pack used to hunt three days in succession with the same horses and the same hounds. South country hunting men if they ever see these memories [will] say, "My word, he is drawing a long bow!" Well facts are facts, and this practice still continues, though since the war fixtures are held on two days running, and another within the week, thus making a regular three days a week. Well to cut the cackle and get to the "osses", to stand this in a country of hills and precipices, they must be as nearly clean bred as possible. An original pony about 14 h.h., crossed with a thoroughbred, is about the best stamp, and the Border Nimrods have them. A half bred horse would collapse altogether after a couple of long hill and bog days, so "Blood, and Blood all the time", it ought to be.

[Ferguson also mentions that the Border Terriers are up with the hounds and in at the kill, having followed the hounds all the time.]

On Rabies in the 19th Century

Ferguson makes an observation on rabies which demonstrates how virulent the disease then was and how little it was understood.

1874 January 27th. After a very good day from Gibshield "Marquis" bit a man and was said to be mad, so all the hounds except a few favourite bitches were destroyed. . . .

Those in towns and cities were especially reluctant to credit the reality of the disease, as the following letter by my grandfather, a Dumbartonshire veterinarian, makes clear.

RABIES AND THE MUZZLING OF DOGS (To the Editor of *Helensburgh & Gareloch Times*)

Sir,

A considerable amount of dissatisfaction appears to exist among owners of dogs, caused by the County Council and the Local Magistrates having issued an order for the proper muzzling of dogs, for the better protection of the public.

Those having pet animals consider the muzzling a very great hardship, causing considerable annoyance and being a source of continual irritation to their favourites. There also exist among us a number of gentlemen holding prominent positions in society, and even members of the medical profession, who do not believe in the existence of such a disease as hydrophobia. For the condolence of the former, and the edification of the latter, I think it well to place before your readers a few facts that have happened in our neighbourhood within a very short period.

On the 10th June last I was requested to see a dog at Camis-Eskan that had bitten the gamekeeper and his son the previous day. I saw the dog the following day, and declaring it to be a case of canine madness, I ordered it to be destroyed, which was accordingly done. As I considered it was of the utmost importance for the safety of the gamekeeper and his boy, I requested the owner of the dog to send them both to the Pasteur Institute, Paris. They were dispatched at once, and they have great reason to be thankful for this kindness. They came home in three weeks, and are now enjoying good health.

About the same time a mad dog about Kirkintilloch bit two persons before being destroyed. They were also sent to Paris, received treatment at the Institute and are now in the possession of good health. A boy at Kilsyth was bitten about the same time; but whether those in authority did not believe in the efficacy of the cure or the existence of such a disease, or whether it was due to the want of a philanthropic mind the boy, sad to tell, died of that frightful and fatal disease, hydrophobia.

I have also destroyed several dogs suffering from this disease, but as they did no harm to anyone I will pass over them to other cases. On the 11th September the carcase of a spaniel was sent to me from Kilmahew Kennels, Cardross, for examination. I made a careful post mortem and reported to the owner it was a case of rabies. I was also informed that two other dogs in the same kennel had been bitten by this one. In a very short time they both developed the disease, and were destroyed. On the 8th September I was requested by the County Council of Dumbarton to go and report on a case at Old Kilpatrick. On going there I found a fox terrier dog that had been shot the previous day. It had come from Glasgow, tearing and destroying all and sundry that came in its way. At Kilpatrick it tore the hand and broke the wrist of George Goldie, aged three years, and lacerated the hand of Wm. Robertson, aged 3½ years and another boy at Yoker. Thanks to the energy and liberality of the County Council and another gentleman in the neighbourhood, the children on the 12th of September, were dispatched with a nurse to Paris, where they received treatment. They are now at home happy and cheerful, and their parents have every reason to be thankful that their children received such attention, seeing what has transpired since that time. At that time there seemed to be some difference of opinion among members of the Council as to whether this was a case of rabies or not. I was instructed to forward the carcase of the dog to the Crown Institute, London, for experiment. This was done on the 11th September, and the report received is as follows:

Crown Institute
Wandsworth House, London, S.E.
October 5th 1883

Sir, I have performed a series of experiments to determine the presence or absence of the virus of rabies in the carcase of the dog, sent by you and received by me at the Institute on the 13th September last. I regret to inform you that I have tonight obtained conclusive evidence that the dog was suffering from rabies. I should not express so positive an opinion were the experiments not so unanimous in their results and testimony.

I am sir, your obedient servant, (signed) C.S. Shenington, M.D. Professor Superintendent

To the County Clerk, Dumbarton

Apart from the foregoing I may mention that a collie dog, about one year old, the property of Miss McIntyre, butcher, Kilpatrick, was slightly bitten (merely a scratch) by the fox terrier referred to above. I asked the owner to destroy it but she declined. As the Act does not provide for such cases, I was powerless without an order from the Board of Agriculture Section 14, Rule 3 of the Rabies Order, 1892. On the 22nd September the collie refused food, broke a strong chain with which it was tied in the stable, and was shot through a hole in the door on the 24th September. The same day as the collie was bitten, the fox terrier bit another dog, but all endeavours to find the animal have signally failed. The fox terrier also bit an Irish terrier, four years old, which was the means of catching the mad dog before it was destroyed. The Irish terrier belonged to the father of one of the little boys and he took the precaution to have it always chained. The characteristic symptoms of madness having developed on the 13th, it also was destroyed on the 15th inst.

Surely those plain facts should be pondered over by those who fret at our Government making such a law as the Rabies Act, and from time to time altering and improving it (the latest stringent regulation was passed and came into force on the 1st November 1892), and at those gentlemen either on the bench or in the County Council Chambers who have been nominated by the ratepayers to interpret and insist that the law be put into force. The Act was necessary. What would be the use of a dormant Act, or of making regulations if they are to be consigned to the wastepaper basket? Those others I have referred to, whose speech exceeds their prudence, should consider that prevention is better than remedy, and that the preservation of human life is of paramount importance compared with any slight inconvenience to the lower animals. I am, yours faithfully, D. M. Gardner, M.R.C.V.S. Veterinary Inspector for Eastern Division of Dumbartonshire, Springvale, Helensburg, 21st October 1893

A Note or Two about Gypsies

It may be of interest to the reader if we digress a little from the world of dogs to tell a tale of the Faas, who have an historic connection with Border Terriers. (Geordy Faa is mentioned in the letter to *The Field* by Mr. Davidson, in 1878.)

History records that one by the name of Johnnie Faa (who would be an ancestor no doubt of Geordy Faa) was granted a letter under the Privy Seal from James V, dated 15th February 1540, establishing his authority over all the gypsies in Scotland and calling on all sheriffs in the country to "assist him in the execution of justice upon his company and folks". These Egyptians, or Gypsies, travelled all over the south of Scotland and in my boyhood days around the town of Maybole had many camping sites.

In our youth we Minniebolers were reared on a legend that the King of the Gypsies eloped with the Countess of Cassillis, the wife of John, the sixth Earl of Cassillis. Lady Jean, legend has it, was beloved by the gallant young knight Sir John Faa, but politics led her family to marry her to the Earl. The story goes that Sir John came to Cassillis Castle (an old tower on the banks of the River Doon about four miles from Maybole, still in its original state) disguised as a Gypsy, with a band of followers. In the Earl's absence the Countess eloped with him because, in the words of the ballad, "They cuist the glaumourye ower her". (This was supposed to be a powerful Gypsy spell.)

Unfortunately the Earl returned before they had proceeded very far and set out in pursuit. They were all captured at a ford over the Doon (still called the Gypsies' Steps) a few hundred yards below the Castle.

All were brought back to Cassillis Castle and the band of Gypsies, including Sir John, were hanged on the Dule Tree, a splendid plane tree which still flourishes on the mound in front of the Castle Gate. (Dule is an old Scots word for woe.) Legend records that the Lady

Jean was compelled to witness the hanging from a window in the Castle, still regarded as the Countess' room. The sad end of the tale is that after confinement in the Castle Lady Jean was moved to the Castle in Maybole, where an addition had been built for her by the Earl. It was reached by means of a fine projecting staircase, on which had been carved the heads of the band of Gypsies, the head of her lover being rather larger than the remainder.

[Drawn from *The Gypsies of Yetholm* by W. Brockie (Kelso: J. and J. Rutherford, 1884).]

In *The Gypsies of Yetholm* Brockie also includes a note on Will (Piper) Allan (Northumbrian Pipes), who travelled through Northumberland each year. He was a skilled angler and had a passion for otter hunting. He usually kept a dozen dogs; three or four of his special favourites were trained to otter hunting.

Brockie also tells us that Will Allan had a family of six. James, the youngest, became an even better piper than his father, but he appears to have spent the greater part of his life evading the law and deserting from the army. At one stage of his life this Piper Allan became piper to the Duchess of Northumberland. She presented him with ivory small pipes and silver chains when she appointed him her piper, and placed on his right arm, in silver, a copy of the Saracen's crescent worn by Percy during the crusades.

It must therefore have been the son, J. Allan, that Sir Walter Scott met at Kelso races (mentioned in Anne Roslin-Williams' book *The Border Terrier*), as he was wearing the silver crescent on his arm.

Brockie also states that "Will Allan had a rooted and cherished aversion to systematic labour of any kind, not only in regard to himself but to his immediate relatives. The intimation to him that a nephew had been apprenticed to the trade of a weaver threw him into a paroxysm of rage, which did not subside until he had walked miles to where the lad worked and violently dragged him from the loom."

Brockie's description of Will Allan makes it clear why Will is alleged to have refused the tenancy of a farm offered by the Duke of Northumberland in exchange for one of his terriers.

Reversion and Telegony: or Maternal Impression

In the early days of pedigree livestock breeding, where the foundation stock were not far removed from the crosses from which the breed originated and before genetics was understood, breeders were disturbed when the progeny of some matings did not in many ways resemble the parents. In some cases progeny seemed to the breeder to resemble the previous mate. This was called Telegony, or Maternal Impression, and was believed to be due to an infection of the reproductive organs.

Dog breeders were among the most ardent believers in telegony. It was held by some that, for example, if a pure-red Gundog bitch of any breed happened to be mated to a farm Collie in error, then such a bitch was hereafter useless for pure breeding. The theory was that the pups by a pedigreed dog of her own breed would show at least some of the characteristics of the Collie she had mated previously.

This type of thinking was widely accepted even among men of science, until Professor Ewart of the University of Edinburgh conducted experiments using a pure bred mare and mating her to a zebra stallion, then in turn mating her to a pure bred male of her own species.

Border Country Agricultural Shows of Interest: Langholm, Yetholm, Alwinton

Langholm (Eskdale and District Agricultural Society): This show has been in existence for some 136 years. In fact on the 23rd September 1990 the Society held its 142nd Annual Show. In the early days of the Border Terrier breed, this show was regarded by the older breeders as worth winning. Unfortunately the dog section of the show, run in conjunction with the agricultural show, is not as strong now as it was some years ago. However, one of the strong features of this show is the exhibition of Light Horses or Hunters. Watching the judging would improve one's eye for stock.

Langholm is situated about 21 miles N.W. of Carlisle or some 30 miles N.E. of Dumfries. It is a very old village, dating back to around 1643, situated on the River Esk. There is good fishing and the surrounding country is very scenic, excellent walking country. It is situated on the A7 Carlisle to Edinburgh road.

Yetholm: This was another important show in the early days of the Border and is in the very heart of the Border Country, in the parish of Yetholm in Roxburghshire. It is really made up of two villages, Yetholm and Kirk Yetholm. It is an interesting show to attend as there are many other entertainments in addition to the dog section, including a good athletic contest among the locals, a Fell Run, where the youth run up the hill to a point at the top and then seem to come down in leaps and bounds.

There is usually a good show of Foxhounds from the various local hunts and if the Border breeder is interested in hound judging then Yetholm provides good opportunity to study it. The Haugh where the show is held would be the scene of many of the Gypsy feuds in the early days. 1990 was the 126th Show at Alwinton and the 124th show at Yetholm. It is run by Yetholm Border Shepherds and as far as farm stock is concerned is mainly a hill sheep show. It is usually held in the beginning of October.

Alwinton: This show is also organised by the Border shepherds. 1982 was the 118th Annual Exhibition. Alwinton show ground is on the verge of the hill land. In fact if one looks at the surrounding country it is not too difficult to appreciate why the older breeders who lived in that area wanted a dog on the leg. The show ground is more or less enclosed by the Cheviot Hills.

A feature of this show is the Hound Trail. One gets a very good view of the hounds from the start to the finish as they follow the trail along the side of the hill farm of Barrowburn, where Adam Forster's brother-in-law farmed. Again a feature of this show is the hill sheep section.

APPENDIX E

Description of the Border Terrier (Old Standard)

In the dog world, breeds are generally divided into two kinds, sporting and non-sporting. It is generally admitted that the Border Terrier, besides being one of the most sporting of all terriers, has also all the essential qualities of the non-sporting breeds. This little dog is the most companionable little fellow in the world, and the most intelligent, with an expression which seems to speak at you. He knows all that is going on, and can be the best companion in the world. He is the most extraordinary game dog. The Border should not as a rule be put to a fox until he is at least ten months old, though it is a fact that Borders of seven months old have bolted foxes and done in the hunting field what one might only expect a dog of a year old to do. There is always the danger of a too young a puppy getting too badly punished, with the result that he may afterwards become rather shy. Although the Border is not a large terrier, there are few which are not game and who are not able to draw a fox. He is a bold dog, but his temperament is such that he cannot be thrashed or in any way ill-treated.

It is only in comparatively recent years that the Border has become well known out of the North of England and very much sought after. This is probably due to the fact that the breed was for the most part originated and carried on in the wild hilly country of the Cheviots. Today demands come from all over the world for this game little terrier.

The Border is not a cross-bred, but he and the Bedlington originated from practically the same district. The Border, which is the older of the two breeds, and can be traced back for over 200 years, came from Holystones in Coquetdale, Northumberland.

They are a very hardy type and can stand all kinds of weather. When working underground they are never silent. The size of the Border is all important, as they must be able to get where a fox can. The type and character of a Border Terrier lies chiefly in the formation of his skull and face; the former should be moderately broad and resemble his natural prey the Otter; his foreface, although short, should be powerful, and like that of the Otter and the Fox, built to grip and hold. These characteristics, together with his game alert expression, stamp him as totally different to all other breeds of terriers. His eye should be dark and small with keen expression, the ears small and of moderate thickness and dropping forward close to the cheek bone. In general appearance he is small, active, and hardy looking, 12 to 13 inches high at the shoulder and varying from 15 to 15½lbs in weight. A Border Terrier, when with a pack of hounds, not only has to go to ground in all kinds of places, including deep holes and crevices in rocky hill-sides but frequently has to run with the hounds for long distances; to fit him for the work his frame is more racily built than that of the Fox Terrier, and although comparitively short on the leg, there must be length enough to allow for galloping. The Border coat is of great importance as it must be such that it will stand cold weather. The coat must be hard with a dense undercoat and a thick skin. A good-coated Border can really stand any weather and there is no doubt that they are a hard breed of terrier. The colour is usually red or wheaten, but black and tan and grizzled are not uncommon. He should be narrow at the shoulders, but with a good depth of brisket; straight on the leg with small round feet. The stern should be moderately short, fairly thick at the base, and then tapering, set high and carried gaily.

The description of the Border Terrier is as follows:-

Weight: Dogs between 13 and 15½lbs; Bitches between 11½ and 14lbs.

Head: Like that of an Otter, moderately broad in the Skull with a short strong muzzle, level teeth, a black nose is preferred but a liver or flesh coloured one is not a disqualification.

Eye: Dark with keen expression.

Ears: Small, V-shaped, of moderate thickness and dropping forward to the cheek.

Loin: Strong.

Body: Deep and narrow, and fairly long; ribs carried well back, but not oversprung, as a terrier should be capable of being spanned by both hands behind the shoulder; forelegs straight and not too heavy in bone; feet small with thick pads; stern moderately short and fairly thick at the base, then tapering, set high and carried gaily, but not curled over the back, hind-quarters racing.

Coat: Harsh and dense with close undercoat.

Skin: Thick.

Colour: Red, wheaten, grizzle and tan or blue and tan.

Points

Head, Ears, Neck and Teeth	20
Legs and Feet	15
Coat and Skin	10
Shoulders and Chest	10
Eyes and Expression	10
Back and Loin	10
Hindquarters	10
Tail	5
General appearance	10
	100

Challenge Cups annually competed for (owned by the Border Terrier club)

1. The "Twempie" Silver Challenge Cup.
   Presented by John Smart for the best Puppy dog or bitch to be bred by Exhibitor. The cup to be won three times in all before becoming the property of the winner.

2. The "Lawside" Silver Challenge Cup.
   Presented to the Border Terrier Club by Col. J. S. Couper of Broughton Ferry, for the best Border Terrier (d. or b.) the property of a member of the Club, to be won three times in succession by the same owner or five times in all.

3. The "Harbottle" Silver Challenge Cup.
   Presented by Mr. and Mrs. Forster for the best Border Terrier (d. or b.) holding a working certificate. Maximum weight, dog 15lbs, bitch 14lbs.

APPENDIX F

BATH SHOW:
(BATH CANINE SOCIETY) MAY 11th 1922
BORDER TERRIERS
JUDGE MR. J. R. HADDON

Border Terriers came up in big numbers, in fact, nearly a record, for the West, if not a record.

Class was fairly good, and South of England breeders and exhibitors are creeping up on the Border Natives fast. But there are several points needing overhauling, namely tails want to be shorter in many cases, also wide fronts, light eyes and many were shown in very poor sporting condition. Coats want to be harder. The Northern dogs excelled in hard coats. Size was excellent.

PUPPY (DOG AND BITCH)

1st   Titlington Turk, grand head, the best of legs, front, feet and coat, a shade long in the tail for my liking, will follow his Sire's footsteps with luck to keep small.

2nd   Shotton Rusty, a really good lady, spoiled with a kink in the tail and a little soft in coat at present, ears might be smaller.

NOVICE (D OR B]

1st   Tweedside Red Type, grand body, head and coat, shade strong in ears and long in tail, shown to perfection.

2nd   Tags o' the North. Good bone, plenty coat and fairly good feet. Loses in strength of head to 1st.

3rd   Titlington Turk weak in muzzle, full up to size.

GRADUATE (D OR B)

1st   Tweedside Red Type.

2nd   Daphne, beautiful size but not at her best today, shade light in eye and long in back.

3rd   Tags o' the North.

LIMIT (D OR B)

1st   Themis, one of the best bitches out, but not faultless.

2nd   Tweedside Red Type.

3rd   Daphne.

OPEN (DOG)

1st CH/Titlington Tattler, now a full Champion. A model Border with a little more muzzle and a darker eye. This finishes his show career, never better than today.

2nd Tweedside Red Type.

3rd Shotton Rogue, very fair little dog, will improve a lot yet, nice front, little soft in coat.

Reserve, Clincher, very badly shown, a grand dog spoiled.

Highly Commended, CH/Ivo Roisterer, past showing, still retains his great head and ears.

OPEN BITCH

1st CH/Themis won with little to spare, very alike to 2nd Daphne 3rd Shotton Rusty.

J. R. HADDON (Judge)

Author's Note. The report on the dogs exhibited at the Bath canine show in 1922 is of interest to the modern breeder/exhibitor. This show would be one of the earlier shows of the breed, the first Championship show being at Carlisle in 1920.

The report is of interest as it indicates the defects in the breed at that time. Note the judge's comments in the opening paragraph of his critique. These defects are still with the breed at this date, and some judges have recently made similar comments.

There is one defect that is of interest to the serious breeder, namely in the Puppy dog or bitch class. Shotton Rusty "spoiled with a *KINK* in tail".

The Kinky or Screw Tail

It may be that some of the younger breeders or newcomers to the breed have not come across this condition. It can best be described as a Kink in the lower portion of the tail. At first one is inclined to think the tail has been broken.

The first time I came across the defect I wrongly came to the conclusion that it was due to the way the pup had been lying in the womb previous to birth. This defect is noticeable at birth, by drawing your hand along the tail. I queried from the older breeders if they had come across this type of thing. Some admitted they had and added the observation that it had appeared when a litter was a large one. This observation seemed logical: if a large litter, the amount of room in the womb would be less than when there are fewer pups. If, of course, it was a genetic defect then the greater the number of pups the greater chance there is of getting a defective pup.

Some time later on a visit to an Ayrshire herd I saw a cow with what was described in genetic literature as a Wry tail (Angle). Screw tail is used when the condition is more severe, or in extreme cases.

A study of the genetic literature on the subject in cattle (mice are also affected by a similar condition) indicates that the tissue which should develop into the disks between the vertebrae fails to form normal fibrous tissue on the side of the Kink. The gene causing the Kink in the tail is inherited as a recessive. It is found in other breeds of cattle and pigs.

The judge's report on the Bath Canine Show in 1922 draws attention to the fact that this defect has been in the breed practically from its foundation. He draws attention to the fact of the Bitch puppy Shotton Rusty b. 12/21 "being spoiled by having a kink in her tail". The defect has not been listed in the Breed Standard and as a result has not been selected against by breeders. (A gene is accepted as a recessive when the defect appears and the sire and dam do not show the defect. In such cases they are carriers of the gene.)

The frequency (that is the proportion of gametes carrying the particular gene) of the gene condition i.e. Kinky Tails has become noticeable in recent years and I believe this is due to an increase in the carrier population.

Some breeders and judges make the point that it is not noticeable, and does no harm, as it is only when you draw your hand along the tail you feel the kink.

But then some judges fault a dog for having an irregular incisor tooth and this is not noticeable until you open the dog's mouth. Again the task of judging is approached in an illogical manner. Viz, one judge informed me that he had turfed out a dog because it had a Kink in its tail. But the same judge, when it came to judging a group, placed the dog in the top position.

Recessive genes are very difficult to control (see chapter on the recessive gene as found in Galloway cattle).

If you have a dog with a Kink in its tail, then you can identify the sire and dam at least as being carriers, so if you trace the lineage back it will give you an idea of the carriers. The same line of breeding will be on both sides of the pedigree.

APPENDIX G

From the Gallovidean Annual 1933 Illustrated Magazine for Galloway & Dumfriesshire published Annually. The Dumfriesshire Otter Hounds 1889 by J. Bell-Irving MOH.

Mr. Wilson Davidson, 1st huntsman of the pack, used Borders exclusively in 1933, but at first had whites. First was Tom, smooth working fox terrier type, with a strong jaw showing the bull terrier blood in his veins. A son of his, Spring, who lost his nose, but lived for many years, though did no more hunting, sired many good terriers. Among them was Venom, a white bitch, harsh coated black round one eye the other eye a wall one. She worked many years. One of a family of three bitches, from an old fashioned pedigree smooth coated fox terrier Topsy. (My father owned the other two, Varmint and Vixen.) Granddaughter of Varmint was Button the last of the breed died about the end of the War. Vixen had hysteria though it was put down to fits at the time; this was about 1902/1903. When I hunted hounds in 1919 we had a wonderful Red Terrier, Rock. He was Border but smooth coated and had a bull terrier jaw and cheek.

A nailer to ground and could swim the foil of an Otter like a hound.

That same year there was one Black Sandy, the hardiest dog alive and in spite of the awful punishment he received he lived to a great age. Years after when pensioned off and watching hounds from a car who were marking at a root, he dived into a small rabbit hole 10 yds away and a bout of blood curdling yells were heard, out came the Otter and Sandy with a twinkle in his eye and blood streaming from his nose; he was 12 years old at the time and hardly a tooth in his head. Tinker was the next and was a hard little dog though careful, very excitable and turned on Ginger when getting out an Otter once and damaged Ginger's nose. Another time I picked up Tinker as we usually do the terriers during a worry. In his excitement he got me by the face and shook me like a rat.

Old Sandy was a marvel and lost his lower jaw but could still bolt Otters. My Uncle David was first Master until 1908. Then his son William who was killed during the War in a flying accident. My younger sister Mrs. Fergus Graham took over in 1915 and then my elder sister from 1917 to 1923. In that year I became Master.

The first meet took place at Millhouse Bridge on the Annan, on the 20th May 1889, when an Otter was found, hunted and killed.

Since the formation these hounds have accounted for 645 Otters, and as a sign the Otters are not being entirely stamped out the past season 1933 produced a record Viz. 32 kills, which as yet should be, as there was never a summer like it. There were 63 meets advertized, and hounds were able to hunt on 61 days.

Wilson Davidson was huntsman for 25 years, when Joe Parker took over and died in 1918. William Scott took over in 1919 from being 2nd whip with W. Thomson's Otter hounds.

They usually had four terriers running loose with the hounds and gamer beast never lived.

Author's note

In chapter 4 of the first edition of this book I discuss some aspects of breeding livestock in general. I emphasize the need for the breeder to fix on his mind the type of animal he/she wishes to establish. In livestock breeding it is on the overall type of the results of the breeding programme that the breeder is judged by his fellow breeders. In general livestock breeding, the greater number of breeders who admire the type of stock being produced, the greater is the demand for your stock.

In dog breeding there are really two types of breeder. One is the commercial breeder who is in the game for profit, and that only is their concern. It is their hope that out of the considerable number of pups produced they hope that they will obtain a winner to keep their name to the fore and the misfits (from the exhibition side) are disposed of for whatever the market price allows.

On the other hand, we have in the dog game the hobby breeder whose sole interest is to try and improve his own stock first. This type of breeder's only interest in competing in the show ring is to compare his stock with those on exhibition. The judges' opinion of this type of breeder does not influence his ultimate aim, although he hopes to get a judge who may consider his exhibit (Type) does indeed satisfy the requirements of the Breed Standard closer than the exhibit of his competitors. After all the best judges do try to interpret the Standard of the breed to the best of their ability.

The photographs of the MAXTON dogs are included in the hope

that they may exhibit to the younger breeders a Type they may wish to seek to produce.

There are of course some in the breed who are critics of the Inbreeding programme I have followed. If they look at the matter with an open mind they should come to the conclusion that it is not as disastrous as they would wish to portray. At least in the breeding policy adopted we had, in 1966, our stud dogs and brood bitches tested for P.R.A. (progressive neuronal abitrophy) and X-rayed for hip dysplasia (they were found clear). Thus we showed some responsibility for breed improvement for future generations. I personally would not advise those who do not understand the problems to attempt inbreedings of their dogs or even line breed. Inbreeding and, to a degree Line Breeding, either system brings to the surface the unknown factors in your stock. Inbreeding has been defined by some as line breeding gone wrong. On the other hand inbreeding and line breeding where carefully handled by the breeder have been the foundation of all the successful breeding of all the important stocks in this country, in all breeds of stock.

The greatest critics of the system are those who do not understand genetics.

APPENDIX H
The Border Terrier by Montagu H. Horn
Characteristics

The Border Terrier is an original dog in many ways, and it is noticeable that it has many characteristics differing from other breeds. Whether at work or play, a Border is never quarrelsome, excluding, of course, the usual squabbles during puppyhood. When hounds and other terriers stand around an earth awaiting the bolting of Reynard, it never becomes aggressive. In the Show Ring all is peace and quiet, and these terriers give the impression that they are there only for a brief interlude from their more serious job in life. Unlike the majority of terriers in the close confines of a Show Ring, it appears to be on very friendly terms with its competitors. Neither the judge nor the exhibitors desire them to adopt the keen, alert, varminty attitude of other breeds of terriers.

This peaceful and serene attribute goes some way towards balancing their inbred love of hunting, so marked that they are always liable to go off alone, sometimes for days together. There are many notable Borders which have vanished on such hunts, never to return. Within recent years they include such winners as Ch. Grakle, Ch. Not So Dusty, and Finery.

If a Border cannot find a fox on these lone expeditions it is not averse to lesser vermin, and one of the dangers of allowing a Border to stray away, quite apart from the possibility of its loss, is its liability to turn to a quarry other than vermin, such as cats and poultry.

One of the best unorthodox cures for a roaming dog is a chance encounter with a goat, especially if the latter has already had experience with the canine species.

Whether the expression is an asset is doubtful, but the Border cannot be called a "one-man dog." The average specimen completely disregards strangers, but those with whom it is acquainted are always afforded a welcome, and it possesses an uncanny knowledge of those who hunt, whether wearing "scarlet" or the garb of the more humble earth-stopper. It is obvious that a Border regards itself as of equal importance to the hounds themselves, and, having its particular favourites with the pack, shows no sign of jealousy if another Border is lent for the day's hunt.

The Border has the advantage of occupying little space. Exercise, as with most dogs, is essential, and, as far as youngsters are concerned, here is the advice of a breeder whose terriers always excel in their action and general fitness. His method is to take all puppies for exercise on a thin lead, along a quiet pavement at five weeks of age. The distance travelled at first need not exceed fifty yards, his contention being that exercise upon a lead strengthens their hind action to such an extent that at maturity good movement is guaranteed.

Both the Border Terrier kennelled in its native hills and kept mainly for hunting, and the dog intended to share the hearth and home of its city owner solely as a companion, should have regular exercise at certain hours. As a breed usually free from canine ailments on the whole, its weather-resisting coat and height of leg tends to keep it clean under whatever conditions it may have to live. It is as likely to incur unfortunate habits as other breeds if allowed to roam either the hills and woods, its natural playground, or the back streets and gutters of a city.

Borders have been known to make great and lasting friendships with horses, and there is a remarkably close association between this breed and racing stables. A noted writer relates that the only dog he ever saw inside that "Holy of Holies," the weighing-room of a racecourse, was a Border Terrier.

The History of the Breed

Of the long era prior to the recognition of the Border Terrier as a distinct breed we know comparatively little. For the scant knowledge that is authoritative we are ever indebted to the energies of the late Mr Fred Morris, who spent many years sorting facts from a mass of fiction concerning its early history.

As it was not until 1920 that the Kennel Club admitted the existence of the Border, it may well be described as a very young breed. On the other hand, it must be one of the oldest indigenous to Britain; in fact, there are several owners who claim that their families have been breeding Borders for over four hundred years. Be that as it may, there are many who aver that the breed might have received an even more appropriate title than it did. The name "Robson Terrier" has been suggested frequently, in honour of the family which did so much to foster the breed and preserve it as a pure-bred variety.

That the Border is akin to the Lakeland there is little doubt; nor that there is still great, through most friendly, rivalry between owners of this breed in the Lake and Cheviot districts.

It is popularly supposed that the breed contains a mixture of the blood of the Dandie Dinmont and the Bedlington Terrier; but it is much more likely that both these breeds descended from the stock of the original Border, by whatever name it was then known. During the early years of this century, some Borders were known as the "Coquetdale Terriers," after the Northumbrian valley which claims to have been the birthplace of the breed, and owners in this locality claim to have perfected it from a breed now nameless and extinct.

The Bedlington was formerly known as the Rothbury Terrier (as well as the Northern Counties Terrier), and Rothbury is the only town of any size in Coquetdale which strengthens the claim that the ancestors of both these breeds were related. The only feature which the Border shares with the Bedlington today is its abundance of spirit and courage.

The word breed can be used very easily without due regard for its meaning, and before any mixture of blood or canine strains can merit the name, it must be certain that any two specimens can product their like. For example, the mis-alliance of two dogs of different breeds produces cross-breeds, yet if this mating is repeated frequently, and the resulting offspring mated to the offspring of parents of the same two breeds, they will eventually produce a strain of dogs with similar features. Care will have to be taken to mate only those cross-breeds which bear the joint appearance of both parental original breeds, otherwise in the early stages of the invented cross-breed it is certain that some will bear stronger resemblance to one than to both the parent breeds.

We must presume that experiments of this type must have taken place in the founding of the Border, and that they were not conducted by one man alone. Opinions would have differed, factions no doubt divided, and probably only a few were united about the plans for the future of the newly-created breed.

There is plenty of evidence that at one time a white-coated dog appeared in the pedigree of the Border. Either this was a hastily-remedied mistake, or, in the compounding of the breed, a white-coated dog was considered to be essential at the time. In any event, the sight of any white in the coat of a Border is an abomination to breeders today, and to those who claim descent from the originators, it is a reminder that the task commenced by their forefathers is not yet complete.

There was, of course, the Redesdale Terrier, of which nowadays we know little, but it is suggested that there was little difference between it and the modern Border, incidentally it is but a walking distance from the Rede to the Coquet rivers.

It is at this junction that we come to the long connection of the breed with the Robson family, who have been connected with farming and hunting in the Border Counties for over twelve hundred years.

It is almost a century ago that the late Mr John Robson's father moved his hounds from East Kielder to Byrness, in Redesdale, which amalgamated with another pack hunted by a Mr Dodd, of Catcleugh, which were known as the Redeswater Hounds before they adopted their present title, the Border Hounds. Since Border Terriers have been used by this hunt for a very lengthy period—indeed, exclusively for the past sixty years—their title was assumed from the name of that pack. In addition, the late Messrs Robson and Dodd have been prime sponsors for this breed of terrier from the time when interest was first aroused in it as an earth-terrier.

It is but fair to mention the Ullswater and Elterwater Terriers, which take their names from the Lake District, where they were raised. Often has it been claimed that they also were of the same breed as the Border, or that from them came the Border. Whether rightly or wrongly, all these dogs were the epitome of gameness, and, at a time when outward appearance was of negligible importance, we may be sure that breeders would be concerned solely with the intensification of that spirit.

Today we owe a great debt of gratitude to these pioneers for so cementing this most valuable trait, their errors we can correct, but from whatever source it was gained the character of the Border is permanently fixed.

It is frequently stated that Borders are descended from a strain of terriers which were bred at Lowther Castle over two hundred years ago, and that they were worked in the early days of the Cottesmore Hunt. In support of this theory was a picture in the possession of the late Lord Lonsdale, although he himself never claimed that the Lowther Terrier was a forerunner of the Border. There is also in existence a painting by the noted animal artist of the early 19th century, Abraham Cooper, which depicts the breed of terrier used by the Cottesmore, but this has no resemblance whatever to the Border.

We do meet with enthusiasts living at various distances from the Cheviots who assure us that it was their father who owned the first Border Terrier, but such yarns can only be related at the same time as that of the pitman who assures us that the two dogs which accompanied Noah on his voyage were Bedlingtons.

Turning to the time of the recognition of the breed, this was brought about by repeated urgings from all parts of the North, and in 1920 official notice was taken of the breed, and in the following year a specialist club was formed. From that time onwards the breed has increased in popularity year by year, and specimens have been exported as far afield as America and Sweden. It is interesting to hear from their new owners that, despite the change of climate and quarry, the Border shows the same active love of sport as in its native hills.

Standard Description

(The following standard was laid down by the Border Terrier Club in 1926)

The Border Terrier, being essentially a working terrier, and, it being necessary that it should be able to follow a horse, must combine activity with gameness.

Weight.—Dogs between 13 to $15\frac{1}{4}$ lb, bitches between $11\frac{1}{2}$ to 14 lb.

Head.—Like that of an otter, moderately broad in the skull with a short, strong muzzle, level teeth, a black nose is preferred, but a liver or flesh-coloured one is not objectionable.

Eyes.—Dark, with keen expression.

Ears.—Small, V-shaped, of moderate thickness and drooping forward close to the cheek.

Loin.—Strong.

Body.—Deep and narrow and fairly long; ribs carried well back, but not oversprung, as a terrier should be capable of being spanned by both hands behind the shoulders; forelegs straight and not too heavy in bone; feet small, with thick pads; stern, moderately short and thick at the base, then tapering, set high and carried gaily, but not curled over the back, hindquarters racy.

Coat.—Harsh and dense with close undercoat.
Skin.—Thick.
Colour.—Red, wheaten, grizzle and tan, or blue and tan.

Head, ears, neck, and teeth	20 Points
Legs and feet	15 Points
Coat and skin.	10 Points
Shoulders and chest.	10 Points
Eyes and expression	10 Points
Back and loin.	10 Points
Hindquarters	10 Points
Tail	5 Points
General appearance.	10 Points
Total.	100 Points

It will be seen that the above standard was compiled in the early days of the post-recognition period, but today members of the Committee which was responsible realise that it is in need of amendment and some additions. There is, for instance, no mention of the size of the dog, and much more could be defined more particularly. When the occasion offers a new standard will be drawn up to be of greater use to owners.

It is quite possible to have a Border complying with the standard as to weight, but to be too large in size as to remain a balanced terrier.

The Border should have a perfectly flat head, any roundness between the ears, pronounced occiput, or apple-headed specimen is wrong. The muzzle should be proportionately short and blunt.

It is doubtful if "keen expression" is quite apt, as the eye of the Border should be round (not oval, varminty, or almond-shaped, as with some of the Scottish breeds), and the actual expression while still remaining keen could be better defined as mild and steady.

The ears should be described as dark brown in colour, it is a definite drawback to have a Border with ears of any other colour, and light tan ears are a definite defect. Few puppies are born with true dark ears, nor do they deepen to the desired shade until almost mature.

Note will be made of spanning the terrier with both hands behind the shoulders. This is an old huntsman's trick, for he knows from experience that if a terrier cannot enter an earth with his belly flat to the ground, it will turn sideways, the girth of a Border being less from ribs to ribs than from back to belly.

No Border should excel in bone, unlike the general run of terriers, and the set-on of tail should also be dissimilar. The thicker the base of the tail the better; when standing or walking, this should be held at "halfmast," not erect, nor curled over the back. It is permissible for the tip of the tail to curl slightly upwards, and wave from side to side, when walking, akin to the foxhound.

The desire for a harsh and profuse coat with dense undercoat cannot be too strongly emphasised, nor can the thick hide, for obvious reasons, for any working terriers, but Borders in particular.

After officiating at a championship show, Sir John Renwick, ex-Master of the Sinnington Hounds, wrote: "Not enough attention is being paid to coat, and hide, which is most essential. There are also some Borders being exhibited with white toes or white feet, which are certain signs that there is a cross of Fox Terrier in their breeding. A true Border never had white feet, although a little white on the chest is quite usual in a true-bred Border."

Red is the colour most frequently met with, although in recent years grizzles have gained numerically. There is always the possibility that grizzle can become so dense that it can only be described as black, and there are some Borders with a large proportion of black in their coats. The colour is not permitted, and, once introduced into a strain, is most difficult to eradicate owing to the excess of pigmentation.

In breeding, to intensify or to eradicate a colour, it must be born in mind that the colour of the sire usually predominates, that being an unwritten law in all livestock breeding. If, therefore, a lighter colour is required, it is advisable to use a lighter-coloured dog than the bitch parent. There is no such thing as a "brindle Border." Shades introduced in the description of colour which are not mentioned in the standard usually cloak black.

The Border at Work

Border owners may be divided into two sections—those who require their dogs solely for work, and those mainly concerned with breeding and exhibiting. The former are usually huntsmen, and, while they have little regard for the pedigree of a dog, they are certain to require it to be sound in essential characteristics. No huntsman has any use for a terrier with a poor coat, thin hide, or one that is too big or too small for his purpose, and he demands a terrier with sound action and freedom of movement. The huntsman has a rigid code to which he sticks with unfailing tenacity and he despises a terrier showing weakness. Did the exhibitor follow these practices with the same bias and refuse to breed from any inferior stock, the Border would be a much sounder breed.

Although the huntsmen of the Border Counties show the greatest respect for a slightly larger dog than usually seen in the show-ring, this desire balances the present urge in other spheres, which is to reduce the size to conform to the usual terrier characteristics of compactness.

It must be appreciated that most of these hunts run their terrier with hounds, and no short-legged, compact little dog could keep up with hounds for any distance in the hill country of the Cheviot district, let alone be expected to go to ground at the end of the run and bolt his fox. It will be seen that when a huntsman of the Border Country makes his awards in the Show Ring, he always shows preference to a terrier of longer leg, even though it may fail slightly in some other respect. The terrier with the well-barrelled body and cobby appearance is likewise his aversion.

It will be seen from the foregoing that those Borders which are owned and worked by huntsmen most nearly conform to the general requirements of the breed, for the terrier which cannot work in the way required is a bad Border. A great many of the famous winners of the past have enjoyed still greater fame as workers.

Those who were responsible for the founding of the breed never intended it to be other than a working terrier which would bolt a fox. It was neither expected to kill nor to hunt, those being the pursuits of hounds. Nor was it intended ever to face anything but a fox, neither the otter nor the badger came into the picture at all, though the Border has since been used with great success in otter-hunting, mainly through the efforts of the late Mr Tom Robson, Master of the Northern Counties Otterhounds. Unfortunately, there is a minority who regard the actual killing of a badger as the supreme test of the ability of a Border Terrier.

This is not the place to defend the badger as harmless, however much our sympathy may lie with this maligned animal, but its killing requires a dog with characteristics quite alien to that of a Border Terrier, and, as the breed was never intended for this sphere of action, nothing can be gained by any attempt to test its spirit and convert it into anything but a legitimate worker to fox.

When working, a dog may suffer sufficient punishment from a fox to result in disfigurement, but no Border should be penalised in the show-ring on account of scars which have been honourably gained through combat with fox. Torn ears, scarred jaws, or even the loss of a tooth should not debar it from the highest honours. It is quite understandable that, with other breeds such a disfigurement could make winning an impossibility, and it has been argued that any such scars tend to detract from the appearance of a terrier. However, in the case of a working breed, they are the hallmark of its worth and should rather enhance its value than be regarded otherwise.

Within recent years, some strange excuses have been put forward by certain breeders to cloak the very serious defects of Border Terriers which they themselves have bred. As explained previously, yellow eyes, white chests or white legs are to be discouraged, and are such serious defects as to debar dogs from the award list under any specialist judge of the breed at any show. Emanating from some kennels come the explanations that dogs with yellow eyes see better in the dark, and that unless a Border bears a sufficiently large patch of white coat, it is liable to be mistaken by the hounds for the fox itself. Such stories are only suitable for repetition to the feeble-minded, but they are retailed with such persistency that it is of interest to refer to statements made by such noted workers of the Border as Sir Alfred Goodson, M.G.H. (College Valley Hunt): "I have never seen a terrier worried by hounds and have seen hundreds of foxes killed, and almost always some terrier in at the death."

"I have had Border Terriers for over fifty years, and in that time have only once seen a hound mistake a terrier for a fox, they both came out of an earth together, and, as each was covered with moss and soil, the colour of the dog was immaterial," as Mr Simon Dodd (Border Hunt) remarked a short time ago.

There is also a mistaken belief among breeders who lack any actual experience of working a Border that an immature young dog will take readily to bolting foxes, and they do not hesitate to describe the progeny of their kennels as "promising workers." The training of a terrier, and the experience necessary to bolt to perfection, are lengthy processes, and do not come as readily as we are led to believe. While all Borders are imbued with a sporting spirit and may inherit the abilities of their ancestors, the youngster which will bolt a fox at the first time of asking is a rarity, and by far the best training for a young dog is to follow an experienced terrier.

It is seldom known to either huntsman or terrier how many foxes there may be in an earth, and the wiles of an old fox, young fox, tired fox, fresh fox, or rogue fox, differ vastly.

It is only on too rare occasions that the huntsman of the Border Counties can be prevailed upon to judge at any distance from their homes, but there are many annual shows within sight of the Cheviot where the dog classification allots two classes for Borders, and here their services are always available. Such events have nothing of the glamour of the championship shows, but they do bring out the wealth of the breed. It is a far greater honour for a dog to win under such a judge than elsewhere, at least with the breeders of that district.

"The Border Terrier is being spoilt by those who are only concerned with the Show Ring, because they are producing them too thick in body and too short in leg. For following hounds over heather and rough country we require a rather narrow, leggy dog." Such is the opinion of yet another M.F.H. from Northumberland. In face of his accusation there can be no excuse for the continued production of the wrong type of terrier.

Although the Border was produced for the sole purpose of bolting foxes, when circumstances preclude hunts from enjoying their full complement, and hunting is so curtailed that vermin cannot be kept within bounds, the Border can not only hunt and bolt, but kill its fox.

The full debt which agriculture owes to this little terrier may never be computed, but some hundreds of foxes have been exterminated, and the ravages of the greatest foe to the sheep farmer have been considerably reduced.

Sport is good entertainment for both man and dog, and at such times even in those localities where foxes are not numerous, stoats, rats, weasels, and other vermin all come within the compass of the Border.

The terrier which satisfies a Master of Hounds that it is capable of going to ground and bolting a fox is awarded what is known as a Working Certificate, providing that the owner applies for such a document. This is by no means the ornate affair of the Challenge Certificate, and may not even be written on the official letter-heading of the hunt, it may only be a scrap of blood-stained paper torn from a diary, but is held in the greatest esteem.

There were special classes at several shows some years ago which were confined to Borders holding Working Certificates, and it is to be regretted that written proof of their work fell into abuse through the carelessness and generosity of one or two huntsmen. So many certificates were issued without ever the dogs being seen, let alone seen working, that even the genuine certificates became valueless.

Efforts are now being made to have these guarantees of the merit of earth-terriers issued and authorised by an Association whose signature will be beyond reproach.

The actual uses to which a Border can be put are diverse, as will be seen from the following anecdote of the early history of one of our most fashionable hunts. It occurred when hounds were trencher-fed (that is, kennelled singly or in couples by hunting farmers), and they were called on hunting mornings by the youthful Master pulling and nipping the ears of his Border-Terrier.

Those who have heard the effects of this cruelty will appreciate the probability of the story. However, the noise was so great that it came to the ears of the Master's uncle, a certain bishop, who threatened him with "bell, book and candle" so that other and more humane means were invented.

Some idea of the tremendous stamina of this game little breed may be gained from an exceptional run which is recorded in the annals of the Border Hunt. A fox was found at 8.30 one morning, and run until four in the afternoon, a distance of over forty miles. The fox went to ground and a Border Terrier, which had run with the hounds all day, was entered. Not until the next day was the terrier recovered, but the fox was found to be dead.

Border Terrier Pedigrees

The two dogs which figure most prominently in modern Border pedigrees are Revenge and Rival, and they were kennelmates, by different sires; they were both from Coquetdale Vic, one of the most famous bitches ever bred.

Bred by Mr Adam Forster, and litter sister to the dam of Ch. Titlington Tatler, owned by Mr George Sordy, which was one of the first champions in the breed, Coquetdale Vic laid the foundation for half the kennels in the country.

Long before the Border Terrier Club was formed, there existed the Northumberland Border Terrier Club, which possessed several challenge cups with the usual stipulation that, before being won outright, they must be won three times in succession. Accomplishing this feat, Coquetdale Vic became the first of her breed to win a cup outright. Although never appearing at a Championship Show, she had a lasting impression on the breed, despite having the whole of the flesh of her jaw torn away by a fox.

Her first litter was by a dog owned by the late Mr Carruthers, of Barrow Mill (Mr Forster's father-in-law), when she produced Flint, Dash, and Winnie. The former was only once at a Championship Show, where he won the certificate. This being at a time when owners never gave a thought to shows more than fifty miles from their own homes. Flint was the sire of Rab o' Redesdale, sire of Rival, sire of Ch. Ranter, in turn the sire of Ch. Grakle, the sire of Ch. Oakwood Pickle.

Rival was bred by Mr "Jack" Carruthers, and there was always a great friendly rivalry between the two brothers-in-law. It was on a visit to the latter's farm that Mr Forster noticed a mangy little puppy to which he took a fancy, and exchanged it for a bitch puppy of his own. Both parties felt very certain that each had got the better of the other over the deal.

The dog puppy, recovered from his mange, became Rival, while the bitch was named Suzanne. On several occasions one headed the dog classes at a show, while the other was at the top of the bitches; so that neither owner could boast of having got the better of the other.

Subsequently, Coquetdale Vic bred Little Midget, who in turn produced that wonderful sire, Revenge; though it was only by a provident "accident" that he appears in the Border pedigree at all. The story is interesting and worthy of repetition.

For some time, Mr Forster had been tormented by a friend who wanted a puppy to be reared solely for working. Tired of repeated requests, the friend was allowed to choose one from a litter, which he did. Very soon afterwards he returned, wishing to exchange it for a bitch puppy, and, as Mr Forster saw that the dog he had given away was actually the better of the two from a show point of view, he readily agreed. A few months after the exchange, the dog puppy, which was named Revenge, won both his classes, and the cup for best puppy at the Royal Show, held that year at Newcastle. Back came his former owner in the hope of reclaiming him in place of the bitch, but under the circumstances a second "swop" was too much to expect.

Revenge sired no less than five champions; Ch. Bladnoch Raider, and Ch. Benton Biddy, as well as the litter from Mr John Renton's Causey Bridget, which included Ch. Tod Hunter, Ch. Happy Mood, and Ch. Blister.

Mention has been made of the late Mr Carruthers, who deserves the greatest praise for his energies in keeping the breed pure and distinct. He was one of the pioneers of the Border, associated with the breed from childhood, and for over sixty years. Where he rendered such good service was that he would never cross his Borders with anything but Borders, and his terriers never changed in appearance. It must be remembered that this was during the period when the Border was kept solely for hunting and when gameness (not show points) was the sole aim of breeders.

When she was quite a young bitch Coquetdale Vic was nearly lost when out one day with the Border Hunt. A fox was run to ground at Hindberries, a noted stronghold, and Vic was entered, and although she could be heard she could not be drawn, so that she was left for the night. Next day saw the start of digging, but it was not until the third day that she was reached. The earth was a rock hole and had filled up with small stones and rubble. Vic was recovered, and with her the bodies of two foxes and four cubs, she was showing the effects of her ordeal and was carried to a keeper's house until she recovered.

Some details of the descendants of these two dogs are of interest, the following were full champions and winners of certificates.

REVENGE

Ch. Tod Hunter, by Revenge.
Ch. Benton Biddy, by Revenge.
Ch. Happy Mood, by Revenge.
Ch. Bladnock Raider, by Revenge.
Ch. Blister, by Revenge.
Ch. Not So Dusty, by Ch. Blister.

Ch. Share Pusher, by Stingo, by Ch. Blister.
Ch. Finchdale Lass, by Stingo, by Ch. Blister.
Ch. What Fettle, by Ch. Bladnock Raider.
Ch. Gay Fine, by Ch. Bladnock Raider.
  Dipley Deans, by Ch. Bladnock Raider.
  Puffin, by Ch. Bladnock Raider.
  Speed of the Wind, by Ch. Blister.

RIVAL

Ch. Ranter, by Rival.
Ch. Grakle, by Ch. Ranter.
Ch. Oakwood Pickle, by Ch. Grakle.
Ch. Dinger, by Gem of Gold, by Rival.
Ch. Brimball of Bridge Sollars, by Ch. Dinger.
Ch. Barb Wire, by Ch. Dinger.
Ch. Bess of the Hall, by Randale, by Rival.
Ch. Aldham Joker, by Ch. Barb Wire.
Ch. Ranting Fury, by Furious Fighter, by Ch. Ranter.
Ch. Swallowfield Garry, by Ch. A. Joker.
Ch. Boxer Boy, by Ch. A. Joker.
  Epigram, by Ch. Dinger.
  Finery, by Gem o' Gold.
  High Jinks, by Ch. Grakle.
  Vanda Daredevil, by Moor Jock by Ch. Dinger.
  Fire Fighter, by Fearsome Fellow, by Furious F. Swallowfield
    Shindy, by Ch. S. Garry.

A very successful kennel of borders was founded by the late Mr J.
Johnson, which owed much of its success to the inbreeding of the
Revenge-Rival lines. The initial purchase was Ch. Bladnock Raider,
bred by Mr McEwan, from a bitch called Red Gold. Before gaining
his title the dog had many victories in the North when in the hands of
Dr. Lillico, of Wigtown; his certificates being won at the Joint Terrier, Kensington, and Darlington Shows under Messrs McCandlish,
Nicholls, and Morris, respectively. He also had five reserve certificates to his credit.

Mr Johnson purchased the bitch Red Floss, by Dr. Fullerton's
Gem o' Gold, out of Hunty Gowk, which was one of Mr John Renton's breeding. Gem of Gold was by Rival from Ch. Benton Biddy (a
daughter of Revenge), while Hunty Gowk was by Whitrope Don,

hence her great suitability as a mate to Ch. Bladnock Raider, and the inbreeding of these two lines did much to produce the two Champions, What Fettle and Gay Fine.

The former won seven certificates at Cheltenham (MrsPacey), L.K.A. (Mr Nicholls), Blackpool (Mr Chris Houlker), Edinburgh (Mr H. Bonsor), Kensington (Mr Sam Crabtree), Blackpool (Mr Simmonds), and Richmond (Mr Nicholls).

Ch. Gay Fine won her first award at Leeds under Mr Harry Calvert, soon afterwards taking her title by wins at Harrogate and London.

A short pedigree of these two winners is worthy of study:—

BUTTIE	BRANTON MICK
REVENGE	FLOSS
LITTLE MIDGET	JOCK
	COQUETDALE VIC
Ch. BLAD RAIDER	
BLADNOCK TWINK	Ch. BEN OF TWEEDEN
RED GOLD	BLADNOCK GYP
TAYNISH	RATTER
	MONSIN JUDY
RIVAL	RAB o'REDESDALE
	TIBBY
GEM OF GOLD	
Ch. BENTON BIDDY	REVENGE
	MOLLYWAY
RED FLOSS	
WHITROPE DON	RED ROCK
HUNTY GOWK	LIDDESDALE NETTLE
LIDDESDALE BUNTY	ARNTON BILLY
	HAWWOOD LADY

Shortly after his purchase of Hunty Gowk, Mr Johnson crossed her with Ch. Blister, and bred Ch. Not So Dusty, which had an even more distinguished record, winning no less than eight certificates. Unfortunately this bitch met with the fate of many Borders and wandered away on a lone hunt from which she never returned.

A great many kennels have been founded on the progeny of two dogs, which take us back to the infancy of the breed, Miss Bell Irving's Tinker, and the late Mr J. Dodds' Ch. Grip of Tynedale, which are closely linked in many pedigrees, and it is obvious that Mr Walter Irving, one of the foremost of the Scottish owners of Border Terriers, has relied a great deal upon these two lines for his success.

It is not necessary to look far before meeting with Ch. Station Masher, by a son of Ch. Grip of Tynedale. One of her first litters provides a good example of good breeding, for she was mated to Ch. Barney Bindle, himself by Ch. Grip of Tynedale, and the result was Ch. Kineton Koffey, which was one of the first of the more famous Borders to appear at shows in the South of England, having been purchased by Capt. C. R. Pawson, and was also one of the first of the Southern champions to gain a working certificate.

Mated to Tinker, Ch. Station Masher produced Arnton Billy, the sire of Hunting Boy, Toit Fancy, and Liddesdale Wendy, as well as Dandy Warrior, which Mr Renton had to withdraw from exhibition through being badly mauled by a fox.

Liddesdale Wendy produced Liddesdale Nettle, the dam of Whitrope Don, who was mated with Ch. Station Masher, and gave Mr Irving his famous Ch. Joyden, which was winning challenge certificates at the advanced age of nine years old, a tribute to the lengthy show-life of a Border.

Tinker appears in most pedigrees honoured with the title Champion, but he was not actually entitled to this distinction, as two of the three certificates which he won were secured under the same judge—a Champion must, of course, win three challenge certificates under different judges.

It is impossible to trace through many pedigrees without meeting with the prefix "Newminster", owned by Capt. Sir John Renwick, Bart., who did so much to help the breed through many difficult periods when both numbers and quality had been seriously depleted.

The first Border that Sir John owned was a grizzle dog, Flyer, given to him by the late Mr Tom Robson, who was Master of the North Tyne Foxhounds fifty years ago. He remembered that when staying at Bellingham as a boy with Mr Robson, he took one of his host's bitches to be mated with a dog which Mr Carruthers owned.

Ch. Grakle, which won nine certificates for Sir John, was bred by Mr J. Dodds' Queen of the Hunt (by Tally Ho from Foxie).

Ch. Jedworth Bunty, one of the most successful bitches of her time, was by Pincher (the sire of Ch. Station Masher), from a bitch called Doodles; and mated to Mr Septimus Renwick's Sandy, she produced Newminster Rummy, which made his debut at Bellingham Show, a noted stronghold for this breed, where he headed all his classes. On the following Monday the Border Hounds were meeting, and he was taken along with his dam. A fox was found and run to earth in an old quarry on Mr Dodds' farm, and Rummy went to ground, spending the rest of the day there. He bolted no less than seven foxes from this quarry, and later became a very prominent worker with both the Border and North Northumberland Hunts.

Mated to Fairy Footsteps, litter sister of Ch. Grakle, he bred Ch. Newminster Rose.

In comparatively recent times Furious Fighter (by Ch. Ranter-Romance) has upheld the traditions of this kennel, both at stud and as a worker.

Reference has already been made to the five champions sired by Revenge from his matings to Causey Bridget, and Ch. Blister, owned by Capt. Hamilton, who was Chairman of the Border Terrier Club, was the most prolific sire of any, a winner of no less than fourteen certificates. Ch. Blister was not only the sire of Ch. Not So Dusty, but also of his owner's Stingo, which in turn produced Ch. Share Pusher, which won four certificates under Messrs Hamilton Adams and John Renton, Miss Vaux and Sir John Renwick, before being sold to America.

Of Mr Renton's brace, Ch. Tod Hunter matured very quickly, being what is known as a "good-doer," taking her first certificate at the surprisingly early age of nine months; whereas Ch. Happy Mood, her sister, went to the other extreme, being only just eligible for the junior class before entering the ring. However, she made up for a late start by winning over two hundred firsts, mostly in breed classes, which must constitute another record for the breed.

Details of the direct descendants of Ch. Grip of Tynedale, Tinker and Whitrope Don are as follows:—

CH. GRIP OF TYNEDALE

Ch. Barney Bindle, by Ch. Grip of Tynedale.
Ch. Station Masher, by Pincher, by Ch. G. of T.
Ch. Kineton Koffey, by Ch. B. Bindle.
Ch. Jedworth Bunty, by Pincher, by Ch. G. of T.
Ch. Newminster Rose, by Ch. Jedworth Bunty.

TINKER

Ch. Ben of Tweeden, by Tinker.
Ch. Heronslea, by Stirrup, by Ch. Ben of T.
Ch. Wedale Jock, by Ch. Heronslea.

WHITROPE DON

Ch. Joyden, by Whitrope Don.
Ch. Fox Lair, by Rab o' Lammermuir.
Ch. Dipley Dibs, by Ch. Foxlair.
Duskie Maiden, by Rab o' Lammermuir.
Ch. Bladnoch Spaewife, by D. Dusty, by Ch. D. Dibs.
   Portholme Mab, by Devonside Diversion, by Rab o' L.

In addition to all the famous lines and strains of Border Terriers, there is the "stolen strain," a plea which is commonly put forward to account for the absence of pedigree. It is a mysterious expression, usually uttered in a whisper, and if elucidation is required there follows a strange story which tells in romantic fashion how the service of a famous dog was obtained unknown to its owner, and only through the kind agency of a gamekeeper, or some such worthy. The probability of such a yarn is remote, for the owners of famous stud dogs (in this breed, anyway) are ever ready to place their services at the use of an owner, however humble he may be.

Obviously no name of any sire can be mentioned which makes tremendous increases to the pitfalls which await an owner breeding from such a bitch. In all good faith, she may be mated to her own sire, or to a litter brother, close inbreeding which holds too many chances concerning the success of the mating.

Far from a puppy being bred from a stolen strain, it is much more likely that it comes from unregistered parents, or the result of mating a Border with some other breed. There is only very slight opportunity of a service being obtained in this way. Border Terriers of note do disappear from time to time, but the probability of their theft for the purposes of breeding is so remote that it can be disregarded.

GEOFF	FLINT
NORTH TYNE GYP	WASP
WANNIE OF	PINCHER
TYNEDALE	NETTLE
CH. DAPHNE	PIPER

LANCE
MIDGE
TIBBIE

LANGHOLM GUESS
PINCHER
WASP

Breeder—(The Late) Miss DODD

BUTTIE
REVENGE
LITTLE MIDGET
CH. BLADNOCK RAIDER
BLADNOCK TWINK
RED GOLD
TAYNISH

BRANTON MICK
FLOSS
JOCK
COQUETDALE VIC
CH. BEN OF TWEEDEN
BLADNOCK GYP
RATTER
MONSIN JUDY

Breeder—Mr McEWAN

CH. BEN OF T.
STIRRUP
ROSIE
CH. HERONSLEA
ARNTON BILLY
TOIT FANCY
L. WASP

TINKER
BETTY
(UNKNOWN)
(UNKNOWN)
TINKER
CH. STATION MASHER
REDDEN
COLTERSCLEUGH BETTY

Breeder—Mr A. REID

RED ROCK
WHITROPE DON
L. NETTLE
CH. JOYDEN
PINCHER
CH. STATION MASHER
JED

BURNFOOT JOCK
RAGS
WHISTLER
LIDDESDALE WENDY
CH. GRIP OF TYNEDALE
FLORA FORD
SCAMP
TEVIOT NETTLE

Breeder—Mr W. IRVING

CH. GRIP OF T.
CH. BARNEY BINDLE
BRIDGE END
BEAUTY
CH. KINETON KOFFEY

NORTH TYNE GYP
NELL
GINGER
TIBBIE

PINCHER	CH. GRIP OF TYNEDALE
CH. STATION	FLORA FORD
MASHER	SCAMP
JED	TEVIOT NETTLE

Breeder—Mr W. IRVING

BURNFOOT JOCK	RICCARTON JOCK
RED ROCK	RICCARTON MEG
RAGS	TINKER
WHITROPE DON	WASP
WHISTLER	CH. CULLODEN COMET
L. NETTLE	CH. SCARSIDE BELLE
L. WENDY	TINKER
	CH. STATION MASHER

Breeder—Mr W. IRVING

Selective Breeding

When we come to the written testimony of Border breeding, it is amazing that so many mysterious duplications and blank spaces could have been produced in so comparatively short a time as twenty years.

Perhaps a smaller percentage of Border Terriers are registered with the Kennel Club than other breeds because so many are retained only for work. Owners cannot be compelled to register the name and breeding of every pedigree terrier, and no doubt they regard the registration fee as a needless expense if they have no intention of ever exhibiting the dog. If successful as a worker, it is more than likely that the dog will be used for breeding, and registration should be made so as to enable any future owner, or the owner of its progeny, to have their acquisition officially transferred.

In pre-recognition days the nomenclature of the breed was limited, and in some of the old pedigrees we find Mustard, Jed, Ginger, Rock and Jock in profusion. In some instances the name Ginger in a pedigree refers to the same dog; on the other hand, it is equally likely that any two Gingers will be distinct and quite unrelated dogs.

Border owners suffered from the same conservancy as Mr Dandie Dinmont himself, for to quote "Guy Mannering"—"I have six terriers at hame ... there's auld Pepper and auld Mustard, and young Pepper and young Mustard and little Pepper and little Mustard."

Then there is the Ginger owned by one hunt which passed into the hands of a neighbouring hunt and was re-named Jock. The dog may have sired many litters under both names.

Finally there is the Ginger who changed hands and was then registered, and so we delve backwards into these old pedigrees; and while they provide great interest they can become most provoking.

To quote one instance, there was a dog first known as Rock, purchased by Mr J. Carruthers who re-named it Mick, and exhibited it at a small show in the North. Here it was purchased by Mr T. Hamilton Adams, one of the pioneers of the breed in the South of England, who first showed it at Carlisle under the name Ivo Roisterer. The dog later became a Champion but in some pedigrees it rightly appears as Mick, and in others as Ch. Ivo Roisterer. It was a grandson of Rab o' Redesdale, who himself sired Rival, one of the two most prominent and prolific sires in the breed.

Probing into pedigrees may be very fascinating, but in scientific breeding is only of use up to a certain stage. It may be an incentive to discover that a recent purchase bears a pedigree containing many champions, but if they are several generations back the knowledge avails nothing. In the early years of the post-recognition period Challenge Certificates were for one thing easily gained, and some of the dogs which won them would find their task much more difficult today. It is questionable if a pedigree is of any use in selective mating beyond four or five generations. In a breed of such limited numbers of lines and strains as the Border, it is far better to in-breed judiciously to one line rather than attempt to incorporate the blood of the greatest numbers of champions possible.

Breeding to champions in the hope of producing one is almost certain to result in a dog taking after none of his famous ancestors, for it is an axiom in breeding that it is much easier to accentuate the bad points than the good ones.

The word in-breeding is applied far too loosely, and so frequently is it misapplied also.

There are many people who see one name appearing twice in a pedigree, and without more ado condemn the holder as being in-bred. There are others who lay the cause of every canine complaint imaginable to in-breeding, which is equally stupid.

The meaning of the expression is: To strengthen the good points, or the working abilities, of a certain notable dog by increasing his blood in the parentage of a litter.

It is the adaptation of Galton's Law, "The total heritage of the offspring is derived as follows: the two parents contribute on the average one-half of each inherited faculty, each of them contributing one-quarter of it. The four grandparents contribute one-quarter, or each of them one-sixteenth, and so on."

An excellent elementary example of this may be seen in the pedigree of Rival,

RAB o' REDESDALE	FLINT
RIVAL	DINKIE
TIBBY	FLINT
	BORDER DREAM

in this instance the attributes of Flint are doubled, presumably; and any mating of Rival to a bitch whose predigree contains the blood of Flint will strengthen this line still further.

There can be nothing more misleading than the visual choice of sire, for a breeder may easily select a dog by appearance, or by Show Ring honours which may produce in its progeny all the undesirable characteristics of its remote ancestors. It cannot be said that a remote ancestor has a greater effect upon the results of a litter than the immediate parents by any means, but it's presence cannot be disregarded entirely. There have been many famous winners in Border Terriers which have appeared eminently suitable and keenly sought after as sires, but invariably they pass on some major defect to all their litters.

Dog owners who cannot respect the principles of breeding are very prone to follow the paths of others. Such should altogether be discouraged from breeding. Unfortunately there is a lure about breeding which is attractive and even though their bitch may never have secured an award they have no hesitation in using a sire because they know of some other owner who has done so. Heed is so seldom taken of other litters or comparison made with the pedigree of the dams of those litters and that of their own.

Great and far-reaching harm to a breed is done by such injudicious mating of dogs by the ignorant.

There are people whose sole object in securing a bitch is to turn her into a breeding machine, who have no real interest in the breed selected, apart from monetary gain, and have no hesitation in disposing of ill-bred youngsters at ridiculous prices. The Border owner who boasts of the amount of money made by the litters from every bitch he has ever owned indicates where his interest lies. The safest guarantee, therefore, for a novice purchaser of a puppy is not the pedigree, but the name of the breeder.

The only value an animal possesses as a sire or brood bitch is assessed from the results of its progeny, and this can only be obtained through a system of trial and error. The most popular dog of the year and the biggest winner may be quite useless as a sire of winners. If we could assess the merit of a dog from his Show record alone, or from his pedigree, much of the element of chance would be removed. A great deal can be gained by comparing the puppies sired by a dog, not only for their good points, but also for their inherent defects. They must be seen, and the best place is in the Show Ring, and a comparison must be made of the breeding of their dams.

Exhibiting

Before a dog can be exhibited, it must be registered with the Kennel Club. As mentioned previously, the fee is half-a-crown, and two generations of the pedigree must be inserted on the requisite form. The name chosen in most cases differs from the kennel-name—for instance, the dog may be called and answer to Ginger, but the officially-registered name need not be the same.

There are four main types of dog shows, i.e., Championship, Open, Members-Sanction, and Exemption. Among the former are such notable events as Crufts', the Scottish Kennel Club (always a popular gathering with Border owners), and Birmingham. At such shows there are usually about ten classes provided for the breed, where the judge is a well-known specialist. By "specialist" it is inferred that he judges Border Terriers only. Prize money in each class is £2, £1, and 10/–, with an entry fee equalling the third prize. The Best Dog and the Best Bitch in the breed not only win their awards in every class entered, but also a Challenge Certificate, providing that the judge considers that the exhibit is worthy of bearing the title "Champion." Before such a title is gained, the holder must win three Certificates, each under a different judge. There have been occasions when the judge has awarded the prizes in every class, but has withheld the actual Certificate. He may consider that it is the best dog or best bitch, as the case may be, of those entered at that particular show, but yet not good enough to be a Champion. As the Certificate contains words to that effect, he is quite within his rights in withholding it.

Most Championship Shows extend over two days, the dogs being all benched and the breed classes judged in their respective rings on the first day; while the second day is confined to a few events to determine the Best exhibit of all terrier breeds, and ultimately the Best exhibit in the entire Show.

The dog and bitch which are runners-up to those winning Certificates are awarded what is popularly known as a "Reserve Certificate," and, as with the Certificate itself, no money payment is attached, and the dog receives no title despite the number of such awards that it may win. There is always the possibility—though it is a remote one—that the Certificate winner may subsequently be disqualified, when the Reserve Certificate winner would be advanced to that position.

Open Shows charge an entry fee of five shillings as a rule, and the prize money per class is similarly less. These are one-day events, and no Challenge Certificates are awarded in any breed. The number of different breeds catered for is usually less than at a Championship Show and there are fewer classes for each of them. The judges of the more popular breeds are frequently all-rounders—men who are capable of giving an opinion on all breeds of dogs, or possibly with specialised knowledge of several.

The Members' Shows, as their name implies, are either confined to members of a Club devoted to one breed only, and in that case held annually in conjunction with a Championship, or Open Show, or to members living in one town or district. The annual subscription to such a society is small, and the entry fee per class may be as low as two shillings, with prize money in proportion.

The Border owner will be fortunate to find a local Society which provides a special class for his breed, or a judge of such a show with any knowledge of the Border. Awards at Members' Shows carry little weight in enhancing the value of an exhibit; and, as most classes are open to all breeds, but confined to age, weight, or previous successes, it is obvious that little merit attaches to the Border which wins an award against dogs of other breeds. Such a win might easily be reversed at the next Show under a different judge, even though the same dogs were in competition.

Such shows do have their value in schooling a young dog to the surroundings of a crowded Show Ring at very little cost, however; for there is nothing more disheartening than preparing for a large show, only to arrive in the ring to find that the young dog on which your hopes are centered is so affected by travel, and the crowd of people and dogs, that it fails to look its best at the critical time.

Strangely enough, the Exemption Show concerns the Border more than other breeds, at least in the North of England. Such an event is held in conjunction with an Agricultural, Flower Show, or "charity events," and is limited to four classes only. Dogs entered need not be registered with the Kennel Club, both prize money and entry fees depend on the generosity and finances of the organisers. Held in Northumberland and the Border Counties, these shows attract a large proportion of Borders, the reason being that the judge is either a Master, hunt servant, or member of some hunt, and having a lifetime association with the breed is naturally a specialist.

The Exemption Shows, as far as Borders are concerned, are only applicable to the district already mentioned.

The quality of exhibits can naturally be expected to be the highest at Championship Shows. But, as may be seen elsewhere, there are certain annual Open Shows, Hexham, Bellingham, and Carlisle in particular, where the largest entry of any breeds is in Borders; these shows are within easy reach of many owners who never exhibit elsewhere.

It must be remembered that there are people whose lifelong ambition does not centre round a Challenge Certificate; to beat a friendly rival at one of these Northern Shows is a sufficient honour. Making lengthy visits to other more important Shows is often impossible for these people, who have no yearning for greater glory for their terriers. Quality at the three shows mentioned is usually as good as the quantity, both classification and selection of judge leaving nothing to be desired.

The owner of a Border which had just been made a Champion once went on a long journey to one of these events, hoping to win the

Open Class with ease. His hopes were shattered, for he left the ring cardless. On pointing out to the judge that his dog was the latest Champion in the breed, he was rudely surprised to hear that worthy remark, "Champion?—Man, it isn't even a Border"!

For the benefit of those who fondly imagine that the showing of dogs is a pleasant and easy way of making money, let it be said now that few owners can claim to do so. It will be seen that the exhibit must win a prize in every class to recoup the entry fee alone, and the larger the show the greater the cost of travelling, hotel expenses and incidental items, which more than balance any profit made by the most successful owner. In consequence, an owner who attempts to exhibit at, say, six Championship and six Open Shows during the year must expect to be considerably out of pocket.

It is unfortunate that many people have embarked on dog-breeding and showing without realising the costs entailed, and have made a hasty withdrawal from the ranks. Owners must be prepared to regard the losses on showing as capital invested until such times as dividends commence to flow in, and the capital should be regarded as advertising expenses; for the dog which wins the greatest show-ring honours may be expected to prove a most popular sire; likewise, those puppies born from a bitch which has had similar successes bring larger prices than those of the less fortunate. It has been stressed in a previous chapter that show-ring awards are not the only criterion of successful mating, but it is breeding from winners which pays for the awards that they have gained.

"It pays to advertise" may be translated into, "It pays to exhibit—if you win." The dog which is placed at stud without being exhibited is not likely to be in great demand, nor the dog which has been shown and has never won.

The Border requires very little preparation for the ring so far as actual trimming is concerned, and certainly cannot be included in those breeds which are accused of being carved and chiselled into shape, and it is as near as possible exhibited naturally.

Many specimens are prone to grow a "top-knot" akin to the Dandie Dinmont, which should be removed—in fact, the head above and at each side of the eyes should be trimmed short, likewise any ruffle behind and below the ears should be removed. This is quite easily accomplished without any stripping comb, or elaborate appliance, and is best done by finger and thumb. Dogs are at certain seasons of the year in their best coat; and at others are out of coat. Daily brushing will remove any dead hair in their coat without adopting any other means, and by the time that a ruffle or topknot has grown long enough to be noticeable, the hair will be in such a condition that it can be removed with ease by hand.

No Border born with a coat of poor texture can be improved by stripping. The sign that a dog is starting to come into its poor coat is when it commences to shed hair; daily brushing will reveal this and promote the growth of a new coat. Dogs exhibited when out of coat are at a great disadvantage, and it is better to refrain from showing at that time, however convenient and tempting the event may be.

In order to enter for a Show, a schedule must be obtained; most events are advertised in weekly papers devoted to dog-showing. The entry form must be completed and returned with the appropriate entry fees to the secretary by the closing date. Late entries are never accepted under any circumstances.

Fullest particulars are given in the schedule as to the time when exhibits should be present at the show, which is well ahead of their actual judging.

An exhibitor is expected to be ready to take his dog into the ring at any time; his absence for whatever cause cannot delay judging. Many disappointments are caused by owners who arrive too late, or through having made temporary departure from the benches of the breed just at a time when the judge is busy with their classes.

When in the ring, exhibitors are expected to keep one eye on their dog, and the other on the judge. Being a natural working terrier, a Border does not require "handling" by its owner dropping on one knee, holding up the dog by throat and tail; not is its keenness exaggerated by a small ball, matchbox, or doll which is dangled before it.

The judge may require each dog to be led round him, as he stands in the centre of the ring (this is to observe their action), before lining them up facing him; or he may reverse this procedure. In turn, each dog will be led up to him for examination; and then he will probably ask the owner a question, such as the age of the dog. Whatever the question may be, it should be answered; and no other remark made to the judge at all.

Whatever the result of the class, it must be remembered that by making an entry at a show, the exhibitor does so in order to obtain the opinion of that particular judge. No judge ever reverses his placings when once his awards are made, and complaints are futile. Prizes are given for the appearance of the dog on the day of the show, and not on any past successes that it may have gained.

After their duties are over, and, if time permits, judges at Championship Shows make a tour of the benches, and it is then permissible to ask where he considered a dog to be at fault. Many novices have received very valuable advice at such a time.

Even if an exhibitor is an old friend of the judge, even though they may not have met for a considerable time, it is highly improper for them to converse before judging takes place, and, in dog show procedure, it is one of those things which is just not done. There may be no ulterior motive in doing so, but it is the impression which is created in the minds of other exhibitors which matters.

The novice may be fortunate in securing an award card of any sort at his first show, but whatever the result should not be discouraged; the owner will probably gain as much experience in the art of "ringcraft" as his dog.

There is no hard and fast form in dog-showing: many dogs which are beaten by a certain exhibit at one show may be placed above it at the next—the results depend solely upon the opinion of the judge at each show.

£ s. d.

It must not be presumed that breeding and winning with Border Terriers paves an easy road to riches, for few owners augment their income to any appreciable extent with their dogs.

Until a few years ago, good specimens of the breed changed hands for the proverbial old song; most owners were concerned only with hunting, and fox-hunters are notably generous. If a hunt was known to be in need of a good terrier, many members were only too eager to supply one, for most kennels were started with a gift dog. Notable workers were lent from one hunt to another, stud services were generally free, and the furtherance of sport could not be hindered by the lack of money.

It was quite possible to procure an experienced worker, a winner at Championship Shows, bred by a Champion from a bitch which had won a certificate, and a proved breeder, for about five pounds. The stud fee of a Champion was seldom more than a couple of pounds, and puppies were sold from the nest for a sum equal to the stud fee of their sire.

There were isolated instances where dogs changed hands for quite ridiculous figures in comparison—nobody blamed the vendor for striking a good bargain. It was only the buyer's fault if he was a fool.

Perhaps those days have passed, but it is doubtful whether for the benefit of the breed. At the present time there are Borders which have never seen a fox, whose owners do not believe in allowing them any sport whatever—not even a taste of rat! In consequence, interest in the breed is far removed from that of the original Border owners. To debar a terrier from participating in sport for fear that it may lose its value as a show specimen is ridiculous, when we recall that scars of combat are disregarded by judges of the breed.

It is to be deplored that a distinct "type" of Border Terrier is ever created by non-sporting owners which is alien in attributes to the original; and an animal bred in contradiction to the standard, whose deficiencies are cloaked by weird stories, produced solely for the benefit of sale.

Every Border owner does not rear his terrier for the sake of hunting, now that ownership has been extended far from the natural home of the breed, but every owner can maintain his dog as a sporting terrier. Nor is it his wish to lose money intentionally. Times change, but it should be possible to purchase a puppy from the nest at a cost of £5 to £10, according to its breeding and the success (in both earth and show-ring) of its parents. Stud fees should be less than half this figure.

A great deal of business is effected at Championship Shows, as they are the recognised meeting-place of breeders, and are therefore attended by many whose interests are not confined to exhibiting. Novices will do well to recall the advice tendered previously that the name of the breeder is a more reliable guide than the pedigree of a puppy, and no heed should be paid to stupid stories circulated to shield the deficiencies of badly-bred stock, offered for sale at exorbitant prices.

Great credit is due to those who wish to learn as much as possible about a prospective, or recent, acquisition, and it is deplorable that a minority of breeders should descend to practices which have never been associated with this breed.

Timely warning is perhaps not out of place, as so many young dogs have been sold to novices by owners who are yet to make their names as breeders, that when exhibited under Border judges (to use a term employed by Northumbrian owners to assess the value of a poor specimen) price themselves at a shilling.

Glossary of Canine Terms

Apple Headed.—A rounded skull instead of flat.

Brisket.—Forepart of the chest.

Beefy.—Big hindquarters, showing lack of exercise.

Broody.—A likely whelper.

Blood.—A well-bred dog, pedigreed.

Character.—Points distinguishing one breed from another, or one dog from another.

Cow-hocked.—In-turned hocks, like those of a cow.

Cat-foot.—Short, round foot with good knuckles.

Cheeky.—Well-defined cheek-bones.

Condition.—Synonym of good health and appearance.

Dewlap.—Loose skin beneath the chin.

Domed.—Rounded skull.

Expression.—Determined by the size, colour and outlook of the eye.

Flat-sided.—Flat, not rounded ribs.

Hare-foot.—Long and narrow.

Loins.—The body between ribs and hindquarter.

Listless.—Dull and sluggish in appearance.

Length.—The body from nose to tail.

Occiput.—The prominent bone at the top of the skull.

Overshot.—Front teeth of the upper jaw protruding over the lower front teeth.

Out at Shoulder.—Shoulder set on outside like a Bulldog.

Out at Elbow.—Elbows turned outwards.

Pastern.—Lower part of leg below hock, or below knee.

Pad.—The underpart of the foot.

Racy.—Slim in build and long in leg.

Roach-back.—Arched loins like Dandie Dinmont.

Stifles.—Upper joints of hind leg.

Stop.—An indentation between the eyes.

Snipy.—Too pointed and narrow in muzzle.

Stern.—The tail.
Short-coupled.—Shortness of back and loins.
Undershot.—Lower front teeth protruding over upper.
Up to Size.—A term meaning too big.
Wall eye.—A light blue, or white eye.

APPENDIX I

Border Lines

Early Champions and Breeding Lines of the Border Terrier

This old breed is becoming increasingly popular and although most people will agree that the Border has been smartened up in appearance and that fronts, tails, eyes and certain other points have been improved, we must be careful not to lose any of the essential characteristics of the original terrier, which was bred in the early days entirely for work in the rocky and difficult country of Northumberland and the Borders. Therefore, the conformation of the Border must at all costs remain the same as that laid down in the standard of the breed which was drawn up with the greatest care by those who had bred and used them for many generations, and who knew exactly what was required of a terrier for underground work in the most difficult places, and they have been most carefully bred with this in view.

The first show at which Challenge Certificates were offered for the breed was at Carlisle on Sept. 30th, 1920, and the placings in the Open Classes were:—

Open Dog:—1, Tinker; 2, Dan; 3, Teri.

Open Bitch:—1, Liddesdale Bess; 2, Nett; 3, No award.

The other shows at which there were Challenge Certificates in 1920 were: The Kennel Club Show at the Crystal Palace on Nov. 3rd and 4th.

Open Dog:—1, Tinker; 2, Dan; 3, Flint.

Open Bitch:—1, Winnie; 2, Dot; 3, Riccarton Meg.

And at the Scottish Kennel Club's Show on October 6th and 7th:—

Open Dog:—1, Teri; 2, Dan; 3, Gyp.

Open Bitch:—1, Winnie; 2, Bet; 3, No award.

It will be seen that Tinker and Winnie each won two certificates. Tinker won three in all but two of them were gained under the same judge so that although he comes in many old pedigrees as "Ch Tinker" he never actually gained the full title. It is interesting to note that Gyp, better known as North Tyne Gyp, and Dot were brother and sister as were Flint and Winnie.

In 1921 Challenge Certificates were awarded at the National Terrier Club's Show in January, at Birmingham in February, Ayr in April and the Kennel Club's Show in October. Teri, KCSB 854 AA and Liddesdale Bess KCSB 842 AA became respectively the first Border dog and bitch champion in this year.

During the first ten years after the breed was officially recognised and listed as a separate breed by the Kennel Club in 1920, there were twenty seven champions made up, and to those or to their near relatives, brothers, sisters, etc., nearly all of our best known Borders trace back. Perhaps it will be interesting to list these early champions and then trace back their breeding to see how the blood lines mingle and finally merge into the comparatively few original strains.

Starting in 1930 the champions were:—

Ch Ranter (1060 JJ) the sire of Ch Grakle, Renton, Furious Fighter, etc. This is one of the strongest champion producing lines. He was born on June 1st, 1927, and was by Rival, by Rab of Redesdale, by Flint (mentioned above) by Ch Ivo Roisterer. His dam was Coquetdale Reward, by Tug, by Ivo Roisterer and Coquetdale Reward's dam was Little Midget × Coquetdale Vic × Nailer II × Nailer I.

Ch Kineton Koffey (38 KK) born on the 8th of Feb., 1928, by Ch Barney Bindle × Ch Station Masher.

Ch Jedworth Bunty (41 LL) born on the 28th of July, 1928, by Oxnam Pincher by Ch Grip of Tynedale × Doodles (unregistered) by Tinker by North Tyne Gyp. Doodles was × High Level Sting × Dale Wasp × Fury.

Ch Dryburn Kutchuk (28 JJ) born on the 23rd of January, 1927, by Ch Barney Bindle × Ch Daphne.

In 1929 we get the Champions:—

Ch Station Masher (1476 GG) born on the 11th April, 1924, by Oxnam Pincher (the sire of Ch Jedworth Bunty) × the unregistered Jed who was by Scamp by Piper by Newton Rock. Jed's dam was Teviot Nettle (by Ch Teri) × Spitfire, litter sister to Ch Liddesdale Bess. Ch Station Masher was the dam of Ch Kineton Koffey, Ch Joyden, Arnton Billy and many other very noted ones.

Ch Troglodyte (1154 HH) born on the 26th June, 1926; he was by Tornado by Blackadder, by High Newton Flint by Newton Rock × Tertius.

In 1928 came:—

Ch Benton Biddy (1155 HH) born on the 30th July, 1925; she was by that great sire Revenge by Buittie by Branton Mick by Jack × Molly-way by Redden by Ch. Titlington Tatler. Mollyway's dam was Aldersyde Maid by Titlington Rap by Titlington Jock × Vic × Bess × Nellie. Benton Biddy was the dam of Gem of Gold.

Ch Southboro' Stray (2295 HH) is rather a mystery; he is registered as "Breeder, pedigree, date of birth unknown," and there does not seem to be any trace of his descendants.

Ch Ben of Tweeden (359 HH) born on the 26th July, 1925, was sired by Tinker by North Tyne Gyp and his dam was the unregistered Betty by Jackie of Newlands (by Ch Teri) × another unregistered bitch called Betty, which is as far as one can trace his female line.

1927 produced four Champions:—

Ch Rustic Rattler (358 HH) was born on the 28th June, 1925, and was registered as Foxtrot, but his name was changed later. I believe that he was exported, but he left a daughter behind called Wasp and she was the dam of Tommy Brock. Rustic Rattler was by Crosedale Jock by Allan Piper by North Tyne Gyp and his dam was Crosedale Judy by Ch Titlington Tatler × Priestfield Gyp who was a daughter of North Tyne Gyp and Jean of Tynedale so that she was a sister to Allan Piper.

Ch Tertius (1305 GG) born on the 21st April, 1925, dam of Ch Troglodyte was by Sniper by Titlington Jock × Ch Themis.

Ch Betty of Scarside (1306 GG) born on the 21st October, 1924, was by Ch Cribden Comet × Ch Scarside Bell.

Ch Tweedside Red Topper (129 FF) was a son of Ch Dandy of Tynedale and Ch Tweedside Red Tatters. He was born on Sept. 13th, 1923.

The year 1926 produced:—

Ch Barney Bindle (1487 EE) who was the only one to gain his title. Mated to Ch Station Masher he sired Ch Kineton Koffey. Born on the 18th of July, 1923, he was by Ch Grip of Tynedale × Bridgend Beauty (unregistered) by Ginger (by Newton Rock) × Tibby × Wasp (untraced).

1925 brought three Champions:—

Ch Cribden Comet (527 EE) born on the 21st of Jan., 1921, he was first registered as Dazzler, and the bitch Thimble was sired before his name was changed. Later mated to Ch Scarside Bell he produced Ch Betty of Scarside and Whistler. Whistler was sire of Liddesdale Nettle, and she, mated to Red Rock produced Whitrope Don and

Foomert and by a mating to Ch Grakle, Miss Grakle, Halleath's
Piper and Ch Oakwood Pickle, and by yet another mating this time
to Ch Blister Stung Again. Cribden Comet was by Sandiman
(brother to Ch Titlington Tatler) by Titlington Jock and his dam was
the unregistered Posski × Wasp (untraced); Barndale Jock the grand
sire of Ch Dinger was litter brother to Ch Cribden Comet.

Ch Scarside Bell (1052 FF) born on the 28th of Sept., 1923, was by Ch
Grip of Tynedale × Honeycomb by Dan of Rawfoot French by Rock
by Pinch by Flint unregistered. Whether this is the same Flint as the
grand sire of North Tyne Gyp and Ivo Roisterer, I am not sure.
Honeycomb was × Nellie (untraced).

Ch Tweedside Red Type (1225 CC) born on the 7th of October, 1920,
was the same way bred as Ch Tweedside Red Tatters.

In 1924:—

Ch Dandy of Tynedale (1212 CC) born on the 1st Nov., 1921, and
mated to Ch Tweedside Red Tatters sired Ch Tweedside Red Topper
and many other good ones. He was by North Tyne Gyp × Otterburn
Lass and she was by Dan (sire of Honeycomb) × Redewater Lass
(untraced).

Ch Daphne (1213 CC) born on the 26th of April, 1921, was the dam
of Ch Dryburn Kutchuk, her sire was North Tyne Gyp and her dam
Midge (unregistered) by Lance (sire of Jean of Tynedale) by Tim.

1923:—

Ch Grip of Tynedale (1216 CC) born in June, 1920, he was sire of Ch
Barney Bindle, Ch Scarside Bell and Oxnam Pincher (sire of Ch
Station Masher and Ch Jedworth Bunty). He was by North Tyne
Gyp × Nell (by Rock, untraced) × Nellie who was a sister to Geoff
(sire of North Tyne Gyp).

Ch Tweedside Red Tatters (1224 CC) born on the 11th Dec., 1921.
She was dam of Ch Tweedside Red Topper and was closely related to
Ch Ivo Roisterer through his dam Flossie. She was by Ch Titlington
Tatler × Chip by Ingram Beetle by Newton Rock and Chip was ×
Flossie × Floss I.

Ch Themis (1223 CC) born on Oct. 8th, 1920, was by North Tyne
Gyp × Lesbury Tatters by Branton Mick (sire of Buittie) by Jack ×
Betty (untraced). Ch Themis was dam of Ch Tertius and by a mating
to Battling Robert, often mis-named Rattling Robert in old pedigrees, a brother to North Tyne Gyp, she produced Teri Trumpeter

and Typhoon in 1922. Teri Trumpeter was a blue and tan grizzle and through him come many good Borders of today. He sired Compounder and from her in direct female descent comes Ch Teddy Boy. Mated to Blackadder (Newton Rock male line) Themis produced Tantalus, ancestor of Ch Finchale Lass and Ch Swallowfield Garry.

Ch Ivo Rarebit (433 CC) born on the 12th of Aug., 1920, was by Ch Teri from a bitch called Floss (untraced).

Ch Titlington Tatler (924 BB) born 5th of April, 1919. He was one of the best sons of Titlington Jock × Gippy by Barrow Jock by Mack.

Ch Ivo Roisterer (930 BB) born on the 5th Aug., 1915 by Jock (by Flint sire of Geoff) × Flossie × Floss I.

1921:—

Ch Teri (845 AA) born on the 21st of April, 1916, by Titlington Jock × Tib by Cheviot by Rock by Dagg's Rock. Tib was × Chickie by Rock (sire of Newton Rock) by Whaup.

Ch Liddesdale Bess (842 AA) born 9th Aug., 1917, by Liddesdale Nailer by Piper (brother to Tinker's dam Daisy) by Rock. Liddesdale ·Bess' dam was Pearl by Sandy. Ch Teri and Ch Liddesdale Bess were mated on several occasions and one of their offspring was Priesthaugh Venom the grand dam of Ch. Heronlea's sire Stirrup.

These twenty seven champions go back to North Tyne Gyp sixteen times, to Titlington Jock fifteen times and to Newton Rock seven times, and these three dogs seem to be the chief male lines from which our present-day Borders come.

North Tyne Gyp was born on the 17th of March, 1917, and he was registered as Gyp (431 BB) but he is always known and comes in most pedigrees as North Tyne Gyp. He was by Geoff (1913) by Flint unregistered × Wasp unregistered. His dam was Wannie of Tynedale by Pincher by Adam. Wannie of Tynedale's dam was Nettle × Birkie × Bess I.

Titlington Jock was born in June, 1909, but he was not registered until 1921, so that most of his puppies are registered and come in pedigrees as "sire Jock." Besides those already given one of his best sons was Longhurst Pepper the grand sire of Ch Blister, Ch Todhunter, Ch Happy Mood, etc. He was by Weddels Rap (Ginger × Newton Bessie) × Tatters (Swinbourne Piper × Rags).

Newton Rock was born on the 17th of March, 1914, by Rock I (by Whaup × Wasp) × Tib (by Snap × Floss).

The four chief bitches to which I have been able to trace back are Flossie, Chickie, Nailer II and Bess I. The bitches are much more difficult to find out about and many of them are not yet traced.

Flossie (dam of Ch Ivo Roisterer, Chip, Buittie) was by Jim × Floss I. *Chickie*, dam of Tib (Ch Teri's dam) Jimmy (sire of Newton Pinch) and Blackie (dam of Rawfoot French) was sister to Newton Rock. *Nailer II*, dam of Coquetdale Vic, (dam of Little Midget) Tino (great grand sire of Ch. Twempie Tinker) and Gippy (dam of Ch Titlington Tatler and Sandiman) Nailer II was by Rock (untraced) × Nailer I and she was by Rock (by Twig × Pep) × Gowanburn Bess. *Bess I*, born in 1900, was the dam of Venus (grand dam of Tinker) of Piper (grand sire of Ch Liddesdale Bess) and of Birkie (grand dam of North Tyne Gyp) and many other lines go back to her as well. She was by Twig × Fury (by Flint by Rock by Rock by Flint!) × Vene.

The Breeding of the Modern Border

By "Red Card."
(Reprinted by permission of the *Hexham Courant*).

I.

Any dog of a strange breed imported to this country from a distant land finds immediate favour, and the more unusual its features, the more publicity it will receive. In the last few years we have seen strange breeds without tails, without pedigrees, some even without a name which have risen to fame as soon as they have been released from quarantine, but no breed has acquired such notoriety as that very "canny" little dog, the Border Terrier, since it has travelled from the immediate district of its natural home.

It is only in very recent times that it has appeared at Southern shows, and there are many districts in England where it is still unknown, but from the demand from as far afield as Eire, America and Scandinavian countries. It promises to rank among the most popular terriers in those far off lands before many years have passed, and much though we regret the departure of many of our notable winners, foreign owners are wisely founding their kennels with the highest quality of breeding stock.

As expected by those who have enjoyed a lifetime's intimacy with the breed, Borders readily adapt themselves to new surroundings, and their activities are by no means confined to successes in the show ring, as reports received from their new owners indicate that they have resumed the more serious business of their lives with considerable distinction, whatever the quarry.

Long Show Life

Few breeds exhibited in this country have a longer show-life than the Border, and a dog which in any other variety would be considered far past his prime is quite capable of winning the veteran class, and the challenge certificate at the same show, while dogs of eight and nine years of age are frequently seen at the head of the open classes.

Much has been written on the probable origin of the breed, although many writers appear to overlook the fact that the Border is not what can be termed an original breed, but like many popular terriers, the outcome of selective experimental blending of other breeds, known and nameless, and is therefore purely man-made.

It is frequently stated that the Border is descended from a strain of terriers bred at Lowther Castle, over two hundred years ago, and worked with the Cottesmore, and in support of the theory is a picture in the possession of Lord Lonsdale, although he himself has never claimed that the breed were the forerunners of the modern Border.

There is also in existence a painting by the celebrated canine artist of the early 19th century, Abraham Cooper, of a breed of terrier used by the Cottesmore, which has no resemblance whatever to the Border. It is in fact, a long-haired, erect-eared dog, larger than the Cairn, shorter in back than the Dandie Dinmont, but apparently akin to both breeds. So that it is a great stretch of the imagination to assume that there is a very close connection between the Lowther breed (which has never been registered with the Kennel Club), and the Border, although the former may have been used in some of the final experiments to put a last "polish" to the establishment of the breed.

Early History

We do know that somewhere in the early history of the Border, a white-haired breed was inbred, and though the fault is by no means as common as it used to be a small percentage of Borders have white hairs, either white feet or a white blaze down the chest, and this defect is an outcrop from some breed used in the making of the Border. The defect is not confined to Border Terriers alone, and can be entirely eliminated if all future breeding excludes the use of either sire or dam with white markings, as has been successfully accomplished in certain other terriers, but the outcrop of white in an otherwise red breed may best be explained by the simple form of Mendalism,

	White Sire			Red Dam	
	(		)		
W	WR		WR	R	
		(	)		
	WR	WR	R	R	
		(	)		
	WR	R	R	R	

Unfortunately there are stud dogs bearing white which as far as possible are otherwise perfect, and they are used by a section of owners who pass lightly over such a defect, but in fairness to those who claim a connection between the Border and Lowther terriers, the latter strain bear a high percentage of pure white coated dogs.

It is always a matter of opinion how far back a pedigree need be traced before it is useless. We have seen pedigree forms bearing the names of champions in red ink, but the latter colour is never used when only one champion is included and that probably seven generations back. The majority of live-stock breeders consider that three to four generations must be studied before a contemplated mating, but if any useful information can be gained from any knowledge of the original strains used in perfecting a breed, it is so slight that no reliance can be placed on its accuracy in future breeding.

Important Detail

In the matter of colour breeding, a rather important detail in connection with Borders, it is well to remember that the sire predominates, therefore if the sire is darker than the dam, it may safely be assumed that the majority of the puppies born will be darker in colour than the bitch, and if the bitch is already too dark, a lighter dog must be used to eradicate the shade.

In pedigree breeding, it is usual to trace descent in male line, and in Border Terriers it is very much easier to do than in other terrier breeds because of the persistency with which breeders repeatedly used the same sires. Indeed they would have been exceedingly foolish to have done otherwise considering the regularity with which champions and certificate winners were produced, and without such sires as Revenge, Rival, and Whitrope Don, to mention only a trio, it is doubtful if the Border would be as near universal perfection as it is today.

In modern pedigrees no dog figures more prominently than the famous winner. Revenge (by Buttie—Little Midget), and his progeny include Ch Bladnoch Raider, Ch Benton Biddy, and the litter from Mr. Renton's Causey Bridget which included Ch Blister, Ch Tod Hunter, and Ch Happy Mood. Ch Bladnoch Raider, now the property of Mr. J. Johnson, has already sired Ch What Fettle, Ch Gay Fine, and the certificate winner, Puffin. Ch Blister, an equally popular sire, has given us Ch Not So Dusty, and Speed of the Wind which also has a certificate to her credit, while Ch Tod Hunter bred Ch Barb Wire, the sire of Aldham joker, another dog on his way towards the title, and Ch Benton Biddy bred Gem of Gold, sire of Ch Dinger, who in turn sired the South Country winner, Ch Brimball of Bridge Sollars.

Taking Revenge as the "A" line—it would be useless to trace further back as neither his sire nor dam were descended from any very notable winners—we have the following four generations:—

Revenge

1st: Ch B. Biddy, Ch Happy Mood, Ch B. Raider, Ch Blister, Ch Tod Hunter; 2nd: Gem of Gold, Ch What Fettle, Ch Gay Fine, Ch Not So Dusty, Ch Barb Wire; 3rd: Ch Dinger, Ch Share Pusher; 4th: Ch B. of Bridge Sollars.

II.

It was only by a very provident "accident" that Revenge figures in the pedigrees of the modern Border at all, as his breeder, Mr. Adam Forster was being tormented by a friend for a Border puppy to be used solely for fox-hunting. Tired of the repeated requests, Mr. Forster allowed him to pick one, and Revenge was chosen. A short time afterwards, the friend returned and when he saw the bitch puppy which he had rejected, wanted an exchange, and Mr. Forster, seeing that the dog puppy was actually the better of the two, readily agreed. A few months after this exchange had been effected, the Royal Show was held at Newcastle where Revenge won his two classes and the cup for best puppy. Back came his former owner with the bitch and asked for yet another exchange, but this was not granted.

Turning to that other notable sire from the same kennel, Rival, we are obliged to travel backwards some years to Coquetdale Vic, also bred by Mr. Forster, which was litter sister to the dam of the famous Ch Titlington Tatler, which brings us to the official recognition of the breed, and to the founding of the Northumberland Border Terrier Club. The club possessed several challenge cups with the usual stipulation that they had to be won three times in succession before becoming the property of the winner, and accomplishing this feat, Coquetdale Vic became the first Border to win a cup outright, and she had an almost unbeaten record in the ring.

She never appeared at a championship show; at that time there were plenty of terriers in Northumberland well worthy of the title but a win at a small Border show was always considered of greater merit than at the larger events of the year. In fact it is a debatable point whether the older Border breeders do not still hold this opinion. Be that as it may, Coquetdale Vic did continue her victories in other directions, and mated to a dog owned by Mr. John Carruthers, she bred Ch Winnie and Dash, which were successfully exhibited by Major Appleyard, of Birtley, and in the same litter, Flint, a dog which was only once entered at a championship show when he headed all his classes and won the certificate at Darlington. He was the sire of Rab o' Redesdale, which in turn produced Rival.

Damage by Fox

Coquetdale Vic, one of the gamest workers in the country, had the misfortune to have the whole of the flesh of her underjaw torn away by a fox.

Rival, taken as the "B" line bred Ch Ranter, another of Mr. Forster's famous sires, which in turn produced Ch Grackle (the property of Sir John Renwick, Bt.), from Mr. Dodd's bitch, Queen of the Hunt, which in turn sired Ch Oakwood Pickle, so we have RIVAL, sire of Ch Ranter, sire of Ch Grackle, sire of Ch Oakwood Pickle, and this line is linked with the "A" line of Revenge by the mating of Coquetdale Vic to a dog called Jock, resulting in Little Midget, dam of Revenge.

The very select kennel of Border Terriers owned by Mr. J. Johnson owes much of its success to inbreeding of these two lines through his purchase of Ch Bladnock Raider which was bred by Mr. McEwan, in April, 1932, from the bitch Red Gold. Before taking his title the dog had many victories on both sides of the Border when owned by Dr. Lilico, of Wigtown. His certificates were won at the Joint Terrier, Kensington and Darlington shows under Messrs. McCandlish, W. J. Nicholls and F. W. Morris, and during 1934 to 35 he also took the reserve certificates at Darlington, the Joint Terrier, Roundhay (twice) and the Crystal Palace.

Ch Bladnock Raider has been used extensively as a stud and has sired many notable winners, including Mr. Johnson's brace, Ch Gay Fine and Ch What Fettle, Puffin, winner of the Roundhay '38 award, Dipley Deans, Wild Lucy, Klondyke, and the big winner at Northern shows, Daphne, which has recently been sold to Mrs. Twist.

Mr. Johnson purchased the bitch, Red Floss, by Dr. Fullerton's Gem of Gold, out of Hunty Gowk, bred by Mr. Renton. Gem of Gold was by Rival out of Ch Benton Biddy, a daughter of Revenge, while Hunty Gowk was by Whitrope Don, hence her great suitability as a mate for Ch Bladnock Raider, and the consequent inbreeding to the "A" line gave the two champions, born in January, 1935.

The dog, Ch What Fettle, has won seven certificates at Cheltenham (Mrs. Pacey), L.K.A. (Mr. Nicholls), Blackpool (Mr. Houlker), Edinburgh (Mr. H. Bonsor), Kensington (Mr. Sam Crabtree), Blackpool (Mr. A. Simmonds) and Richmond (Mr. Nicholls), and has also accounted for the reserve certificates at Crufts and Richmond.

First Award

Ch Gay Fine won her first award at Roundhay under Mr. Harry Calvert, soon afterwards taking her title at Harrogate and the Alexandra Palace, under Miss Vaux and Viscountess Portman. A fourth award was gained at Edinburgh when she completed a double event with her brother, and she has also had the reserve awards at Crufts and Glasgow.

A short pedigree of these two winners, showing the inbreeding, is worth studying:—

		Revenge	
		Rival	Ch Benton Biddy
Revenge	Red Gold	Gem of Gold	Hunty Gowk
Ch Bladnock Raider			Red Floss
	Ch What Fettle and Ch Gay Fine		

Shortly after his purchase of Hunty Gowk, Mr. Johnson crossed her with Ch Blister, still keeping to the "A" line, and in October 1932 bred Ch Not So Dusty, which has an even more distinguished record winning certificates at the Palace (Mr. George Thompson), Round-hay (Mr. P. R. Smith), Darlington (Mr. F. W. Morris), the Joint Terrier (Sir J. R. Renwick, Bt.), Crufts (Mr. Hoskins), Edinburgh (Mr. Lawrence), Harrogate (Mr. Houlker), and Olympia (Miss Vaux).

We meet with the "A" and "B" lines in the Pedigrees of notable winners in many other kennels, and without doubt they are two of the most formidable sires among modern Borders, and without them it is highly doubtful if the breed would be in the strong position it commands at the present time. Fortunately there are several young dogs yet to start their breeding careers which look capable of continuing the successes for many years to come.

III.

A great many Border kennels have been founded on the progeny of two dogs which take us back many years, Miss Bell Irving's, Ch Tinker, and Mr. J. Dodds', Ch Grip of Tynedale, which are closely linked in many pedigrees. It is very obvious that Mr. Walter Irving relied a great deal on these two lines when establishing his famous kennel.

It is not necessary to look very far in Border pedigrees without meeting Ch Station Masher—which we take as the head of Family I—although she was bred by a son of Ch Grip of Tynedale (line C), and it was in breeding back to that line, and to Ch Tinker (line D) that she played such a great part in making the present-day Border Terriers.

One of her first litters provides a perfect example of inbreeding; she was mated to Mrs. Potts', Ch Barney Bindle, himself by Ch Grip of Tynedale from his owners' Bridge End Beauty, and the result was Ch Kineton Koffey, which was incidentally one of the first of the more famous Borders to appear at Southern shows, having been purchased as a puppy by Captain C. R. Pawson, and was one of the first Southern champions to gain a working certificate.

Mated to Ch Tinker she produced Arnton Billy, the sire of Hunting Boy, Tiot Fancy and Liddesdale Wendy. The former has played a great part in the foundation of the "Dipley" kennel, owned by Mr. J. J. Pawson. He sired Kineton Minx, a wonderful worker which has never failed to throw a good litter although in most of her matings she has been put back to the same family, either through Dandy Warrior, another of Arnton Billy's sons, which Mr. Renton was unfortunately obliged to withdraw from the show ring after he had been badly mauled by a fox, or through Ch Heronslea, a son of Tiot Fancy.

Mr. Reid's Ch Heronslea, mated to Ch Shaw's Lady produced Ch Wedale Jock, our latest champion, now the property of Mrs. Twist.

Liddesdale Wendy, another of the Ch Tinker—Ch Station Masher breeding, produced L. Nettle, the dam of Whitrope Don, and although he never attained the highest rank in the show ring, when mated back to Ch Station Masher gave Mr. Irving his famous Ch Joyden, which at eight years of age can still meet and beat the best of her breed. She has won six certificates under Messrs. Garrow, Simmonds, Houlker, Nicholls, Black, and Percy Smith, her most recent success being at Blackpool this year.

Whitrope Don has also bred Hunty Gowk from Liddesdale Bunty, another Arnton Billy bitch, and mated to Mr. Irving's Din Shield, which had two certificates to her credit, produced a dog which was exported to Maryland, U.S.A. Previously it was mated to Brandy Snap, litter sister to Ch Blister—the only reversion apparent to the A line—giving Rob o' Lammermuir, the sire of Ch Fox Lair.

Bred by Mr. Stevenson, in 1934, Ch Fox Lair has a unique record, now also the property of Mrs. Twist, during the last three years he has taken eight certificates, in 1936 at Crufts (Mr. McCandlish), Glasgow (Mr. Garrow), Roundhay (Mr. Harry Calvert), and the Kennel Club (Mr. Craig), in 1937 at Crufts under Mr. Garrow again, and at Glasgow under Mr. Irving, while this year he had the distinction of completing the hat-trick at Crufts under Mr. E. Hoskins. At his last outing in public at an open show at Maidstone, Sir John Renwick made him best in show.

Ch Tinker also sired Mr. Barton's, Rags, sire of Red Rock, sire of Whitrope Don and mated to a bitch called Betty (it is doubtful if she was registered) produced Ch Ben of Tweeden, grand sire in male line to Ch Heronslea.

As explained above, Ch Grip of Tynedale was the grand sire of Ch Station Masher, and from the interbreeding with Ch Tinker, lines C and D result in the following notable descendants of:—

Ch Grip of Tynedale and Ch Tinker, Ch Station Masher, Ch Joyden, Ch Kineton Koffey, Ch Barney Bindle, Ch Ben of Tweeden, Ch Joyden, Ch Heronslea, Ch Fox Lair, and Ch Wedale Jock.

IV.

It is impossible to trace through many pedigrees without meeting with the "Newminster" strain, owned by Capt. Sir John Renwick, Bart, who has done so much in recent years to help the breed through a very difficult period when both numbers and quality had been seriously depleted.

The first Border that Sir John owned was a black and tan dog Flyer, given to him by the late Mr. Tom Robson, master of the North Tyne Foxhounds nearly 50 years ago. He remembers when visiting Bellingham as a boy, his host, Mr. John Robson telling him that many years before, his father had carried a Border puppy on his horse over the moors to give to the late Mr. Carruthers, who later became so successful in breeding the very best working Borders.

Sir John is very emphatic in urging breeders to pay more attention to coat, undercoat, and tough hides which are most essential. He maintains that far too many of the present-day Borders are soft in coat, and that there are far too many dogs exhibited with the white toes or white feet, a certain sign that there is a near cross of Fox Terrier blood in their pedigrees, and deplores the use of suich animals in breeding.

Champion Grackle, which won nine certificates for Sir John was bred to line B, from Mr. Jim Dodds' beautiful bitch, Queen of the Hunt (by Tally Ho, out of Foxie), while his son, Newminster Rock traces back through his dam, Newminster Wisp, to lines C and D, as she was by Worry 'im, by Arnton Billy, from the Ch Tinker—Ch Station Masher litter. Unfortunately Rock was disfigured by his encounter with foxes and judges persisted in putting him down in consequence, thus depriving him of taking his place at the top of the breed, which he would certainly have done otherwise. All the New-minster dogs were bred for the sole purpose of working (show bench honours being of secondary importance) and at stud produce the dead gameness so essential.

Many of Sir John's bitches are in direct line from the outstanding Ch Barney Bindle, which did so much good service for Mrs. Potts, hostess of the Fox and Hounds, at Bellingham.

Ch Jedworth Bunty, one of the most successful bitches of her time at the leading championship shows was by Pincher (the sire of Mr. Irving's Ch Station Masher), from a bitch called Doodles, and mated to Mr. Septimus Renwick's, Sandy, produced Newminster Rummy which made his debut in the show ring at Bellingham where he headed his classes. On the Monday following, the Border Foxhounds were meeting there, and he was taken out along with his dam. As usual in this part of the country a fox was soon found and was run to ground in a set of rocky earths in the old quarry on Mr. Dodds' farm, The Riding. Newminster Rummy was put to ground there for the first time, and accompanied by his dam, spent the rest of the day there. Between them they bolted no less than seven foxes although both were severely mauled in the process. Messrs. Calvert, Butler and J. Anderson, who had judged at Bellingham were both impressed by the performance, but Rummy could not fail to be otherwise than "dead" game as his sire was often described as the gamest of the game with both fox and badger, and was one of the best known dogs with the Coquetdale and North Northumberland hunts.

Mated to Fairy Footsteps, litter sister to Ch Grackle—B line again—Newminster Rummy produced one of the finest examples of the correct type of the present day, Ch Newminster Rose, a bitch which had a meteoric rise to the highest honours in quick time although her classes contained many champions, actual and poten-tial. She was made-up at Glasgow under Mr. Walter Irving in 1937.

Furious Fighter, another of Sir John's Borders, which was equally famous as a worker was yet another of the B line, being by Ch Ranter out of Romance, and was also prevented from the highest honours in the show ring merely by his battle scars, but he has successfully com-peted in working terrier classes and was for many years a regular win-ner at that prominent Border Terrier gathering by the Thames, Richmond show.

V.

Reference has already been made to the five champions sired by Revenge from his matings to Causey Bridget, and Ch Blister, owned by Capt. Hamilton is probably the most prolific sire of any period. In less than five years he was exhibited at sixteen championship shows and won no less than 14 certificates. His progeny are countless, and at a recent show of the 21 Border Terrier awards, 16 were divided between his puppies, and those of his litter brother, Ch Bladnock Raider. Ch Blister has not only sired Mr. Johnson's, Ch Not So Dusty, but his owner's Stingo, which in turn produced the dog which is now in America, Ch Share Pusher which won his four certificates consecutively at the National Terrier, Glasgow, the Great Joint and the L.K.A., under Messrs. Hamilton Adams, J. Renton, Miss Vaux and Sir John Renwick. From another litter Stingo has also produced Finchale Lass, a young bitch which has been running many certificate winners close and looks capable to moving up one place at an early show.

Ch Tod Hunter, litter sister to Ch Happy Mood and Brandy Snap, mated to Dr. Fullerton's, Gem of Gold gave us Merriment, one of the biggest winners in the South which his owner, Captain C. R. Pawson has used extensively. Among his many winners being, Kineton Niki, Kineton Kilty, and Kineto Minty. It is interesting to note that there are only two strains on the bitch side in this kennel, one coming down through Kineton Susie which Capt. Pawson has had from mother to daughter for over 30 years, and the other being from Parkhead Vic, which was the dam of Mr. Walter Irving's Din Shield, two certificates, and grand-dam of Rab o' Lammermuir. In the same family come many of the "Winstonhall" dogs, owned by Miss M. Long, of Stowmarket, and from which descends Miss Williams', Puffin, which is one of Ch Bladnock Raider's off-springs.

Good Doer

Of Mr. Renton's brace, Ch Tod Hunter matured very quickly, being what is known in the terrier world as a "good-doer," and took her first certificate under Mr. Walter Glynn at the surprising age of nine months, whereas her sister, Ch Happy Mood went to the other extreme and was only young enough for the junior classes before she took her first award; however, she made up for a late start by winning over two hundred firsts, mostly in her breed classes of course which must be getting on towards a record in Borders.

Close inbreeding is happily unknown in the breed, at any rate in the Northern kennels, although there is much to be said for a careful blending of two or more of the strains headed by those five famous dogs, Revenge, Rival, Ch Tinker, Ch Grip of Tynedale, and Whitrope Don. Two good examples being Puffin, referred to above which is by Bladnock Raider and includes on his dam's side, Rival (twice, through her sire, Randale), and Tinker twice, through Ch Heronslea and Arnton Billy, and Mrs. Twist's kennel foundation, Ch Fox Lair, whose pedigree below prompts to question how could he be anything but a winner.

Whitrope Don—Din Shield

Knowe Roy

Revenge—Causey Bridget

Brandy Snap

Rob o' Lammermuir

Ch Fox Lair

Quintet of Sires

Champions and recent certificate winners descended from this quintet of sires are appended below, and provided that the progeny of such dogs are bred back to the same lines there is no reason why the list cannot be extended yearly, but it will be necessary to retain the original blood and the attending qualities.

Line A—Revenge.
B—Rival.
C—Ch Grip of Tynedale.
D—Ch Tinker.
E—Whitrope Don.

In male line descent:
LINE A.—

Ch Tod Hunter by Revenge.
Ch Bladnock Raider by Revenge.
Ch Blister by Revenge.

Ch Benton Biddy by Revenge.
Ch Happy Mood by Revenge.
Ch Not So Dusty by Ch Blister.
Ch What Fettle by Ch B. Raider.
Ch Gay Fine by Ch B. Raider.
Ch Share Pusher by Stingo by Ch Blister.
Puffin by Ch B. Raider.
Speed of the Wind by Ch Blister.

LINE B.—

Ch Ranter by Rival.
Ch Grakle by Ch Ranter.
Ch Oakwood Pickle by Ch Grakle.
Ch Dinger by Gem of Gold by Rival.
Ch Brimball of B.S. by Ch Dinger.
Ch Barb Wire by Ch Dinger.
Ch Bess of the Hall by Randall by Rival.
Aldham Joker by Ch Barb Wire.

LINE C.—

Ch Barney Bindle by Ch, Grip of Tynedale.
Ch Station Masher by Pincher by Ch G. of T.
Ch Kineton Koffey by Ch B. Bindle.

LINE D.—

Ch Ben of Tweeden by Ch Tinker.
Ch Heronslea by Stirrup by Ch B. of Tweeden.
Ch Wedale Jock by Ch Heronslea.

LINE E.—

Ch Joyden by Whitrope Don.
Ch Fox Lair by Rob o' Lammermuir.

Since the War the following have achieved championship status:—

Dr. Lilico's Ch Bladnoch Spaewife.
Lady Russell's Ch Swallowfield Garry.
Mr. W. Irving's Ch Rising Light.

Mrs. Mulcaster's Ch Portholme Magic.
Mr. W. Hancock's Ch Alverton Fury.

Type—by Wm. Lilico.

One of the commonest remarks one hears, from newcomers to the breed, is that they have difficulty in appreciating what exactly is the type required. Just recently I have—as I have always done when time permitted—watched the judging in other breeds, with the idea of comparing the evenness of type in some of those breeds with that shown in the Border ring. And I must say that the impression left on my mind is that difference of type is not confined entirely to our particular breed. In addition when I remember the variation of fashionable types in some of these breeds during the time I have been interested in them, I am the more certain that this is so. After all our breed is one of the most recent of the terriers to be exhibited, and whilst its popularity seems to be steadily rising it is still to the eyes of many something of a novelty.

When one comes to think of it a great many of the terrier breeds are on very stereotyped lines, with many common characteristics, and it is just on these lines that the Border shows up in violent contrast. So that anyone coming from another terrier breed to the Border may well find himself at sea for a time. I say "for a time," because from personal experience I can vouch for it that the newcomer will soon appreciate the things that are wanted. Of course as in all things mundane the personal element comes very much into play, and I am quite prepared to admit that my idea of a Border terrier is very much my own, and only corresponds broadly with the ideas of my friends in the fancy. That our ideas do correspond broadly has been, I think, amply proved by the fact that whilst recently individual placings have no doubt varied, the same dogs and bitches have appeared pretty consistently in the prize list.

A poorer criterion than the usual list of "breed points" can hardly be imagined, and naturally so, because such a list is a lifeless thing, and at that, the list without comparison with the living animal, would be interpreted in as many different ways as the number of people reading it. So we must take it that the list of "breed points" must be taken as a rough standard, to be used after making the acquaintance of as many specimens as possible. I grant you that all this is not very sat-

256

isfactory and not very illuminating, but I hope it will make my point that only experience of individual dogs and a comparison of winning exhibits are likely to help in making one's idea of type.

I have no intention of going over the list of points, but I do think it might be helpful if I refer to some of my pet notions, not with the idea that others will necessarily agree with them, but only because they have been guides to me in my breeding and showing.

First then is the question of the "otter head," a most difficult thing to describe or define. The head should be broad and flat between the ears, with wide cheek bones to accommodate the very powerful jaw muscles. It is also wide between the eyes, and the fore face should be short and thick, with no pronounced stop in looking either from above or in profile. If the head is not flat between the ears you tend to get an apple head, and if there is much drop in front of the eye the result is a Pom. face, neither of which is desirable. As one would expect from the jaw formation, the teeth should be very strong. The correct mouth anatomically is one where the upper incisor teeth just overlap the lower ones with no gap between. Often one or other or both of the lateral incisors of the lower jaw meet or just overlap the corresponding ones above, a small fault that in my opinion might be overlooked or only lightly penalised, whilst the occasional case where the teeth meet edge to edge is treated as correct. The under-shot mouth is a different matter altogether, although I think the tend-ency among judges in other breeds is not to penalise too heavily minor degrees so long as the mouth condition does not interfere with the dog's work. The over-shot mouth often escapes notice in its minor degrees, tho' it is the weakest mouth and the worst of the lot.

As regards the vexed question of size, I have no hesitation in saying that I like the small ones. I do not mean by that that I like a toy one or a weakly undersized one, but I do think that the standard adopted by all the clubs gives ample scope in the upward direction, and that any relaxation of it would run the risk of losing one of the principal charms of the breed—its handy size. I can hardly imagine a terrier of any use at his job that could follow hounds in full cry, yet that would seem what some few people desire. Such a dog would require to be as big as a hound to have the necessary speed and stamina, and that would, of course, put him out of count altogether for going to earth, which ordinary people like myself take to be the work of a terrier.

The question of colour crops up now and again, and I am sorry to see that in some quarters a prejudice seems to exist against the blue and tan, or as I prefer to call them, the saddlebacks. Now it is perfectly legitimate to have a preference for any one colour, but I hardly think it legitimate to damn any other without a substantial reason. Blue and tan is one of the colours recognised by all the clubs and whilst a judge may prefer a red or wheaten, he is not entitled to dock a dog of points because he is a blue and tan, nor do I think any judge would do it. Personally I like a saddleback, but apart from that, I think it of value to preserve them. It would be wrong to say that you always get a good coat in a saddleback—I have seen more than one soft coated one—but if you do get one with a hard coat, then it is indeed a hard one, and what is more, it is usually associated with a grand hide. I am convinced that it is of value to use occasionally a blue and tan stud dog or to breed from a blue and tan bitch, both to improve the texture of the coats and to secure sound reds.

One other point that seems worth remark is that of fronts. Whilst one does want good straight forelegs, tight shoulders and close elbows, I do not think we should aim at the gunbarrel fronts that some of the other breeds encourage. It seems to me that by doing so, we should risk getting a short stepping, stilted action in front, quite different from the easy and free movement that is or should be a feature of the Border terrier.

WM. LILICO

Advice to a New Enthusiast about to Purchase a Border Terrier

by M. RICHMOND, Bicknoller Border Terriers.

Remember that a Border is essentially a working terrier. He has to go to ground, very often in difficult circumstances, either among rocks or down very narrow earths. He therefore must not be oversized and should be a compact terrier full of quality. If the novice remembers to judge a Border as one does a weight carrying blood hunter, he will not go far wrong. For the benefit of those who do not know a blood horse, here are some points to remember.

The Border must have a quality head with dome of skull and strength of muzzle which should be as short as possible. Care must be taken to see that the mouth is good. The eye should be of the full type, a dark brown but not black. The ears should hang close to the head, as small as possible and of a fine texture. There should be good spring of neck and lie back of shoulders, depth of chest and spring of rib, racy hindquarters and dock (tail) not dropping off the end of the back but well set on and of very medium length. A slight curl is permitted but preferably should be straight, thick at the base, tapering to a natural point. Bone naturally must be much heavier in a dog and feet need particular attention. They should have thick pads, round in shape, and up on their toes.

There appear to be many terriers today up on the leg and lacking in depth of chest, feet are often bad being long and quite flat. One sees whip tails and terriers oversized. The texture of coat should be dense, weather-resisting, a good undercoat and really harsh on top. Allowance must be made in summer for jacket, the winter months, naturally, producing a better texture.

To preserve type, line breeding is essential.

A Few Characteristics of the Border

In response to the request to write some notes on the Border Terrier, I do so in the hope that the "Old Brigade" will consider I have endeavoured to profit from their teachings, and that newcomers to the breed will find something useful and constructive in my remarks.

The Standard laid down by the Border Terrier Club begins "The Border Terrier is essentially a working terrier, and it being necessary that it should be able to follow a horse must combine activity with gameness." Perhaps one may say "Well, that doesn't tell us much" but on reflection one will appreciate that it emphasises the three most important things to breeders. First, we must never forget the Border is a working terrier; secondly, he must be active so as to get about to do his job; and thirdly, he must have the right spirit to complete the job when he has got there.

The Standard was drawn up by a band of stalwarts who had long experience of the breed, and knew the best sort of terrier for killing foxes in their difficult country. Can the Standard be improved upon? I should say the answer is a definite "No" as regards the essentials. One might enlarge at more length on certain points, although it is difficult to picture a dog fully from a mere written description. The head for instance is the outstanding characteristic of the Border Terrier, but I fear there is a danger of losing this point. Many people seem to be under the impression that a coarse, thick-skulled type of head, with a broad muzzle, is the correct head, but I don't think so. Read the Standard again: "Like that of an Otter, moderately broad in skull with a short strong muzzle." The proper Border Terrier head is a very pleasing one; it doesn't look like a coarse-headed wire Fox terrier, but has a charm of its own. The strong jaw, well protected with skin but not too heavy in jowl—a working dog doesn't want a lot of loose skin that will get damaged in a scrap—the eye not too large or bold, yet full of expression and intelligence, the ears neat and V-shaped, and not set on high like those of the usual terrier breeds; this with a moderate amount of whisker gives the Border a head unlike any other terrier. I have noticed that a few being exhibited have heads almost Griffon-like in appearance, and coupled with protruding eyes one gets an impression that is far from pleasing and utterly foreign to the breed. Another fault is that a number of bitches have quite nice heads as regards make and shape but they are not sufficiently large or powerful enough. If one studies the reproduction in Mr. Rawdon B. Lee's book "Modern Terriers" of Mr. Jacob Robson's Borders one is immediately struck by the very strong heads which the dogs possess. This book was published in 1896 and the description given of the Border Terrier is closely akin to the dogs we see today.

We are all aware of the fact that undershot mouths are fairly common in the breed at present, and it behoves us to do our best to breed the fault out. It will have to be done gradually as a bad mouth seems to crop up occasionally whatever strain or stud dog we may be using, but it will be eliminated if we are determined not to breed from bitches that are definitely undershot, however good they may be in other respects.

I first came into contact with the breed about 20 years ago, and owned my first Border a few years later. In that time they have improved a lot as regards body, shoulders, legs and feet. Coats don't seem quite as good and there could be improvement in hind action. Type is more uniform although we have quite a bit to go before newcomers to the breed cease to be puzzled by the difference in appearance that one sees amongst Borders in the ring. Another point that the ringsiders cannot understand is the different sizes of Borders being shown today. One of our most experienced breeders in Mr. A. Forster referred to this in the Southern B.T.C. Year Book for 1947, and in the course of his article said "If judges repeatedly put dogs down because of their size, then we would all be seeing to it that we bred them to the correct size." I heard an equally experienced breeder say in Edinburgh Ch. show last year that a number of the Borders were too big. This point was stressed by two other authorities in Dr. Wm. Lilico and Mr. J. J. Pawson in the canine Press during the War, and although I cannot speak with the experience of these people yet I do know what the Standard gives for weight, and have been very disappointed that certain judges have awarded Challenge Certificates during the past year to dogs that were much above the prescribed size. I must say in fairness to the old school that I cannot remember any of the older breeders encouraging this fault. Bitches seem a much more uniform lot both as regards type and size, and this is a good omen for the future. Not only do these big Borders lack the activeness of the smaller ones but they could never reach their objective owing to their size. I know a number of game-keepers who will not consider a dog as suitable for work unless he is much smaller than some of the dogs that have recently been high in the awards. The Standard gives plenty of scope for slightly different sizes of Borders, but a really large Border to me lacks what I most look for in the breed, viz.:—Character, amazing vitality and activity, coupled with that wonderful stout heart and determination which is remarkable when encompassed in so small a frame.

It behoves us therefore to always bear the Standard in mind, and not to be misled by what I hope is a passing phase, namely, the awards given to over-sized Borders that do not comply with the sizes laid down by the early stalwarts of the Border Terrier.

Good luck to the breed, and long may he retain that type, character, and individuality, which makes the Border a charming companion, and a glutton for work when called upon.

Size, Eye and Coat

by DAVID BLACK.

That small insignificant word "SIZE" again appears to be the subject troubling most Border Terrier enthusiasts. True, at many of the big shows of late, we have had a variety of sizes, small, medium and big. But are Borders the only breed so affected. I emphatically say NO. Take Fox terriers, Bedlingtons, Cairns or Dandies and there are other varieties of terrier where you get just the same variety of size.

I contend the Breeder has the remedy in his own hands. Pretty nigh, most of the crack judges know the size they want and that is the medium size, giving that neat typical appearance which catches the eye in the ring at the first glance. Breeders would be well advised to breed for size. If you have a smart sized bitch and she is bred to a dog full up to size or oversize, the chances are some of your puppies are also going to be oversized. Smashing looking puppies at six weeks are not often the world-beaters you expect them to be at six months.

I quite agree size is one of the leading features in the show Border, but there are two others I consider of just as equal importance viz., EYE and COAT. In all terrier breeds except the Dandie, the eye should be small (not full) and well-sunk, the darker the colour the better. With such an eye you get the real "varminty" terrier expression.

I also think not enough attention is being paid to coats. At the last c.c. show I judged, very few good and correct coated specimens were on view.

I have given what I consider the three most important make-ups of a Show Border, viz.:—Eye for expression and size and coat for general appearance. If you are strong in these, hope the other points will drop in and you will not be far wrong.

The pamphlet *Border Lines* was published in 1948 by Shiach & Co Ltd, Carlisle.

THE BORDER COUNTRY

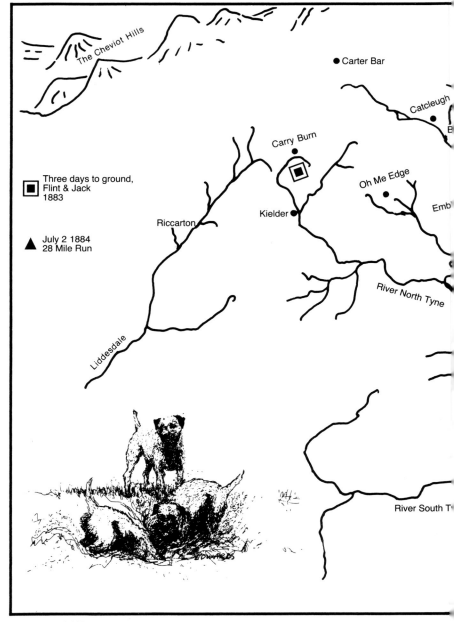

The Cheviot Hills

Carter Bar

Catcleugh

Carry Burn

Three days to ground,
Flint & Jack
1883

Oh Me Edge

Emb

Kielder

Riccarton

July 2 1884
28 Mile Run

River North Tyne

Liddesdale

River South T

Scale 1″ = 6 Miles

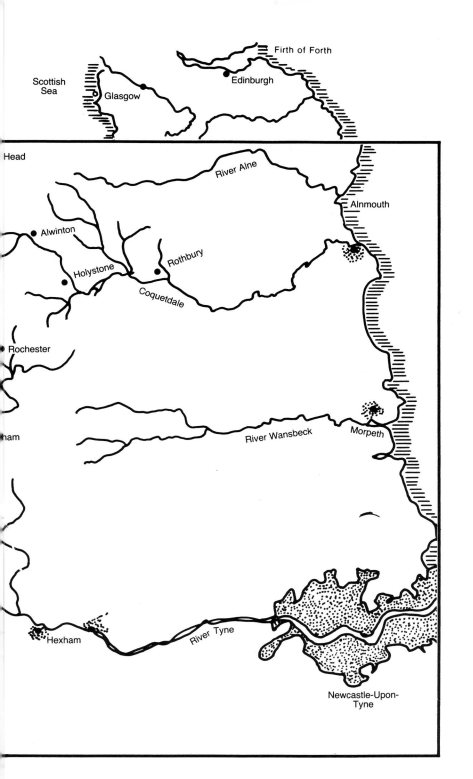

Firth of Forth

Scottish Sea

Edinburgh

Glasgow

Head

River Alne

Alnmouth

Alwinton

Rothbury

Holystone

Coquetdale

Rochester

River Wansbeck

Morpeth

ham

Hexham

River Tyne

Newcastle-Upon-Tyne